De-Stress at Work

Burn-out, excessive hours, office politics, handling complaints, isolated remote working, complex and inefficient processes – this book addresses the full complexities of chronic stress at work. It explains the potential for emotional and physical illness resulting from work, and importantly, presents ways in which occupational health and wellbeing can be enhanced through strengthening chronic stress diagnosis and promoting resilience. The latter is a win-win, for the worker, for the organization, and for society in general.

Drawing on 40 years of research in collaboration with some of the best-known occupational stress gurus (including Cary Cooper, Susan Jackson, the late Ron Burke and Arie Shirom), Simon L. Dolan translates abstract concepts of chronic stress into practical guidance for enhancing resilience in a VUCA world. The ILO and many governments recognize stress as a principal cause of emerging physical and mental disease and one of the strongest determinants of high absenteeism, low morale and low productivity. While important advances have been made in the diagnosis of acute stress, the field of chronic stress in the workplace remains less clear. This book seeks to address this by presenting a wealth of diagnostic tools, including "The Stress Map". The text is brought to life for the reader by short vignettes in the form of anecdotes and stories.

This book will be of particular interest to HR professionals, consultants, executive coaches, therapists and others who wish to help employees and clients better manage their own and others' stress and to build resilience that leads to a more productive and healthier workforce.

Simon L. Dolan is a respected international speaker, author and scholar in human resource management, organizational behaviour, work psychology and cross-cultural competences. He has written over 80 books that have been published in various languages on themes connected with values, people management, coaching, leadership, stress-wellbeing and the future of work. He has more than 40 years of research and teaching experience at leading universities in the United States, Canada, France, China and recently Spain. He is also the honorary president of ZINQUO, an international centre for values-based training and president of the think tank foundation, The Global Future of Work.

De-Stress at Work
Understanding and Combatting Chronic Stress

Simon L. Dolan

LONDON AND NEW YORK

Cover image: © Getty Images

First published 2023
by Routledge
4 Park Square, Milton Park, Abingdon, Oxon OX14 4RN

and by Routledge
605 Third Avenue, New York, NY 10158

Routledge is an imprint of the Taylor & Francis Group, an informa business

© 2023 Simon L. Dolan

The right of Simon L. Dolan to be identified as authors of this work has been asserted in accordance with sections 77 and 78 of the Copyright, Designs and Patents Act 1988.

All rights reserved. No part of this book may be reprinted or reproduced or utilised in any form or by any electronic, mechanical, or other means, now known or hereafter invented, including photocopying and recording, or in any information storage or retrieval system, without permission in writing from the publishers.

Trademark notice: Product or corporate names may be trademarks or registered trademarks, and are used only for identification and explanation without intent to infringe.

British Library Cataloguing-in-Publication Data
A catalogue record for this book is available from the British Library

Library of Congress Cataloging-in-Publication Data
Names: Dolan, Simon L. (Simon Landau), 1947– author.
Title: De-stress at work : understanding and combatting chronic stress / Simon L. Dolan. Other titles: Destress at work
Description: Milton Park, Abingdon, Oxon ; New York, NY : Routledge, 2023. | Includes bibliographical references and index. |
Identifiers: LCCN 2022039113 (print) | LCCN 2022039114 (ebook) |
ISBN 9781032109008 (hardback) | ISBN 9781032109015 (paperback) |
ISBN 9781003217626 (ebook)
Subjects: LCSH: Job stress. | Burn out (Psychology) |
Work–Psychological aspects. | Psychology, Industrial.
Classification: LCC HF5548.85 .D639 2023 (print) |
LCC HF5548.85 (ebook) | DDC 158.7/2–dc23/eng/20220908
LC record available at https://lccn.loc.gov/2022039113
LC ebook record available at https://lccn.loc.gov/2022039114

ISBN: 978-1-032-10900-8 (hbk)
ISBN: 978-1-032-10901-5 (pbk)
ISBN: 978-1-003-21762-6 (ebk)

DOI: 10.4324/9781003217626

Typeset in Bembo
by Newgen Publishing UK

This book is dedicated to my outstanding colleagues who have co-authored books with me throughout my professional career

Contents

Preface ix
Acknowledgements xi

    Introduction 1

1 Work, Stress, and Health: An Overview 7

2 The Who's Who in the Field of Stress: Principal Models and Concepts of the Pioneers in the Field 22

3 Understanding Stress from an Individual Angle: The Key Role of Personality, Self-esteem and Other Personal Characteristics 53

4 Stress, Coping, and Consequences: Individual and Organizational 87

5 Understanding Stress from an Organizational Leadership Angle 105

6 Work and Family Triangle Synchronization as Resilience to Stressful Work–Family Conflict 123
    Garti Anat and Tzafrir Shay

7	The Stress Map as an Emerging Gamification Tool and Methodology to Combat Chronic Stress	144
8	A Kaleidoscope of Individual and Corporate Remedies to De-stress and Enhance Resilience and Well-being at Work	161
9	Workplace Stress and the Future: Looking Beyond	209
Index		251

Preface

I cannot believe that by completing this book I have accumulated authorship (or co-authorship) of over 80 published books. While writing this book and dealing with the concepts of DE-STRESS and resilience, I truly understood why I keep on writing. A man needs to have a meaningful project in mind to feel fulfilled. In addition, as being an altruistic person as I am, I truly hope that my writings will genuinely help humanity (namely readers, be they students or professionals in various fields). And, if you are lucky (as I have been over the years) to collaborate with wise people for which the process of book production becomes a process of learning, relearning, satisfying your intellectual curiosity and constantly growing, I think this is a recipe for rejuvenating. True, not all my 80 books are about stress. The books were written for different classes of readers ranging from university students to professionals and even a book for children (a tale about values). What´s important is that I think I am finally discovering the secret for resilience; "*Always have a book project that keeps you massaging your brain, develop positive attitudes, help you grow and boost your self-esteem*". Once a book project is over, I do understand the urge to prepare a new one; thus, a new project becomes alive. I think that the cycles of writing books (and articles) challenge my level of curiosity especially when it is combined with the opportunity to collaborate and perhaps add value to mankind.

Just to ensure that it does not sound arrogant, let me say that amongst my 80 books, many are new editions of older books (certainly these include a series of textbooks destined to university students). Then there are books that have been translated into other languages; although in most cases a local author-collaborator was added, and the content was adjusted to the given culture. And, recently, some of the books are entirely digital. So actually, my 80-books shelf contains a mix of media, readership and co-authorship. The themes of my books range from Managing Human Resources and Organizational Behaviour (i.e. very academic), to managing, leading and coaching by values, to cross cultural management and naturally to the understanding and managing stress (destined to professionals and practitioners).

Which brings me to the essence of the present book. The first book I have ever written in the early 1980s was on stress. It was co-authored with Dr André Arsenault of the Montreal Institute of Cardiology. It was written in French, and published by

ERI (Monograph 5), the University of Montreal. Over the years it has sold almost 200,000 copies. The reason that it became an instant bestseller was perhaps because it was prefaced by the famous stress guru: "**Hans Selyé**". Remember that in the 1980s, neither myself nor André Arsenault were known amongst the community of stress researchers. Our fame has developed years later following the appearance of many published papers in some of the leading scientific journals and a series of media appearances on local and national Canadian media (TV, Radio and newspapers). Additionally, I attribute the success of the first book in French to the amazing non-nonsense writing style of André Arsenault who manages to communicate complex concepts in parochial and simple manner; I think that all that has captured the readers' attention. Another plausible explanation of the great success/sale of our first book on stress was perhaps the mere fact that the book was simply cheap (13$ CDN). The title of the book was: *Stress, Health, and Work*.[1] Ever since, we have developed a solid reputation in the scholarly stress research community and had the chance to collaborate with the "who's is who" in the occupational stress field. The latter became instrumental for me in negotiating the publishing of similar titles with reputable publishers in other countries and languages (i.e., McGraw/Hill or Pearson, or Thompson or Palgrave MacMillan or Routledge). For example, we have published a Spanish version of the book with McGraw Hill in Spain in 2005 (i.e. co-authored with Salvador Garcia and Miriam Diez Piñol); I had published by myself a book with Palgrave-MacMillan in English (in 2007), which later was translated to Portuguese. In 2009, André Arsenault and myself have decided to revise our initial book and have published the new updated version in French with a commercial publisher: **PUQ** (Presse de l Université du Québec). These days my colleague Eric Gosselin has joined us to write the 2nd edition (which was released in March 2022).

Today, we live in a VUCA world (**V**olatile, **U**ncertain, **C**omplex and **A**mbiguous) and stress is becoming explosive again. The COVID-19 pandemic combined with the possibilities of another world war (i.e. Putin invasion of Ukraine) added new facets. Now, not only are people in organizations stressed, but it has spread to a large chunk of the world population. Thus, I have decided to republish the book on stress with a different focus and include all the necessary updates so that it will be helpful to the general population, on one hand, and to professionals working in organizations, on the other hand. The real dilemma I had prior to writing this book, was wondering if another book on stress is really needed, especially with the proliferation of authors and books on the theme. A quick search on Amazon bookstore with the term "**stress**" yielded more than 60,000 hits. I read some of these (but obviously not all) and following a long and serious reflection, have decided that my added value and my angle will be different. And, for a resilient person like myself, it was another opportunity to undertake serious research and become current with the latest in the field. After all, you learn a lot when you prepare a new book.

So, I wish to dedicate this book to the many colleagues with whom I had the pleasure of collaborating and undertaking research projects in the field of occupational stress (and related themes) in the past 40 years or so. Each co-authorship was enriching. I hope that I have not forgotten anyone in my acknowledgement.

---

1 Dolan S.L. Arsenault A. (Préface pour Hanse Selyé): ***Stress, Santé et Travail***. Monographies #5 (ERI – Université de Montréal).

Acknowledgements

First, I wish to acknowledge the great assistance of the late Professor **Arie Shirom** (of Tel Aviv University – Israel), who has "discovered" my scholarly potential and pushed me to pursue my doctoral studies. Arie was instrumental in convincing me to abandon the corporate world and reorient my career towards research and the academia. He also connected me with several universities in the US, enabling me to finally pursue my doctoral studies at the University of Minnesota. The late Arie Shirom has also arranged for me to receive a scholarship from Tel Aviv University. I learned from Professor Shirom the importance of conducting rigourous research on stress. He also taught me that, albeit our training was in social and behavioral science, a multidisciplinary perspective can significantly enhance the understanding of this complex phenomenon. I kept in touch with him until his passing away a few years ago. Like many others who knew the person and his conduct, it has been difficult not to admire him as a scholar and as a humble human being. While he is no longer with us, his work and publications are still being cited. His (**SMBM**) burnout measure, for example, developed jointly with Prof. Melamed, is still being used by thousands of researchers. This tool captures burnout by measuring three components (physical strength, emotional energy and cognitive liveliness).[1]

I also wish to acknowledge the opportunity given to me by the late Dr **Hans Selyé**, who many consider to be "*the father of stress*", to accept me into his research lab and mentor me during my initial academic work in the field.[2] He has entrusted me to develop models of chronic stress amongst humans in work situations. Remember that in his laboratory, prior to our arrival, stress has been studied only with animals and in purely experimental laboratory designs. I was lucky to regain this level of trust as a junior researcher and was more than happy to be invited by him in 1979 to participate in the 2nd International Conference on the Management of Stress (Monte

---

1 See: Shirom–Melamed Burnout Measure (SMBM) (arabpsychology.com).
2 For more on Selyé see in Wikipedia (https://en.wikipedia.org/wiki/Hans_Selye)

Carlo-Monaco). This was a prestigious conference that brought together eminent scholars that only the *"Hans Selye Foundation"* could have organized. Amongst the Nobel laureates and distinguished researchers, I had the chance to personally meet and talk and dine with people like the late Linus Pauling[3] or Jonas Salk.[4] I also benefited from a lithography prepared by Salvador Dali for this symposium, and later used it as a cover page to my book *Stress, Self-Esteem, Health and Work* (2006).[5] The fact of being associated with Selyé, helped me boost my brand ten times faster than usual. I do explain my life and experience with Hans Selye in one of the chapters (vignettes) of this book.

The late Doctor **André Arsenault** from Montreal (a physician and nuclear medicine specialist) was my principal collaborator for almost 22 years while I resided in Canada. Jointly, and after the death of Hans Selyé, we managed the *"**Center for Occupational Health and Stress**"*, at the University of Montreal. André had several outstanding skills. He wrote eloquently, had a great capacity to synthesize complex concepts, and was a brilliant mathematician–statistician who used the latest techniques in his/our research. I have to admit that the voyage with André has marked me significantly hence my learning has never stopped. Those who knew André will agree with my observation that he was a great humanitarian and a super sensitive person. He cared about patients, about people who were poorly treated, about the environment and about the future of the world. In addition to book writings in French, we have collaborated in doing pioneering research on stress and burnout in Quebec creating the first multidisciplinary team of researchers. Our work was a remarkable piece of research in the health (hospital) sector, which was sponsored and financed by the then newly-established Quebec Research Institute on Occupational Health and Safety (**IRSST**).[6] André later became one of the first Directors of the **IRSST** research arm. One of our team members at that time was Dr **Lucien Abenhaim**, who later on rose to become the Surgeon General of France.[7] I wish to thank Lucien for his friendship throughout the years.[8]

During the 1980s and the 1990s I had close contacts and collaborations with two great occupational stress researchers: the late Prof. **Ron Burke** (York University, Canada), and Prof. **Cary Cooper** (University of Manchester in the UK). With Ron I had years of collaboration in conferences and book chapters, and in recent years we also published a couple of scientific papers together. Ron was perhaps the best-known researcher on occupational stress in Canada. And Cary Cooper is perhaps the scholar who has written more about stress than anyone that I have known. He helped me publish in journals with which he has been associated as an editor or co-editor and endorsed several of my published books, as well as writing the Preface to my former and first book on stress in English (Palgrave-MacMillan, 2007).

3 Linus Pauling – Wikipedia.
4 https://en.wikipedia.org/wiki/Jonas_Salk
5 www.amazon.com/Stress-Self-Esteem-Health-Work-Dolan/dp/0230006426
6 Occupational stress and its effects on the individual and on work organization (irsst.qc.ca).
7 Lucien Abenhaim – Wikipedia.
8 While writing this section, the sad news arrived about the death of Andre on March 18th. I had to change this paragraph to so that it will also be a memory to our relationships.

Professors **Susan Jackson** and **Randall Schuler** are dear friends and outstanding scholars. At the time we first met, they were both on the faculty of psychology and management respectively, at New York University. Both were interested in themes similar to mine (managing human resources, I/O psychology and of course occupational stress). Both were co-authors of our HR books in Canada (both in English and in French). Later, they also collaborated on the writing of the HR book in Spanish. They have moved to Rutgers University to pursue their academic careers. Susan Jackson was involved in the original validity studies of the famous Maslach Burnout Inventory (**MBI**), which was developed in 1981 by Christina Maslach and Susan Jackson. Randall Schuller, on the other hand, published one of the first outstanding papers in the 1980s labelled: ***Definition and Conceptualization of Stress in Organizations***. Our relationships are still alive and well and both have written the Preface to our latest edition of "Managing people and talent" textbook in Spanish (McGraw Hill, 2022).

As of the early 2000s, I moved to Spain, and have spent my career communing between Barcelona and Montreal. In Spain, I met a young physician who has decided to exit traditional medicine to become an organizational specialist. Dr **Salvador Garcia** was my collaborator and provider of incentives to publish our first book on values, called "***Managing by Values***" (in Spanish) by McGraw Hill 2003.[9] Salvador is a very creative person, a true philosopher and in addition writes very eloquently in Spanish; no doubt these were the reasons that our first book on values became very well known in the Spanish speaking communities throughout the world. Actually, the book became a bestseller in the McGraw Hill series. In a later edition of the book in English, published in 2006, we invited **Dr Bonnie Richley** to join us and the "*Managing by Values*" concept became a household concept to scholars and practitioners; the book became so popular that it has been translated to multiple other languages such as French, Portuguese, Russian, Hebrew, Chinese and others. In this English version of the book, we mentioned for the first time our concept of the ***triaxial model of values*** that years later became very known and has been used by coaching communities around the globe. The triaxial model was reflected in the subtitle of the book: *A Corporate Guide to **Living, Being Alive and Making a Living in the 21st Century**.*[10] In 2005, Dr **Salvador Garcia** and Dr **Miriam Diez** joined me in co-authoring the first book on stress in Spanish (McGraw Hill-Madrid). It became a best-selling book in the McGraw Hill series.[11] I am grateful to Salvador and Miriam for being there and for fomenting continued collaboration in research and publications to the current day.

While in Spain, I got to know Prof. **Ramon Valle** who was at that time the Dean at the University of Cadiz and later the Dean at Pablo de Olavide University (Seville). What started as a pure professional collaboration ended up in close and intimate friendship. Together we have organized several international workshops in Cadiz and Seville and co-authored several editions of a classical textbook on managing people

9 Garcia, S., and Dolan (2003) *La dirección por valores*. Madrid, McGraw Hill.
10 Dolan, S.L., Garcia, S., and Richley, B. (2006) *Managing by Values: A Corporate Guide to Living, Being Alive, and Making a Living in the 21st Century*.
11 Dolan, S.L., Garcia, S., and Diez-Piñol, M. (2005) Autoestima, Estres y Trabajo. Madrid, McGraw Hill.

in organizations (McGraw Hill). Prof. **Alvaro Lopez** has joined us in preparing the 4th edition and continued to help us complete the 5th edition of the book (currently in press, 2022). Ramon (and his wife Concha) are authentic friends. With all modesty, I can attest that Ramon is the best academic scholar in the HR field in the Spanish-speaking hemisphere. While collaborating with him I have learned plenty and have invited him to become the co-founder and member of the board of the "**Global Future of Work Foundation**". I wish to acknowledge his contribution to me as a person and as a scholar.

For many years my research interest was in understanding life and behaviour of people in organizations. Until I met **Dr Mario Raich**, who has convinced me that the time has come to spread the word about values and perhaps move from management and organizations to the larger society concerns. Mario is a future thinker, and with him we have published books like *Beyond: Business & Society in Transformation* (Palgrave MacMillan, 2008). The book was translated into German, Polish and Russian in addition to Spanish and Portuguese. Years later, we invited **Riane Eisler** (a true paradigm breaker) to join us in writing another futuristic book: *Cyberness: The Future Reinvented* (2014, Amazon.com). Mario also led the joint publication of more than a dozen articles dealing with the future. Collaborating with Mario is a nonstop journey of development hence the ideas are fresh and innovative. Mario is not a person that is bound by the rules of strict academic criteria; he is not afraid to publish breakthrough ideas about the future even when it goes against the mainstream. Mario is part philosopher, part dreamer and part concerned citizen who cares about the future of civilization. He was also one of the pioneers in pushing me to create the **Global Future of Work Foundation**. Thank you, Mario, for being part of my life.

Prof. Shay Tzafrir from the University of Haifa, Israel, has been a dear friend and co-author of numerous articles, namely on TRUST. We have also co supervised numerous doctoral theses together and I am in debt for his loyalty, collaboration and ingenuity. Along with Dr Anat Garti, he was sufficiently generous to contribute to this book by writing Chapter 6, discussing the interface of work stress and family stress.

Dr **Kristine Kawamura** was my associate editor and section editor while I was at the helm of Emeralds' *Cross-Cultural Management Journal*. Following years of collaboration in the journal and beyond, we have also published a book on *Cross Cultural Competence: A Field Guide for Developing Global Leaders and Managers* (Emerald, 2015). Kristine "cares about caring" relationships. Currently she is pursuing a successful academic and consulting career in California. Our friendship is solid and we both hope to undertake future joint projects.

I was also lucky to collaborate and write books (in French) with two of my former doctoral students in Canada: Dr **Eric Gosselin** and Dr **Adnane Belout**. Eric started the collaboration while he was still a doctoral student. He joined us as co-author in preparing the 1st edition of the textbook on work psychology. Over the years the book was re-labelled, and the most recent edition (6th) is labelled: "*Organizational Behavior*" (Chenelier-McGraw Hill, 2022). I have already mentioned that Eric also joined myself and André Arsenault in completing the 2nd edition of our stress book in French (PUQ, 2022). My other former doctoral student is Adnane, who has been my business partner in consulting via "**Groupe MDS**" for over 30 years. Recently, we have decided to venture into book writing, and he led the publishing of "*Organizational Effectiveness and Social Performance*" (in French, Hermes Science Publishing Ltd, 2017). We are currently planning another interesting book for professionals that hopefully will be published in 2023.

I wish to acknowledge the collaboration and contribution of my non-academic associates in ZINQUO (Spain), The Israel Value Center (Israel) and the Global Future of Work Foundation (Spain). With these people, I have published books and monographs that connect values, coaching and stress and is aimed at practitioners. Dr **Anat Garti** is perhaps the best-known family therapist in Israel. She has invited me to write the Preface to her book on "*The parent as a value anchor: A practical guidebook for parents and educators on how to use the 'Value of Values' tools and methodology*." She also helped to develop and design the *Stress Map* that will be presented in a separate chapter in this book. **Avishai Landau** is my brother and my best friend and collaborator. He has co-authored books in Hebrew on managing using values and on coaching using values and is currently preparing a Hebrew version of a book on stress management. He is the co-developer of the "*Value of Values*" game/tool as well as "*The Stress Map*" game/tool. **David Alonso** and **Laura Moncho** are my partners in ZINQUO, a company dedicated to train, certify and develop coaches who have specialized in values and in wellbeing. Their practical experience and wisdom have been integrated into many of my published books in the sense of incorporating and illustrating practical cases of success (see: www.zinquo.com).

And finally, my good friend **Javier de Pablo**. Javier has been instrumental in helping set up the legal entity of the foundation for which he is a founder and acts as secretary-treasurer. Without his help the Global Future of Work Foundation would have not turned into reality. Although he was trained as an economist, he has grasped the essential concepts of coaching, of stress and of leadership and of values. For the benefit of Spaniards, he has translated more than a dozen articles published by the team in English into Spanish. He is the co-developer of DOVA (**D**igital **O**nline **V**alue **A**udit, see: www.mydova.com). Currently, Javier is the catalyst and the co-author of a book on stress and resilience to be published soon in Spanish.

In sum, I feel in-debt to these colleagues for without them I would never have accumulated this impressive number of published books. Thus, in acknowledgement, I dedicate this book to all of them.

Simon L Dolan
Barcelona and Montreal
January 2023

Introduction

The enterprise culture of the twenty-first century helped to transform economies across the globe and led to sustained growth in many countries. This period saw an expansion of the short-term contract culture, major restructurings, outsourcing, global mobility, more monitoring of individual performance and less autonomy, and a long working hours culture throughout the developed world, which has been carried forward during the COVID-19 pandemic in the form of virtual work. To survive in the VUCA world, companies (and individuals) had to reinvent themselves. The result has been a substantial personal cost for many employees; this cost was captured by a single word – **stress.** Indeed, stress has found as firm a place in our modern vocabulary as virtual continuous communication (emails, WhatsApp, Facebook, Instagram, etc.), fast food and food delivery. Add to that, the rise in artificial intelligence, which is threatening many workers who become (or think they will become) obsolete. We use the term casually to describe a wide range of aches and pains resulting from our hectic pack of work and domestic life. People say: "*I feel really stressed*". Albeit the fact that the term is used in a generic and vague manner, it often yields an acute sense of disquiet. "*She's under a lot of stress*", we say trying to understand a colleague's irritability or forgetfulness. But, to those whose ability to cope with day-to-day matters is at crisis point, the concept of stress is no longer a casual one; for them, stress can be a four-letter word, **PAIN.**

This book explores this twenty-first-century plague as we live more frenetic lives, overloaded by work, pushed by new technology, and involved in intrinsically insecure work environments. It highlights the importance of diagnosing chronic stress (which is not easy nor straightforward), the importance of self-esteem (both individually and in the culture of the organization) and explains the methodology and tools that can be used to enhance resilience and positive well-being. This is a class act book which will help you better understand yourself and the organization you work for.

I believe that this book appears at a very fitting time, because the corporate world is being subject to productivity demands that we still do not know how to take on board with a suitable degree of sanity. While many senior managers believe that pushing employees to their limit will increase their productivity, both qualitatively as well as quantitatively, they very often fail to see the hidden costs of stressed employees. They either do not see or neglect to diagnose the impact on their own lives and health resulting from operating in these types of environments. It is obvious that in the twenty-first-century corporate world, we cannot operate in a stress-free environment; this is a utopia. We also understand that while factors generating stress seem to be on the rise, there are also work environments where stimulus is very low, and although this is not a factor in generating stress, it does create boredom, giving rise to a "do-nothing" attitude and bureaucracy.

The common wisdom is that a high level of stress generates a drop in productivity. Hyperactivity may result in more effort being required to get through a task, but it does not necessarily lead to the successful accomplishment of the latter in the long run. As the famous cliché suggests: *"You can be a superman (or superwoman) for a day, a week, or a month, but not throughout your working life"*. Attempting to become a super-person on a chronic basis causes significant **wear and tear** to the body and the soul, and the end result is poor health and poor performance. Being under excessive stress at work also interferes in life outside the workplace, resulting in a reduction of creative ideas and making the attempt at balancing work and private life virtually impossible. Therefore, managing workloads and other stress generating demands is of vital importance.

Among the employees' individual differences that can explain capacities and risk factors in terms of suffering from stress is the individual's personality and self-esteem. Self-esteem varies from person to person, and some authors connect the lack of self-esteem to occupational stress. In my own personal experience, which is based on interviews with hundreds of executives and professionals working in various organizations worldwide, I have noticed that the lack of self-esteem produces more stress because the insecurity that goes along with it is an unnecessary drain on people's energy. In addition, some leaders with low self-esteem become toxic to their teams and organizations, hence they create stress more often than help to manage it. Business environments themselves can often produce "attacks" on people's self-esteem or lead to emotion-generated conflicts, which in turn may lead to stress. People with healthy self-esteem, by contrast, seem to cope better in these circumstances.

An interesting innovation in this book deals with the concept of "Leadership and Corporate self-esteem". I argue that self-esteem can also be analyzed on a collective and business level, and this produces a sensation of pride in belonging to a company. Leadership or an organization that generates such a feeling of pride and commitment among its employees benefits from greater productivity derived from higher levels of motivation and creativity among its members. By contrast, lack of collective pride associated with belonging to a company can produce quite the opposite effect.

But neither can we ignore the fact that there are also organizations that have an excess of self-esteem and pride, which leads to commercial arrogance and lack of humility, limiting their growth given that many potential clients may be put off by just such an attitude. Something similar can be observed in people whose self-esteem is too low, although at first sight this would appear to be just the opposite.

Another personal trait of employees that is connected to generating (or buffering) stress has to do with their personality. In this book, we elaborate on the years of research that focused on Type A personality (a chronic combater) and the perception of control. Apparently, people who perceive more control over their acts, which is the core concept of emotional intelligence, are less stressed and the same applies to people who assume active action and control over their environment.

 INTERESTING TO KNOW

Better.com CEO Vishal Garg reportedly fired the 900 people during a Zoom call. On the Zoom call, Garg told the laid-off employees that the company would provide four weeks of severance and one month of full benefits, as well as other coverage as part of a package.

"If you're on this call you're part of the unlucky group being laid off", "Your employment here is terminated effective immediately", said Vishal Garg.

Source: https://edition.cnn.com/2021/12/05/business/better-ceo-fires-employees/index.html

The observations above provide the framework for this book. It is intended to offer practical models to respond to one of the greatest challenges of our time: *how to go about generating "wealth and health", creating jobs in hypercompetitive global environments without producing excessive stress levels and at the same time attempting to address the issue of our self-esteem as human beings.*

The book takes you, the reader, through an interesting voyage that ends up demystifying the concept of chronic stress and providing no-nonsense understanding and tools from a menu of options about how to manage stress individually, create resilience as well as outlying concrete schemas for organizations in managing stress and promoting employee's wellness.

As is usually the case with books of this particular genre, innumerable quotes from respected researchers, presidents of known multinational corporations and government officials, have been interwoven into various sections of the book to make it richer and more interesting.

At present, the pandemic is still causing havoc and high level of uncertainty, companies are forced to relocate, be involved in temporary or permanent closures, merge with other companies and learn how to manage remotely and search for new markets or even offer new products and services. Many CEOs often repeat the cliché "*our people are our best asset*". Reality, however, demonstrates more and more that this sounds hollow, rhetorical and barely credible, as the same CEOs do not really put their resources into treating people well or showing respect by not pushing them to the edge. While writing this book the social networks are plugged with uncivilized stories about the CEO who fired 900 employees in a single ZOOM call (see vignette). Stress levels at many of the fortune 500 companies appear to be at records that have never been seen before.

Any person that has worked in any firm knows that work and organizational demands are an important source of stress in their daily life. The typical expression nowadays in most organizations around the world is, "*we need the project done by yesterday*". From Monday to Friday, deadlines, emergencies, daily relationships with colleagues, subordinates and supervisors govern the lives of employees on all hierarchical levels, professional categories, levels of responsibility and namely in commercial organizations. During the pandemic, we also learned that the same issues exist in public service organizations such as health and education. At one time, in a society considered as "underdeveloped", people competed with each other and even used physical violence in order to survive. Nowadays, in a society in which physical violence is no longer accepted, controlled by laws and social codes, we are witnessing a new form of psychological violence – subtler and more indirect – but whose results are just the same; in the end people suffer, become ill and even die from it. **This is stress.**

Paradoxically, in spite of all our advances in technology, nutrition, medicine and an increase in scientific, social, legal and behavioural knowledge, those who run organizations are unable to realize that the means that they use every day in what seems to be a fight for economic survival, cause catastrophic suffering, deception, sadness, bitterness, pain and agony among the very people who have built up the organization. Neither do they appreciate that they themselves can become victims of the stress generated amid the corporate culture that they themselves have created. Making the matter more complex, we need to understand that stress in the workplace is a phenomenon that has neither odour nor colour, but its negative effects on the health and well-being, both of individuals as well as organizations, is devastating.

In the first decade of the twenty-first century, a syndrome of epidemic proportions is appearing all over the planet: several billion inhabitants in the most economically and technologically developed regions are suffering from a hidden disorder that prevents them from fully developing their capacity, self-esteem and aspiring to being happy individuals. Stress is universal – it affects billions all around the globe, and this is even worse in countries and regions where other types of stressors have been experienced: intense immigration, wars and belligerent acts, famine and drought, ecological disasters (eruptions, flooding), etc.

Today, in addition to threats posed by advanced technologies, a great majority of workers are forced to do work that they do not consider meaningful. Here we see a steam of evidence suggesting that people are forced to maintain their work for economic reasons, but the latter is not congruent with their core values, wishes and expectations. By contrast, there are the zealous people who happen to do meaningful work, but work becomes an escape from other spheres of their lives, which are unfulfilled. One of the main ethio-pathogenic hypotheses of this atrophic syndrome is based on Aristotelian wisdom: *their excess of work is preventing them from appreciating truth and beauty*. In all likelihood, this excess of work is based on a compulsive need to display their worth to others, due to an increasing fear of poverty and of being excluded from the system. In addition, it comes mainly out of a lack of deep-rooted self-esteem, derived cyclically from a lack of ethical and emotional development throughout their lives.

In other words, at the threshold of the twenty-first century, we may have learned how to work but we do not know how to relax, how to love ourselves, how to live or share our lives as fully developed human beings. There is an old African proverb that is a powerful message to the Western culture: "*We* (the Africans) *have time – you* (Western civilization) *have watches*". In sum, this book sets out to contribute some individual and organizational ways of confronting this new psychopathological mass phenomenon.

This book is not intended to be an example of how to get rid of pressure in the workplace. In fact, there is no simple remedy albeit the quest for panacea. On the contrary, we will present all the complex elements of this phenomenon, as simply and synthetically as possible, so that you (the reader) can understand what stress is, how it relates to your own personal traits, and the options available for reducing your level of stress. We will focus our attention on diagnosis of chronic stress and on remedies to combat it. We will also put forward and demonstrate some examples of personal and organizational policies and strategies that will enhance resilience on one hand and organizational wellness (productivity included) on the other hand. In this book, we pay particular attention to those professionals who display high levels of stress at work. More specifically, the book is organized around nine chapters with the following contents:

Chapter 1 puts forward the bases for reflection between the need for high productivity, quality of life in the workplace, stress and health. This is an overview based on the accumulated knowledge in the field.

Chapter 2 helps understand the evolution of models and concepts in the field of stress. The chapter identifies and presents the "who´s who" in the field and shows the multidisciplinary nature of stress in general and occupational stress in particular, analysing its determining and regulating factors, their symptoms and their results.

Chapter 3 focuses on understanding stress from an individual worker angle. It elaborates on the concept (and importance) of personality, self-esteem and other social/demographic individual factors that operate in the theatre of stress and health.

Chapter 4 discusses life stress, generic coping and distinguishes the manifestations in two levels of consequences: individual and organizational.

Chapter 5 examines stress from the organizational leadership angle. In particular there is a warning of how to get away from toxic leaders.

Chapter 6 looks at the relationships between work, non-work (family and friends) and stress. The chapter, written by Dr Anat Garti and Prof. Shay Tzafrir describes their model entitled: work–family triangle synchronization (WFTS). The work–family triangle relationship consists of a triangle of dyads: the direct dyads of manager–employee and the couple, and the indirect dyad of the manager–employee's spouse.

Chapter 7 is dedicated to the presentation of the Stress map. This is an innovative tool that can be used by either an employee (auto diagnosis tool), by a mental health specialist, or by occupational psychologists within the organization to detect chronic stress and plan individualized strategies to remedy the situation.

Chapter 8 reviews the latest remedies (individual and organizational) designed to manage stress. We label it a kaleidoscope – hence a rich menu of options is described albeit each of them being very brief.

Chapter 9 This chapter looks beyond our immediate horizon. It predicts and even speculates about the context that will bring about stress in the future. This chapter is based on the data accumulated in the past 20 years at the "**Global Future of Work Foundation**" (formerly–the ESADE Future of Work Chair). Worth mentioning that this section is part science and part fiction hence it discusses future distant scenarios. Nonetheless, conclusions can be reached on developing the antidote in the form of resilience.

A personal concluding note. The reflections and key points of action mentioned in this book are largely the result of my personal and professional experience. I was lucky to work, collaborate and learn from some of the world known gurus of occupational stress (i.e., see my acknowledgement section). My interest in the field of occupational stress began after an episode I had experienced at the Mayo Clinic in Minnesota. While still studying for my doctorate degree at the University of Minnesota (back in the 1970s), I was involved in a small survey that studied the perceptions of patients who had survived their first heart attack. All the patients had no previous history of heart disease and were actively working; essentially these were patients who had considered themselves healthy all their lives. Out of the approximately 210 patients, it came as a surprise to corroborate that more than 90% of them attributed the cause of their heart attack to their work. Obviously, this was not a conclusion based on rigorous research design; it only tapped the perception of the patients. Yet, analysing the responses in an aggregate form made you reflect and think: *Is it possible that we are witnessing a new form of toxicity at work*? Something that has no colour and no odour but can kill you. The revelation was sufficiently important for me to spend more than 40 years of my life involved in research in this field. Again, the impetus for this research can be summarized as the following: although work can be positive and increase people's well-being (economically, socially and emotionally), when things go bad at work the impact on health can be devastating. I arrived at the conclusion that in the late twentieth and, of course, the twenty-first centuries, we are dealing with a new form of toxicity; it is colourless and odourless, but its accumulated effect on the individual health and organizational well-being can be devastating. This gave rise to a new interest in an occupational field that was labelled: "**psycho-toxicology of work**".

After attaining my doctoral degree in Minnesota, I joined the international team headed by Hans Selye at the University of Montreal. At that time, Hans was the greatest "**guru**" in the field of stress, and many called him "**the father of stress**". This book is based largely on the work I initially did with Hans Selye, complemented with the co-director of The **Center for Occupational Health and Stress**, Dr André Arsenault, and further developed with other collaborators spanning the entire world, but namely from Canada (the late Ron Burke, Eric Gosselin and recently Kyle Brykman), Israel (The late Arie Shirom and Anat Garti), France (Lucien Abenhaim), the US (Susan Jackson, Randall Schuler, Tony Lingham, Bonnie Richley, Kristine Kawamura and recently Dave Ulrich), Peru (Rachel-Shmueli Gabel), Switzerland (Mario Raich) and Spain (Salvador Garcia, Miriam Diez, Ramon Valle and Ana Perez-Luño).

While working in Spain, I understood the importance of moving from scholarly and academic work to the practitioner world. Thus, I have launched a collaboration with **ZINQUO**, a company that develop and certify coaches and other professionals in using my research tools, amongst professionals (these include David Alonso, Laura Diez and other members of the team). I also collaborate with my close colleagues at the **Global Future of Work Foundation** (Javier de Pablo, Gustavo Piera and others).

My career has been influenced by the collaboration with these distinguished scholars and practitioners and to whom I am truly grateful and appreciative for co-evolving and helping me become a better person and hopefully a better scholar.

CHAPTER 1

Work, Stress, and Health

An Overview

Can the Goal of High Productivity Be Reconciled with the Goal of Quality of Work Life?

The importance of improving productivity and quality of work life is evident to anybody who has ever worked in a company. For many years, workers and organizations believed that they were protected from global competition; therefore, few incentives were devised to increase productivity. However, this panorama has rapidly changed due to the following factors:

- Longer-lasting cycles of economic recession.
- Globalization of markets and increasing international competition.
- The fastest growth of technology.

As companies realize that their survival is at stake, pressures to increase productivity are mounting. A great number of companies face the definitive test of survival that, on the one hand, is related to the economy, and on the other hand, is due to their low productivity levels. A drop in productivity has an effect on people's standard of living as well as the community in general, resulting in companies becoming less competitive. The need to improve productivity coincides with a period in which the workforce is better trained and calls for greater participation in and control over their work. Employees prefer not to be dealt with as just another cog in the wheel, calling for innovative approaches to simultaneously improve the quality of their work life and productivity.

This chapter focuses on the changes in certain aspects of the organization, which can lead to increasing quality of work life without lowering productivity and affecting the well-being of an organization's employees.

In the past, attempts to increase productivity were centered on technological change, which, over time, gave rise to one by-product in particular: the deterioration in the quality of work life for a greater number of employees. In general, people

DOI: 10.4324/9781003217626-2

were asked to work faster, to produce more, to spend less time thinking (that was the task of the machines) and to program their work activity according to the available technology. Although this approach seemed to be effective in the short-term, we now know that this is no longer the case. This has given rise to employees currently trying to exert greater control, having more choices, and participating in all of the aspects related to work that concern them.

Consequently, over the last fifty years efforts have been made to create a more global approach in terms of increasing productivity without having to forfeit the physical and psychological well-being of the workforce. This approach is centered on the concept of quality of work life. We all know that the supreme objective of all companies is their survival, and other strategic objectives include growth and profits which require them to be productive. Interest in quality of work life is based on the supposition that its improvement will result in healthier, happier and more satisfied workers, who are, as a result, likely to be more productive.

It is difficult to define and measure quality of work life. This chapter refers to a process by which all of the members of the organization participate in the decisions that affect their jobs in particular and their work surroundings in general. This is done through open and appropriate communication channels, resulting in workers having greater involvement in their work as well as greater job satisfaction, in addition to lower levels of stress and fatigue. In essence, quality of work life represents an organizational culture, or innovative management style, in which employees have the sensation of belonging, a say in what goes on, responsibility and dignity. Generally, the organization that is characterized as having a high quality of work life promotes industrial democracy: suggestions, questions and criticisms are seen as possibly leading to improvements in one sense or another. In an environment such as this, constructive disagreement is considered a manifestation of concern for the organization instead of being viewed as a destructive complaint. The promotion of this type of participation by management often leads to ideas and actions that increase the efficiency and effectiveness of how the organization is run, improving both working conditions and atmosphere.

Quality of work life (QWL) is a process by which all members of the organization, through appropriate and open channels of communication set up for this purpose, have some say in decisions that affect their jobs in particular and their work environment in general, resulting in greater job involvement and satisfaction, and less stress and fatigue. QWL represents a management style in which employees experience feelings of ownership, self-control, responsibility and self-respect. In an organization with a high QWL, industrial democracy is encouraged; suggestions, questions and criticism that might lead to improvements of any kind are welcomed. Creative discontent is viewed as a manifestation of constructive caring about the organization rather than destructive griping. Management's encouragement of such feelings of involvement often leads to ideas and actions for upgrading efficiency. An idea about the factors contributing to achieving QWL is schematically exhibited in Figure 1.1.

Thus, quality of work life is a concept and philosophy, aimed at improving the lives of employees within organizations. In order to bring this about, its advocates follow several methods, ranging from the strictest and simplest scientific reorganization of

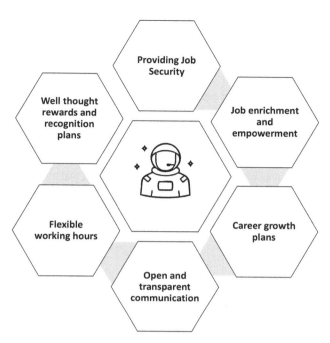

FIGURE 1.1 Factors contributing to achieving a QWL for an employee.

work tasks, as defended by Taylor and his colleagues, to the more complex process of continuous change, introduced by the socio-technical group and the defenders of the more recent system and contingency theories. The quality of work life concept can be translated into operational terms and be applied to the specific context of the organization through programs. Some of these programs are specific and limited in scope, whereas others are intended to produce multiple changes in a wide variety of areas. To better understand the role of quality of work life programs, we will present a brief description of its relationship with other management areas and several theories on work organization.

From the historical point of view, the term "QUALITY OF WORK LIFE" (QWL) originated from a series of conferences sponsored by the US Labor Department and the Ford Foundation in the late 1960s and early 1970s. These conferences were stimulated by the then widely popular phenomenon of *"workers alienation"*.

Many of these factors, and the worker discontent that accompanied them, were on display at General Motors' infamous Lordstown, Ohio, plant. A modern automated plant, Lordstown was designed by automotive engineers in the late 1960s for the efficient production of a small and inexpensive car. General Motors wanted something to compete with the small foreign automobiles that began to eat their way into the American automobile market. The Lordstown plant soon manufactured a possible competitor, the Chevrolet Vega. Lordstown's line speed greatly exceeded that of older plants, and eventually Lordstown came to symbolize the worker discontent and worker alienation of the auto-industrial age – the "Blue Collar Blues". It also epitomized the heady and rebellious youthful working-class militancy of the late 1960s and early 1970s.

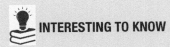

INTERESTING TO KNOW

CMI's research on The Quality of Working Life explored the connections between managers' wellbeing, their motivation and productivity. Based on a survey of 1,574 managers, the results provide insights into the impact of working hours and management style on the productivity challenge faced by the UK. With long hours identified as a major factor in stress and health problems. The report also highlights how our increasingly digital environment could be creating a new form of presenteeism. The Quality of Working Life is evidence of the impact that management and leadership has on well-being. The insights and lessons it offers should help managers understand what they can do to improve the quality of working life in their organizations.

Study by: Worrall, Cooper, Kerrin, La-Band, Rosselli and Woodman, January 2016. For more see: Quality of Working Life - full report - January 2016.pdf (managers.org.uk)

A Youngstown State University oral history project captured the recollections of some of the Lordstown autoworkers. Jim Graham, a Greek-born union activist, expressed the familiar refrain that autoworkers no longer needed brains for their work. When questioned about the early 1970s wildcat strikes, Graham replied that management "came in and said look, when you come in the plant leave your brain at the door, just bring your body in here, because we don't need any other part. Leave your brain at the door, we'll tell you what to do, how to do it, when to eat, when to drink coffee".

So, the series of conferences led to a conclusion that a job is more than a mere pay and repeating routine tasks and following orders. Those who attended these conferences considered that the term referred to more than job satisfaction and that it included other concepts. These concepts included participation in at least some of the decision-making processes, an increase in autonomy for daily work schedules, and redesigning jobs, systems, and structures within the organization, with the aim of stimulating learning and promoting a satisfactory form of employee-backed interest and participation in work issues.

The term Quality of Work Life remained ambiguous for a long time, until in the 1970s a handful of companies expressed interest in putting it into practice, such as Procter & Gamble and General Motors in the United States, and Volvo in Scandinavia. Successful results were achieved with the implementation of programs geared toward improving the quality of work life in their new plants. From the positive results obtained by these companies, in the late 1970s other companies, among them FORD, applied similar projects and also obtained good results. At the beginning of the 1980s, there was a deep recession in the U.S. Asian competition, offering cheap and high-quality products, seriously concerned American corporate executives, leading many of them – along with many public sector organizations – to opt for quality and begin to apply quality of work life programs.

QWL has become a buzzword of the modern time. The QWL has now come to be known as humanization of work. The basic idea of this concept is to treat employees as a human being. The various terms which have now come to be associated with knowledge workers are Intellectual Capital Social Capital, Human Capital, Human

Resource Asset, Talent Investors etc. Although QWL can be defined in many ways, an interesting definition would be the combination of four requirements and perceptions expressed by workers towards their company:

1. **The perception of feeling supported and looked after by the company.**
   Some companies provide employees with a series of services related to their private life, which form part of an increase in employee benefits. For example, in Belgium it is common practice to provide free legal services to employees who are in divorce proceedings.

2. **The need for companies to make employees lives easier.**
   In Sweden, companies have reached a series of agreements with certain suppliers, in such a way that employees can make purchases via the Intranet with the added advantage of considerable discounts and free delivery of goods to the employee's home or place of work.

3. **The need to fulfil personal wishes.**
   Employees increasingly call for their private life to be taken into consideration at work. The company, therefore, provides a series of activities that help to reduce stress and increase employee productivity. For example, the possibility of employees working from home or even making a 24-hour, human resources hot-line available.

4. **The need to maintain good personal relationships.**

   Company recognition for each and every employee helps to maintain a good working relationship, not only with the management, but also among colleagues themselves.

Quality of Work Life and Stress at Work

Quality of work life has significant repercussions on the quality of emotional life and in the socio-emotional and affective balance that may or may not be obtained by individuals. Work is for many one of the fundamental activities of human existence. It is the activity that allows people to produce the goods and services that are necessary and indispensable for modern-day life and enables them to become integrated into the system of relationships that makes up the very fabric of society.

By means of efficient and productive jobs, societies improve the quality of organizational and social life, and through this, workers find the satisfaction they need in terms of their personal, family and social life.

Given the time that people spend at work, we must be aware of the implications and consequences that this has on their lives. The latter is valid for any type of work relationship: a group of professionals, a company of consultants, a micro-company as well as large companies. Certainly, dynamics and the relationships between people will be different in each case since there is an intimate link between the organizational structure and the inherent psychosocial processes.

In terms of personal relationships, obtaining a positive relationship in the workplace has always been an aspiration. Many workers who are proficient in the art of work and friendship – camaraderie – have been and are still daily examples that enable us to renew and reshape our faith and hope in that it is possible to create positive and rewarding human environments in the workplace.

We should bear in mind that the crux of the problem lies in the fact of a perceived hazard or disturbance considered threatening, such as natural catastrophes and emotional loss (the death of a spouse or child, the breakup of a marriage, job-loss, retirement, etc.). Today, however, work-related stress also takes on special significance. Each person may consider stimuli or disturbances in their place of work differently: what some see as a challenge that stimulates them toward self-improvement and development, others may see as posing a terrible threat. This plays an important role in the appraisal of self-esteem, tolerance of frustration, optimism, creativity and the sensation of security – internally as well as externally – through affective, social and economic support networks, amongst other aspects.

Transposing this to work and its relationship with quality of life, there is no doubt that the presence of non-motivating work demands may drastically affect performance and the workplace environment, disrupting personal as well as family and career development. The balance between work-family quality of life, the existence of a good working atmosphere, a satisfactory level of organizational mental health, the existence of good risk prevention programs, and minimum accident and professional illness levels, make it possible to minimize the existence of pathological stress.

Today, we speak of new, emerging causes of work-related stress, increasing job uncertainty for instance, which imply a permanent risk and an exaggerated sense of the short-term goals. Some people talk about the death of long-term career paths (except perhaps for those in the public sector). On the one hand, this clashes with family life projects in the long-term, and, on the other hand, makes it difficult to develop loyalty and commitment (weak bonds), socialization, solidarity, and, especially, trust. We would have to add the need for permanent change, the extreme submission to the computer (the screen replacing person to person contact), and the difficulty in finding a quiet moment amid the accelerated pace of today's technical, economic and cultural events.

Today, there is special significance between the fragmentation of the personal, family and work world and the disappearance of the spiritual and cultural world in work environments, which brings with it an increasing sense of loss of meaning regarding work.

On all levels, life in the last few decades has become accelerated and has exposed people to increasing pressures. In the work environment, employees are expected to produce better quality and more work in less time and using less resources.

The effects of stress upon health are becoming more and more relevant. There are well-documented disparities in health by socioeconomic status and race and ethnicity. Stress has been identified as one of the top 10 determinants of disparities in health (World Health Organization [WHO], 2008).[1] This report presents a state-of-the-science overview of research examining stress as a driver of disparities in health. Stress occurs when individuals experience demands or threats without sufficient resources to meet these demands or mitigate the threats. The WHO report explored biopsychosocial mechanisms that may link stress to health, with a particular focus on disparities in depression, cardiovascular disease and cancer. According to a survey carried out by the European Foundation for the Improvement of Living and Working

1 Stress and Health Disparities Report (apa.org)

Conditions (Paoli, 1997), there has been an important transformation in terms of how work is organized in Europe.[2] According to Paoli, 45% of the 147 million workers in the EU considered that they carried out monotonous tasks; 44% did not rotate tasks; 50% carried out simple and repetitive tasks; 35% stated that they did not have any say in what they did or how they did their work, whereas 54% mentioned that they worked too fast. This data indicates that, if we try to approach the health problems of today's workers, a thorough revision of the concept of occupational health is required.

And here are some interesting observations cited on the website of NIOSH: (STRESS...At Work (99–101) | NIOSH | CDC)

- One-fourth of employees view their jobs as the number one stressor in their lives.-Northwestern National Life
- Three-fourths of employees believe the worker has more on-the-job stress than a generation ago.-Princeton Survey Research Associates
- Problems at work are more strongly associated with health complaints than are any other life stressor-more so than even financial problems or family problems.-St. Paul Fire and Marine Insurance Co.

Diverse opinions exist with regards to whether or not organizations should be concerned about their employees' emotions. By way of a brief, summarized version, we can put forward four reasons why executives and management should be concerned about the emotions of their employees, emotions that might then translate into stress and illnesses:

1. From the perspective of the quality of their work, workers feel more satisfied when their working environments are safe and comfortable.
2. Executives should try to reduce occupational stress because this is a factor that leads to negative results. Specialists in mental health consider that an important proportion of the workforce suffers from depression or high stress levels that will end up affecting their performance.
3. From the enormous economic costs derived from stress, experts consider that the illnesses related to stress represent many millions of euros (or pounds or dollars) a year.
4. The last reason has to do with the recent cases of employees who have taken their companies to court over unpaid compensation for problems derived from stress.

Work, Stress and Health

According to the definition given by the World Health Organization (hereafter WHO), the promotion of health includes all the measures that allow people, groups and organizations to have greater control over the factors that affect their health. The

---

2 Paoli P. (1997). *Second European Survey on Working Conditions in the European Union*. Luxembourg: European Foundation for the Improvement of Living and Working Conditions, Office for Official Publications of the European Communities.

objective of these measures is to improve the health of people, groups, organizations and communities.

For this reason, it can be said that promoting health is a process that allows people to reach a higher level of self-esteem as far as their health is concerned. In this sense, health represents a resource for daily life that allows people or groups to fulfil expectations and desires to act, and, at the same time, take on society at large and change the world.

Promoting health in the workplace is a combined effort involving companies, workers and society at large to improve the health and well-being of individuals in the workplace. This promotion is obtained through a combination of measures:

- Improving the organization of work tasks and the working environment.
- Encouraging active participation in the process.
- Promoting personal development.

An active workforce that is healthy, motivated and well-qualified constitutes a fundamental element of companies in the twenty-first century. Growing evidence demonstrates that health improvements in working environments can represent a key ingredient in a company's efficiency and competitiveness. In innovative companies, the quality of work life and the quality of products or services are part and parcel of the same strategy.

Promoting health in the workplace makes it possible to reduce occupational stress. Its objective is to influence those factors that promote employee health. Its success is due to improving working conditions, encouraging employee participation and bolstering personal competencies. Among the main elements involved in health promotion in a company are the methodological approaches and procedures used. With the purpose of analysing the point of reference, the workloads as well as the subjective effects on well-being have been identified by means of different instruments, including questionnaires, tools for identifying health risk factors and "health circles". Like "quality circles" on which they are based, health circles offer workers the opportunity to participate and to take part, as experts in their own affairs, in the stress reduction process within their capacity. Figure 1.2 represents the U.S>

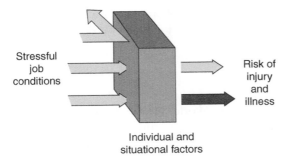

FIGURE 1.2 NIOSH Model of Job Stress.
Source: www.cdc.gov/niosh/stresswk.html

National Institute for Occupational Safety and Health (NIOSH) view of what stress is all about.

Chronic Work Stress and Health

Short or infrequent episodes of stress pose little risk. But when stressful situations go unresolved, the body is in a constant state of activity, which increases the pace at which the biological systems are worn down. Ultimately, this leads to fatigue and/or injury, and the body's capacity to defend itself can be seriously weakened. As a result, this increases the risk of disease or accident.

In the last thirty years, many studies have looked into the relationship between work-related stress and a variety of diseases. Mood swings and alterations of sleeping patterns, gastrointestinal and stomach problems, headaches and changing attitudes towards family and friends, are examples of problems related to stress that develop quickly and which are commonly seen in these studies. These early symptoms of work-related stress are usually easy to recognize. But the effects of occupational stress in chronic diseases are more difficult to diagnose given that these take a long time to develop and can be influenced by many other factors in addition to stress. However, there is increasing evidence to suggest that stress has an important role in different chronic health problems – particularly cardiovascular disease, muscular-skeletal conditions and psychological alterations.

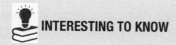

INTERESTING TO KNOW

Work-related Stress and Health: An American perspective

CARDIOVASCULAR DISEASE

Many studies suggest that jobs that are psychologically demanding and which give employees little control over the work results in increased risk of cardiovascular disease.

MUSCULAR-SKELETAL CONDITIONS

On the basis of research done by the National Institute for Occupational Health and Safety (NIOSH) and other organizations, it is believed that work-related stress increases the risk of developing muscular-skeletal conditions affecting the back and lower extremities.

PSYCHOLOGICAL CONDITIONS

Several studies suggest that the differences between the instances of mental health problems (such as depression and exhaustion) for several occupations are partly due to the differences between the levels of work-related stress (The economic and lifestyle differences between occupations can also contribute toward some of these problems).

ACCIDENTS IN THE WORKPLACE

Although more in-depth studies are needed, it is believed that stressful working conditions impede work from being carried out safely and that they cultivate conditions for industrial accidents.

SUICIDE, CANCER, ULCERS AND AFFECTED IMMUNE DISORDERS

Some studies suggest a relationship between stressful working conditions and these health problems. Nevertheless, more research is needed before firm conclusions can be drawn.

- Encyclopedia of Occupational Health and Safety

WORK-RELATED STRESS AND HEALTH: A EUROPEAN PERSPECTIVE

Work-related stress, its causes and its consequences are frequent in the fifteen member states of the European Union. More than half of the 160 million European workers state that they work very fast (56%) and have tight schedules (60%). More than a third of those interviewed have no say in how their work tasks are organized; 40% point out that they perform monotonous tasks.

It is probable that these work-related stress generators have contributed to the present manifestations of disease and illness: 15% of workers complain of headaches, 23% complain of neck and shoulder pains, 23% of fatigue, 28% of "stress" and 33% of backache. They also contribute toward many other diseases, including life-threatening diseases (European Foundation, 2001).

Stress related to prolonged work is a significant determining factor in depressive disorders. These disorders represent the fourth main cause in terms of volume of disease for the entire world. It is anticipated that by the year 2020 this will become the second cause, behind ischemic cardiopathy, but ahead of all the other diseases (World Health Organization, 2001).

In the fifteen member EU countries, the average cost of these mental health problems and other associated problems totals between 3% and 4% of the GDP (ILO, 2000) which totals around €256,000 million per year (1998).

It is quite probable that work-related stress is a significant determining factor of the metabolic syndrome. This syndrome contributes toward heightening ischemic cardiopathic morbidity and type 2 diabetes.

In the EU guideline, examples of ischemic cardiopathy, strokes, cancer, muscular-skeletal and gastrointestinal diseases, anxiety and depressive disorders, accidents and suicides are commented on in detail.

Source: European Agency for Occupational Health and Safety, 2004 http://agency.osha.eu.int/publications/magazine/5/es/index_5.htm

The Great Paradox of the 21st Century: Better Physical Conditions in the Workplace, But Worse Psychological Conditions and More Work-related Stress

INTERESTING TO KNOW

WHAT PEOPLE SAY...

- *I lead a very hectic lifestyle. I work with my husband who is a lawyer, and I am also a housewife. I don't know how to cope with every-day stress, and, in addition, I suffer from kidney problems. I need help.*
- *I'm a sales director and manage a team of 11 sales executives. In our jobs, we have to deal with a lot of pressure as part of meeting our daily targets. I'd like to discover some sort of simple methodology to apply to my work team.*
- *I'm in charge of the Quality Control Department in a clinic and, in some areas, mistakes get made resulting from a lack of concentration, for instance in dispensing medicines, surgical-medical material, etc.*
- *I'm the manager of a Customs Agency, and last week I had a problem with a client. I went home, laid down to rest for a while and started feeling a very strong pain in the chest. I laid back down and when I got up, I felt dizzy again and the pain came back.*

In spite of the enormous tensions and psychological pressures that are experienced every day at work, in most countries we continue to associate occupational health with safety and hygiene. The present fluctuating context of organizations, the uncertainty of the job market and the randomness with which competitive companies have to be run in order to guarantee their existence, nevertheless directly affect the psychological well-being of their workers. The effects of stress on health, for example, are increasingly visible and important. And so, in trying to approach the present-day health problems of workers, there would need to be a thorough revision of the occupational health concept in order to extend it beyond physical well-being to also include psychological well-being.

Work Stress during the Pandemic

So far, we have seen that it is normal for employees to feel somewhat stressed or anxious during normal times. However, during difficult time such as the COVID pandemic, there are several work-related additional conditions that increase stress and anxiety across all workplaces. These conditions include, but are not limited to, the following:

- Adjusting to and managing different workloads, roles and responsibilities.
- Adapting to a different workspace or a new work schedule.

- Adjusting to new communication methods and tools (e.g., technology, virtual meetings) and/or new workplace policies and procedures.
- Balancing work responsibilities with familial or caregiving roles (e.g., difficulties securing childcare, educating children at home).
- Concerns about the future of the workplace and/or employment.
- Financial concerns due to reduced hours, extended time away from work, or unemployment.
- Concerns about securing the appropriate technology and tools to effectively perform work tasks.

In addition to the stressors identified above, essential workers in sectors such as health, have experienced specific conditions in the COVID-19 environment that increased their level of stress:

- Fear or worry about one's own health status, or that of their loved ones, after interacting with the public.
- Increased demands for services, resulting in long, frequent and busy shifts and/or shift work.
- Increased work pressures that require high-level decision-making (e.g., careful precautions while working with high-risk groups).
- Increased exposure to emotionally difficult or disturbing events (e.g., death of a patient).
- Concerns about securing the appropriate infection control supplies (e.g., PPE, hand sanitizer) and/or maintaining infection control practices in the workplace.
- Concerns related to their own family circumstances (e.g., childcare issues, school closures) and a general feeling of lack of control.
- Social avoidance by family members, friends, or the general community as a result of stigma and fear about COVID-19.

So, Now What?

The world of work has changed so quickly in recent decades and the rate of transformation shows no signs of slowing down. What started in the 1970s as a hope for meaningful jobs and good quality of life, continued in the 1980s with a desire for work-life balance and this will most likely will continue in 2020s, with workers caring less about where they work and more about how they work with their leaders and their team.

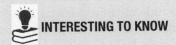 **INTERESTING TO KNOW**

The adoption of new information technologies such as AI in more workplaces is influencing not just employment and wages, but worker well-being such as job satisfaction, stress and health. The finding is based on surveying approximately 10,000 workers in Japan. One

> interesting finding is that the newer information technologies such as AI are adopted, the larger the increase in worker job satisfaction. Conversely, there is a tendency for work-related stress to also increase.
>
> Source: https://voxeu.org/article/impact-ai-and-information-technologies-worker-stress

In a rapidly changing world (some people call it a VUCA world), transparency and information sharing (not off-limits labs and secretive, siloed projects) will unleash the potential of market leaders in this decade. A high percentage of employees say that transparent decision-making boosts their achievement.

Finally, the products and services that will win the hearts of customers will be the ones that are built by diverse teams that harness new technologies and deploy varied perspectives and methodologies.

The impact of AI and new technologies will most likely generate a new type of stressed employees. Our observation, in the Global Future of Work Foundation, is that the future of work will be global, technologically oriented and require new levels of creativity (read the blog: www.globalfutureofwork.com).

Nowadays, there is irrefutable evidence that stress is one of the direct causes of the most common and most lethal psychological and physiological diseases that affect the developed or developing world, including cardiovascular pathology, diabetes, asthma, cancer, hypertension, osteoporosis, anxiety, depression, insomnia, memory loss and premature aging. In the panorama of occupational health and safety, on an international level and especially at a European level, in the last few years we have witnessed the emergence of studies and analyses of what are known as "new risks", and within these, risks considered to be psycho-social in nature.

The Legal Framework

Summarizing the laws on the responsibilities and possibilities on stress is complicated hence it varies from country to country. Here are some facts about some of the legislations in principal countries.

Because stress means different things to different people, in general terms the US legislation employs the reaction to excessive pressure or harassment. In a stress case, workers first have to prove that they have a psychiatric illness ("the injury"). Proving that the psychiatric injury was foreseeable by the employer is a crucial part of any stress at work claim, but it is very difficult to do so. Workers also have to show that it was more likely than not that their employer was to blame as a result of a breach of their duty. This is called the "balance of probabilities".

The European agreement and this guidance are intended to complement existing legislation and guidance available in its members' countries under the European framework directive 89/391, which requires that all employers have a "duty to ensure the safety and health of workers in every aspect related to work" in so far as they entail a risk to health and safety. This duty covers work-related stress and its causes. The EU and the UK approach assumes that failing to undertake measures of alleviating stress not only might end up in courts, but it simply has a straight business logic to cut unnecessary costs and boost production. Each year in the UK there are over half a million instances where work-related stress results in people being absent from work, costing UK employers an estimated £3.7 billion. On average, each stress related absence involves 29 working days lost, a total of 13 million days. This means that work-related stress is the biggest cause of working days lost through occupational injury and ill health.[3]

In sum, there is no one statute specifically and exclusively covering the issue of mental health and stress at work in the EU. The relevant legal duties arise from discrimination provisions, the law of negligence, and express or implied terms in contracts of employment. Much of the law governing mental health and stress has evolved from case law rather than legislation. However, at an EU level, the partners (European employers, trade union and other bodies) agreed to a voluntary framework agreement on work-related stress.

Chapter Summary and Postscript

At present, work organization in most companies is still influenced by the traditional models of management where the focus is on reaching economic goals. Nevertheless, the complexity of the social, economic and cultural changes and the fight to survive is generating a new toxicology in the workplace – occupational stress. Due to globalization of the markets and tough competition, companies are realizing that the road to competitiveness requires innovation and an ability to respond in the same way to clients and employees alike, although the best way to achieve this is not always found.

Although, by and large, workers are better trained, their training becomes rapidly obsolete and they live in constant worry about whether they will be offered continuous training and will they have the competences and abilities to relearn in order to keep current relevant competences. The new generation of workers also has different expectations from work. Work is no longer merely a way of earning a reasonable living. They expect to have jobs that are interesting, that are meaningful, stimulating and valued. Increasingly more is being demanded in terms of taking part in decision-making. An increasing number of positions have to be designed or reshaped in order to satisfy these demands.

Lastly, we are living in an age in which it is increasingly difficult to separate our working lives from our personal lives; families are split up, a greater number of people live on their own and individualism is on the rise. Therefore, the workplace has become, and will continue to become, a place where individuals have the chance to interact, to make use of their abilities, and to contribute to common objectives doing a job that gives meaning to their lives. In general, the workplace will be more and more important as a place where workers' needs in terms of affiliation and self-realization can be satisfied.

If employees are unable to satisfy their job expectations and, in addition, have to put up with an aggressive management style, increases in work-related stress and the proportion of workers who suffer from this new disease will grow. Faced with this

---

3 Source – HSE guide "Tackling work-related stress". Also in: www.hse.gov.uk/stress/assets/docs/eurostress.pdf

new reality in the twenty-first century, we can speak of a new, colourless and odourless occupational psychological phenomenon, which is detrimental to the physical and mental health of workers. The search for a solution to this serious problem is not a luxury – it is a necessity.

ACTION: TEST YOUR QUALITY OF WORK LIFE*

	Aspect	Not at all	Very little	Sometimes	Often	Constantly
1	In general, I can work (including work at home)	0	1	2	3	4
2	My work (including work at home) is fulfilling	0	1	2	3	4
3	I can enjoy my work	0	1	2	3	4
4	I can balance my work with my personal life	0	1	2	3	4
5	After a normal day's work, I sleep well	0	1	2	3	4
6	The things I usually do at work are fun	0	1	2	3	4
7	I am happy with my quality of life at the moment	0	1	2	3	4
8	After a day's work, I'm in a good mood	0	1	2	3	4

Total Score = _____

SCORE AND INTERPRETATION

24–32   You have an excellent level of quality of work life
12–23   You have a good level of quality of work life
0–11   You have a (serious) problem with your quality of work life

* Note: this is a very short quiz. If you wish to undertake a more elaborate assessment, I recommend the one developed by NIOSH and can be downloaded free at: www.cdc.gov/niosh/topics/stress/pdfs/QWL2010.pdf

CHAPTER 2

The Who's Who in the Field of Stress

Principal Models and Concepts of the Pioneers in the Field

Stress: Definitions

Definition of Stress

The word "stress" is familiar to most of us. Almost everyone has felt "stressed out" at times or knows family and friends who complain of stress. Many people believe that we live in a particularly stressful age. But what exactly is stress? What causes it? How do we know it's affecting us? What are its consequences, both for individuals and for organizations? Given the seeming inevitability that everyone will face stress in varying amounts throughout their lives, it is important that we learn about it and learn how to manage it.

Although thousands of articles on stress appear in professional journals and popular magazines, the concept is still poorly understood by the public. Because stress has attracted the attention of researchers in various disciplines from medicine to management, each using its own jargon, models and viewpoints, there are various definitions of stress. We will provide a general definition, but stress has meant different things to different people, and this confusion will likely continue in the future.

Despite Hans Seylé introducing the term over 60 years ago, society has only recently begun to pay attention to the important influence stress has on public health and the economic losses it implies for organizations and companies.[1] Aware of this issue, studies have been carried out and strategies proposed to mitigate what was once considered laziness, reluctance, or lack of will power. From the 1970s onward, the proliferation of articles, seminars and material related to stress management reflects the growing interest in this problem. In fact, stress management has become top

---

1 For example, Selye, H. (1936) A syndrome produced by diverse nocuous agents. London, *Nature*, 138, 32; Selye, H. (1952) *The Story of the Adaptation Syndrome*. Montreal, Quebec, Canada: Acta Inc. Med. Pub.; Selye, H. (1958) *The Stress of Life*. New York: McGraw Hill; Selye, H. (1955). Stress and disease. *Science*, 122, 625; Selye, H.(1975) *Stress Without Distress*, N.Y., New American Library. https://openlibrary.org/books/OL25128749M/Stress_without_distress.

DOI: 10.4324/9781003217626-3

priority in companies, implying the creation of ever more workshops designed to help employees.

A brief definition of stress is *"the non-specific response to all the demands made"*. This simple definition implies the interaction of the organism with the environment, whether it is another organism or the environment in which we move. As such, stress can be defined according to:

(a) the stimulus; (b) the response; or (c) the stimulus–response concept.

(a) **According to the stimulus**: Stress is the force or stimulus which acts on the individual and which leads to a tense response.

(b) **According to the response**: Stress is the physiological or psychological response which an individual manifests in a stressful environment.

(c) **According to the stimulus – response concept**: Stress is the consequence of the interaction of environmental stimuli and the individual's idiosyncratic response.

INTERESTING TO KNOW

A stressor is anything that throws the body out of allostatic balance. Allostasis is a range of measures appropriate for situations (sleep vs. bungee-jumping, heat, cold, illness, injury, hunger, etc.)

Homeostasis is the maintenance of single optimal level between subsystems of a larger system.

We can broaden the brief definition of stress above by adding that any demand, whether physical, psychological, external, or internal, good or bad, produces an identical and stereotypical biological response within the organism (see illustrations in Figure 2.1). This response produces quantifiable hormonal changes which can be measured by laboratory data and changes which these hormonal secretions produce in our organism, and which are responsible for our reactions, whether functional or organic, when faced with stress.

Although stress is generally considered harmful, life without stimulation would be monotonous and boring; people would be missing out on the creative force which can be a source for motivation and the step prior to achieving goals.

Occupational Stress

Over the years, the concept of workplace stress has evolved in its definition and scope to comprise a far more complex phenomenon.

Today, **workplace stress**, also known as **occupational stress**, is seen as *the entire process in which people perceive and interpret their work environment in relation to their capability to cope with it*. Under this definition, stress is present when the environment

FIGURE 2.1 The stress mosaic.
A: Acute physical stressor – The explosion B: Chronic Physical Stressors – Drought
C: Psychological-social stressors – Traffic D: Psychological-Social Stressors – Relationships

poses (or is perceived to pose) a threat to you, either in the form of excessive demands or in the form of insufficient resources to meet your needs.

There are many types of situations that can be physically or psychologically demanding, such as a fast-paced job, getting married or divorced, having children, being fired, or even receiving a promotion or winning the lottery. Any event or situation that puts a demand on a person is called a **stressor.**

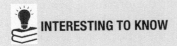 **INTERESTING TO KNOW**

THE INTERNATIONAL LABOR ORGANIZATION (ILO) DEFINES WORK RELATED STRESS

For the ILO stress is the harmful physical and emotional response caused by an imbalance between the perceived demands and the perceived resources and abilities of individuals to cope with those demands. Work-related stress is determined by work organization, work design and labor relations and occurs when the demands of the job do not match or exceed the capabilities, resources, or needs of the worker, or when the knowledge or abilities of an individual worker or group to cope are not matched with the expectations of the organizational culture of an enterprise.

Source: A collective Challenge: WORLD DAY FOR SAFETY AND HEALTH AT WORK 28 APRIL 2016 p.2 (wcms_466547.pdf (ilo.org)

Stress generally occurs when the individual is unable to respond adequately or efficiently to the stimuli of his/her environment or when it is only achieved by affecting the organism's health. Occupational stress is, then, the imbalance between the individual's hopes and the reality of his/her working conditions or, in other words, the perceived difference between the professional demands and the individual's ability to carry them out. This definition coincides with all motivational theories in that motivation will only be present when the worker perceives that there is a chance for his/her needs to be met at work. If this were not the case, there would be no motivated behaviour. Additionally, occupational stress is the individual reaction to a threatening situation related to his/her job, whether or not this is due to having the necessary means at hand to satisfy his/her needs.

An organization's results and efficiency are normally evaluated in terms of economic profit, market position, product or service quality and competitive possibilities in the medium and long-term. Well-being and an individual's illnesses are not generally seen as organizational results, not even partially. In a situation where primordial competitive advantage stems from the quality of the available human resources, offering quality of work life is one way of ensuring greater employee commitment to the organization's mission and objectives.

Stress: Different Models

Over the years, several distinct models of stress were suggested. Like in any field, there were some pioneer works that the reader needs to know about. For example, the work of Walter Canon, Hans Selye and others. Also, in presenting the model we will distinguish the different focuses: medical and physiological focus and/or psychological-cognitive focus. We will also clearly explain the advantages and challenges in understanding models that target acute stress vs chronic stress. We will end up connecting the model to occupational settings.

The first documents on stress tried to discover a common origin: doctors believed that it had a common physical, chemical or bacteriological origin; psychologists felt that the originating factors were exclusively psychological or social responses to stress. Today, it is frequently accepted that stress has its origin in multiple sources, and is of multidisciplinary nature; stress is an interaction between the person and the environment. Chronic stress is highly subjective , some people amplify it (and have higher stress) and others filter it (and have lower stress).

The Physiological Aspects of Stress – Canon and Selye's Pioneering Concepts

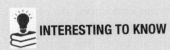 **INTERESTING TO KNOW**

THE PHYSIOLOGICAL CHANGES THAT CHARACTERIZE THE FIGHT OR FLIGHT RESPONSE *ARE:*

- *An increased blood flow to the brain and large muscle groups. This increased blood flow makes us more alert and provides us with extra strength to deal with danger.*
- *Vision, hearing and other sensory processes are sharpened, so that we have heightened awareness of the stressor.*
- *Glucose and other fatty acids are released into the bloodstream to provide extra energy during the stressful event.*
- *The pupils of the eye enlarge, to improve vision in a dark hiding place.*
- *The palms of the hands and feet sweat, giving a better grip for running, climbing and holding onto things.*
- *Digestive processes are reduced; for instance, the mouth gets dry.*

The word "stress", like many other scientific terms, existed prior to its systematic use. It was already in use in the fourteenth century to express toughness, tension, adversity, or affliction. At the end of the eighteenth century, Hocke used the word in a physical context, though its use did not become systematic until the beginning of the nineteenth century. The word *LOAD* was defined as an external force, while *STRESS* referred to the force generated within the body as a result of the action of that external force which tended to distort it. *STRAIN* referred to the deformation or distortion suffered by the object.

The concepts of *STRESS* and *STRAIN* persisted and were incorporated into medical discourse in the nineteenth century as antecedents to a loss of health. The word's current use began with Dr Hans Selye, an endocrinologist at the University of Montreal, whose work marked the first significant contributions to the systematic study of stress. In parallel (or even a bit earlier), Walter Cannon published numerous experiments based on the psychophysiology of emotions.

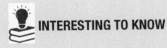 **INTERESTING TO KNOW**

THE WORLD HEALTH ORGANIZATION (WHO) DEFINES WORK RELATED STRESS

Work-related stress is the response people may have when presented with work demands and pressures that are not matched to their knowledge and abilities and which challenge their ability to cope. Stress occurs in a wide range of work circumstances but is often made worse when employees feel they have little support from supervisors and colleagues

> and where they have little control over work or how they can cope with its demands and pressures.
>
> Source: WHO, WORK ORGANIZATION & STRESS, PROTECTING WORKERS' HEALTH SERIES NO 3, 2005 (39608_OMS_Couv (who.int)

Selye considered stress to be a disturbance of the homeostasis when faced with situations such as the lack of oxygen, cold, a decrease in glycaemia, etc. He concluded that this was a non-specific response to practically any harmful stimulus, calling this phenomenon ***General Syndrome of Adaptation*** *(or GSA)* in 1936. A decade later, stress was referred to as an external force acting upon the body or the wear and tear that this action provokes.

Stress according to Cannon – The pioneering work carried out by Walter. B. Cannon is considered essential in analysing the physiological response to a psycho-social stimulus. Using animals as the subject of his study, Cannon was able to elaborate a model of stress which he called the "fight or flight response". According to this model, when an animal tried to obtain the object it desired but was prevented from doing so, the animal suffered stress which was translated into emotional reactions together with sympathetic and hormonal reactions. Due to these experiences, Cannon discovered the secretion of catecholamines (adrenalines and noradrenaline) in situations of stress when the animal prepared itself to either attack or flee.

Currently, there are new contributions to cognitive theory, which describe four fundamental models of primary response to stress: 1) fight, 2) flight, 3) faint, and 4) freeze.

What is the Biological Response to Stress?

The repercussions of stress have an impact on different biological systems, with their associated behavioural correlation. In this behavioural expression, different response models are included – fight, flight, faint and freeze as mentioned – mediated by the locomotive system (up to the pre-medullar system), with the prior activation of the pyramidal system and the striated nucleus. We can observe, for example, how the facial expression is mediated by the skull (trigeminal, facial).

Autonomic expression, characterized by urinary or faucal incontinence, is processed by the vagal parasympathetic system (prior activation of the dorsal nucleus of the vagus vein and the medial hypothalamus). Symptoms, such as sweating, heart palpitations, high blood pressure, mydriasis and/or piloerection, are mediated by the sympathetic system (prior to the activation of the lateral hypothalamus). The hormonal response to adaptation to stress is shown in Figure 2.2.

As such, any external stimulus is perceived by the sensorial or sensitive cortex, and it reaches the thalamic nuclei by various channels where the inputs are filtered and prioritized before activating the amygdaline circuits. Visceral sensations can skip the thalamic filter. The frontal lobe cortex and the cingulate gyrus also play a part in this process and can detain the instinctive responses. It is important to recognize that they are part of the paralimbic system with a hierarchical, preventative and evaluative function.

The tonsils are the "starlet" of the body's responses to adverse situations, while the hippocampus is the permanent prompter. The setting is hemispherical and always

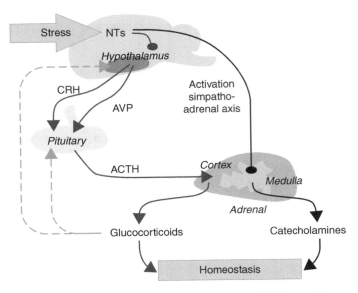

FIGURE 2.2 Stress hormones engaged during stress adaptation reaction.

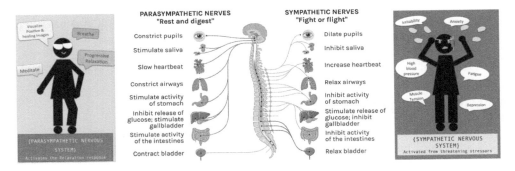

FIGURE 2.3 The sympathetic and parasympathetic responses to stress.

Stress according to the "father" of the phenomenon: Hans Selye

varies depending on the self-psychic and all psychic context for the individual at that precise moment. A synopsis of the responses along the sympathetic and parasympathetic systems is provided in Figure 2.3.

Hans Selye, the great pioneer in the investigation of the physiology of stress, began his work in 1930. He studied the reaction of laboratory rats to physical stressors, such as heat, cold and physical exercise, as well as their reaction to chemical agents, such as injected hormones and steroids.

Seyle observed that, no matter what stressor he used, the animal's reaction was always the same, that is, non-specific. This led him to define stress as: the non-specific response to all stimuli.[4] Supported by his research, he formulated the theory of non-specific response, which he defined as the "General Syndrome of Adaptation". This syndrome refers to the different changes produced within the organism as a result of the more or less constant presence of a stressor. Given that it is supposed that the

PHOTO 2.1 Hans Selye.[a]

[a] *Source:* Division de la gestion de documents et des archives (DGDA) de l'Université de Montréal, image uploaded to Wikimedia Commons as part of the Archives/UdeM project. Image used under Creative Commons licence: Attribution-ShareAlike 4.0 International (CC BY-SA 4.0).

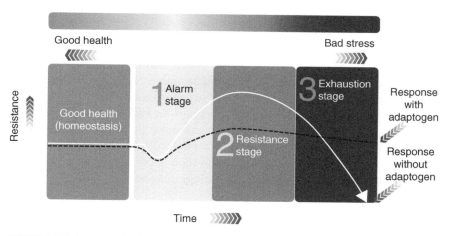

FIGURE 2.4 Selye stages in the general adaptation syndrome.

organism's response is the same when faced with any stressor, all organisms when faced with stress will activate the same generalized and non-specific response. The activation produced in GSA consists of three phases (see also Figure 2.4):

1. Alarm is the first phase, recalling Cannon's observations, and it occurs immediately upon recognition of the threat or of the stressful situation. It is characterized by the release of corticosteroids to provoke the organism into facing and overcoming the situation. The exceptional resources mobilized are aimed at quickly overcoming the stressful situation.

2. If that does not occur, the second phase is triggered. This is the phase of resistance or defence in which activation, although less than in the previous phase, is still high and whose goal is to reduce the stressful situation. This lessened hyper-activation can now be maintained over a longer period of time and, as a result, it provides greater possibilities of overcoming the stressful situation. If this effort succeeds in overcoming the stressful situation, it marks the end of GSA.

3. Should this not occur; the previous moderate period of hyper-activation can't go on indefinitely given that the organism's reserves are being spent more quickly than the rate at which they are being produced. As such, if the stressful situation is not resolved, these resources will disappear and lead to the third phase, exhaustion, in which the organism uses up all its resources and progressively (or sometimes suddenly) loses its ability to be activated (including even normal activation). If, despite all else, the organism tries to stay activated as long as possible, the result will be complete exhaustion with all its negative consequences for the organism, including death. The intensity of the physiological responses demanded by the organism together with the latter's physical condition determine how quickly exhaustion will occur.

Seyle's GSA model encompasses a complete series of complex physiological reactions which all show common characteristics, at least in the experimental situations used by the researcher. However, reality is much more complex when Seyle's model is applied to humans given the great individual differences in the perception and standardization of alarming situations.

According to Seyle, ACTH is the hormone which always increases in stressed individuals. It acts on the suprarenal cortex and produces cortisol (a neuroendocrine response). The hypothalamus, when faced with a stressor stimulus, stimulates the hypophysis, thereby transmitting the stimulus to nerve endings. The central nervous system then projects it onto the rest of the organism and codifies the external and internal stress. This process is known as *heterostasis*. In heterostasis, a specific number of substances circulate within the blood, for example, glucose, which contributes to increasing the consequences of stress and throwing the entire organism into a state of alert, producing a physiological change which then becomes physio pathological.

The organism responds along three physiological axes:

1. *Neural:* The sympathetic and parasympathetic nervous systems are immediately activated. These control respiration, heart rate, muscular tension [toxicity] and movements.

2. *Neuroendocrine:* This is activated slowly and increases the activity of the spine and the suprarenal glands which release adrenaline, noradrenaline and catecholamines. This is a very important step in that it prepares the organism to respond to any external threat by either fighting or running away.

3. *Endocrine:* This is when activity is at its peak, maintained longer and is more intense. When the problem cannot be overcome, this axis controls the release of glucocorticoids [glucose and corticoids], mineral corticoids [especially magnesium], thymus growth hormones [thymus gland and hypophysis], thyroids, vasopresina [increasing pressure] and cortisol [the hormone which produces stress].

If stress is produced due to an excess of activity or overload of the affected organs, it is normal to see this condition in the affected organs. When you learn to control a situation, which produces stress, these symptoms disappear.

Extrapolating from his animal findings to human, Selye describes the GSA model in terms of three distinct response pattern stages:

- Stage 1 – Alarm Reaction (Anxiety or fear; sorrow or depression; shock or confusion).
- Stage 2 – Resistance (aggression, regression, repression, withdrawal or fixation).
- Stage 3 – Exhaustion. (Physiological, psychological or interpersonal).

He also labelled three types of stress (all associated with different hormonal reactions) in humans: EUSTRESS, NEUSTRESS and DISTRESS. **Eustress** according to Selye is the Positive Stress – it motivates, excites and energizes; Distress, by contrast is the Negative Stress – it crushes, oppresses and carries events beyond rational limits.

 INTERESTING TO KNOW

HOW THE "GURU" OF STRESS, HANS SELYE, DIED FROM A LACK OF SELF-ESTEEM AND LOTS OF STRESS IN HIS LIFE: MY PERSONAL ACCOUNT

In 1977, I was a young scholar who had just completed my doctoral studies at the University of Minnesota in the United States. After having some shocking personal experience at the Mayo Clinic in Minnesota, I decided to dedicate my intellectual curiosity and energy over the next couple of years to better understanding stress in work settings. I was fortunate to encounter Prof. Paul Rohan who suggested that I join the team of interdisciplinary researchers affiliated with the Hans Selye International Institute of Stress at the University of Montreal. Paul was a personal friend of Hans Selye (they knew each other from the old continent – Vienna and Czechoslovakia). Paul introduced me to Hans Selye and the rest is history.

Obviously, for me, it was a great honor and an opportunity to pursue my interest in stress research, working with the master himself. Hans Selye was commonly known as the "father of stress". I could not have known then that a few years later the overall balance of working with Selye would not be as exciting and as productive as I had imagined. Our initial contacts went very well and within a very short time I had gained Selye's confidence and developed a very close personal relationship with him. During our many conversations, Hans shared with me his professional dreams and his personal life experiences. Our joint work continued until his death in 1981. After Selye's death, I continued my research on stress and health in Canada and also in Spain

After my initial excitement and the commencement of my work with Selye in 1977, I began to have some doubts about the man, especially in terms of his personality and of his own capacity to deal with stress. To quote from an old saying, "he didn't practice what he preached". What puzzled me the most was the fact that he was a very lonely man, and during his many years of leadership in stress research, he was unable (or perhaps incapable) of establishing a core team of scholars that would stay and continue working with him. On the contrary, I saw eminent names and young scholars coming and going; team rotation was very high and his style of supervision was so annoying that even those who cared and wanted to work with him ended up leaving or facing premature death (i.e., the case of Dr. Jean Taché). Adding salt to the wound, two of his former students and disciples ended up receiving merits and awards (including the Nobel Prize), while he was deeply hurt and disappointed for never receiving this prize (despite having been nominated on two occasions). I noticed that during our relationship his self-esteem was at its lowest, and he constantly needed and looked for gratification and recognition. These were by no means easy to come by.

The answer to the above puzzle was evident after getting to know the man. Hans Selye had a very egocentric and demanding personality (in the work context) and was a very frightened and submissive person in the non-work context. Moreover, he did not tolerate any idea or theory that did not comply perfectly with his early research on the physiological response to stress. I, for one, tried hard to convince him that the stress mechanisms for human's worked differently than that for the cats and mice in his laboratory. I also failed to convince him that in order to understand the multidisciplinary nature of stress, an interdisciplinary team was needed. I noticed that when I mentioned these ideas he was upset and his responses at times were aggressive and antagonistic. There was no doubt in my mind because colleagues and associates decided to desert him and develop their own line of research. I ended up doing the same.

The first 2 years (1977–1979), I subjected myself to Selye's whims by thinking that it was the price that a young scholar had to pay in order to gain recognition and an opportunity to learn from the great master.

During these years we had numerous mini incidents that left a bitter taste in my mouth. Selye was moody, and at times his behavior at work reflected his fear of his tyrannical latest wife. Here is a typical example. One day I received a phone call from Hans and a request to come and see him urgently. My office, located about 200 meters from his office was up the hill. I stopped what I was doing and ran to his office, just to arrive there breathless, in order to find out that the great master was in trouble with his wife because he could not return home that afternoon without taking her new stamps for her stamp collection. While for him this signified a "real crisis", for me it meant another stupid chore that I had to put up with.

These types of "False Alarm" incidents became more common as our relationship grew more personal. I felt pity for the old man and noticed how his self-esteem was getting lower and lower. Obviously, until you get to know a person very well, you will not always notice this kind of behavior.

I have to admit that, apart from these incidents, my experiences of working with Selye were not always negative. He gave me an opportunity by inviting me to participate in the 2nd International Conference on the Management of Stress that our Institute organized in Monte Carlo, Monaco in 1979. This conference gave me a chance to share my initial thoughts about work-related stress with the world's foremost experts on stress, including several Nobel Prize winners. Selye also asked for my editorial assistance in producing a new Journal called "STRESS". For someone with limited, or no publications, revising manuscripts for this Journal and publishing 2 papers (with Paul Rohan) was very instrumental in my career and elevated my own self-esteem. Like many other "Selye" projects, the Journal died with him; he did not prepare a successor, nor did he create a structure to continue this important work. It was after the Monaco Conference and following two more incidents of "abuse of my time" that I realized that I could not count on Selye to help me develop a line of research dedicated to people in work settings, that I had to stop working with him and establish a parallel research centre at the University of Montreal. This was also the first time that I managed to receive substantial research grants from the Quebec and Canadian governments to study occupational stress.

> *Getting back to Selye, in 1979 we had a book project in preparation. I was supposed to provide the leadership for the book and he was supposed to guide and supervise. Once it was completed and there was no feedback from Selye, I invited another physician, Andre Arsenault, to replace Selye. My relationship with Andre Arsenault was very productive and we have jointly managed the research center for the study of occupational stress and health for over 15 years. This collaboration also led to publications of dozens of papers in scholarly journals (in medicine, psychology, and management), which made our work known internationally. Shortly before the book was published, Selye found out about it, called me to his office and insisted that he write the preface. I accepted his offer graciously. It represented a truce in our relationship. The book was titled: "Stress, Health and Performance at Work" (in French), and it was published in 1980 by the University of Montreal; it became a best-seller in French-speaking Canada. Shortly thereafter, Selye asked me to give him a hand in organizing the 3rd International Conference on the Management of Stress to be held in Australia in 1981 and I agreed. Unfortunately, this conference was never held as Selye died just before it started. The great Hans Selye died a very lonely man, agonizing for not having received the Nobel Prize, subject to the tyranny of his last wife and completely isolated from other people and scholars who could not work with a man who was not a team player. It is my conclusion that Selye's self-esteem at the end of his life was extremely low. The last straw which perhaps triggered the "master of stress" death was the beginning of an inquiry by the Canadian Tax authorities into alleged tax improprieties, namely, the failure to report income received for various conferences and speeches he gave around the globe.*
>
> ***Note:*** *I admit that the text written above is a biased and subjective account, representing the way I saw and interpreted the last years of Hans Selye's life. My memories are based on the period that I worked with him at the University of Montreal. I am still in debt to him, and this book is dedicated amongst others to his memory.*
>
> Simon L. Dolan

The Organism's Responses: The Biological Consequences of Stress

The organism's response will vary depending on whether or not it is in an initial phase of tension, in which there is a general activation and in which the alterations produced are easily remissible if the cause is removed or if it improves, or if it is in a phase of chronic tension or prolonged stress in which the symptoms become permanent, leading to illness. Table 2.1 has various examples of the alterations produced.

Stress, Emotions and Diseases

During the past 50 years, many scholars in psychology, management and medicine studied the effect of emotions on human diseases. The cross interest of psychology and medicine gave rise to the filed known as psychosomatic medicine. A field called health psychology (or behavioural medicine) was also developed. In these emerging disciplines the attempt is made to explore, understand and explain the relationships between emotional stress and human diseases.

TABLE 2.1 Examples of some biological consequences of stress

Affected	Initial Phases of strain	Stress Consequence(s)
Brain	Clear and rapid idea	Headaches, migraines, nervous tics, Insomnia
Mood	Mental concentration	Anxiety, loss of sense of humour
Saliva	Reduced	Dry mouth
Muscles	Major capacity	Muscle tension and muscle tic
Lounges	Major capacity	Hyperventilation or Asthma attack
Stomach	Higher level of acids	Indigestion, throwing up
Intestines	Spasms, peristalsis	Diarrhea, pain, colitis
Sexual	Loss of libido	Impotency, frigidity
Skin	Less humid (more dry)	Rushes, dermatitis, outbreaks
Energy	Increase in consumption of oxygen	Getting fast into state of fatigue
Heart	Overuse of cardiovascular organs	Hypertension, pericardial pain

One of the dominant schools of thought connects emotions and stress to human diseases via the immune system. Researchers view the immune system as an autonomic mechanism: a pathological agent in the form of a virus or bacteria that arrives on the scene can trigger the defence mechanism of the immune system. We normally react to such threat via the armory of antibodies and other immunological devices; the immune system recognizes intruders and interacts with various organs, especially hormone systems and the nervous system. Because of the interaction of the two systems, other agents become involved, such as the endocrine system as we had mentioned previously. When the immune system is being "abused", in the case of chronic stress, there is enough research evidence to suggest that its function decreases and thus the susceptibility to infectious disease, cancer and autoimmune disorders increases. In general, Figure 2.5 shows the links and the proposed interactions between, stressors, emotions, the body defence mechanisms and diseases.

But how does the immune system work? The phagocytes, a type of the white blood cells in our system, are mobilized to destroy invading germs. They rely in the process on other white blood cells, namely the lymphocytes, to instruct them to attack the invader. The B lymphocytes, which are called the B cells because they form in the bone marrow, produce proteins called antibodies. The late latch onto antigens (the foreign molecules) such as virus or bacteria and summon phagocytes and circulating proteins to destroy the invaders. T lymphocytes (T cells) act as a killer cell. In addition, special T lymphocytes secrete cytokines, cell signaling proteins such as the interleukins and lymphokines, which regulate the activity of the B lymphocytes and phagocytes. These immune system cells form in the thymus gland, bone marrow, spleen, and lymph nodes, and are released into the blood stream.[2]

---

2 Source. Rozenzweig M.R., Breedlove A.M., and Watson N.V. (2004) *Biological Psychology*. Fourth Edition. Sinauer Publishers, p. 483.

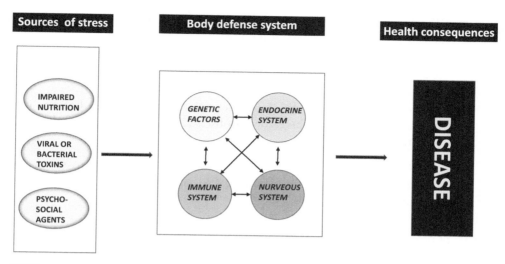

FIGURE 2.5 Stress and the etiology of disease.

Stress as a Psychological and Behavioural Consequence

The Psychoanalytical Approach: The Menninger's Framework

Karl Augustus Menninger was an American psychiatrist and a member of the famous Menninger family of psychiatrists who founded the Menninger Foundation and the Menninger Clinic in Topeka, Kansas.

Karl Menninger does not believe that health and illness are two separate concepts, but rather, that they are psychological phenomena which make up a continuum based on an intermediate state. On either end of the continuum is the dismemberment of the person, the illness in itself. From this perspective, the ego balances the tensions posed by the superego and external reality. In this role the ego is trying to establish a tolerable level of tension, compatible with its growth, development, and expression of its creativity.[3]

An extension of the psychoanalysis has been used by Kets de vries and colleagues in applying principles of psychodynamics to explain the connections between toxic leaders, culture and stress. They have identified a number of constellations of neurotic leaders' behaviour contributing to elevated stress amongst followers:[4]

- *The dramatic leader* – who seeks attention and craves excitement and often touched by a sense of entitlement and tends toward extremes.
- *The suspicious leader* – who is extremely vigilant, constantly on the watch for possible attacks and personal threats and always prepares for a counterattack. This leader is hypersensitive and distrustful.

---

[3] Menninger, K. (1954) Psychological aspects of the organism under stress, 1st and 2nd parts, *Journal of the American Psychoanalytic Association*, pp. 67–106 and pp. 280–310.

[4] See: Kets de vries M., Guillen Ramo L., and Korotov K. (2009) *Organizational Culture, Leadership, Change and Stress*, INSEAD working paper series (coverpage_2009-10 (insead.edu).

- *The detached leader* – who is withdrawn and uninvolved. This leader reduces interaction with other members of the firm.
- *The depressive leader* – who often lacks self-confidence and is plagued with serious self-esteem issues These leaders lacks energy and often tolerates mediocracy and scare away dynamic and active followers.
- *The compulsive leader* – who dominates the firm from top to bottom, insists on conformity and rules. The leader is obsessed with perfectionism, detail, routine and rituals.

Kets de Vries and Miler conclude that neurotic leadership leads to toxic organizational culture as they engage in patterns of social defences and divert energies away from attaining the firms' goals.[5]

The Transactional Model of Stress

Lazarus' Psycho-cognitive Approach[6]

Richard S. Lazarus and his colleagues established a clear distinction between stress, the force applied on the organism, and tension, the result of that stress, which in physics corresponds to a deformation. In other words, there is a correlative internal tension to stress, the external force, which tends to disrupt the established balance. Lazarus uses this notion of stress to explain human behaviour. He emphasizes the interaction between the individual and his/her environment as a generator of symptoms. Lazarus insists on the importance of man's cognitive activity and is interested most of all in the manifestations which become behaviours. This cognitive approach relates the thought process and the mechanics behind the emission of a judgement in the subjective interpretation, which the individual makes of his/her environment. As such, this subjective interpretation becomes more important and significant than the objective reality of the environment. The individual's reaction will therefore be produced by the imbalances at the core of the cognitive structure, which drive the individual to act in order to eliminate those incoherencies and restore the balance.

In this vision of stress there exists an implicit notion of threat, or more specifically, a subjective perception of threat. As a result, the individual differences in the interpretation of what constitutes a threat lead invariably to the presence of personality factors, which determine a particular vulnerability in each situation. Lazarus concludes that individual differences are not the only determinants of stress, but that cultural characteristics, personal value systems and cognitive processes also have a determinant role on behaviour.

To summarize stress, according to Lazarus and his colleagues, is a complex psycho-biological process with three main components:

1. The initial situation in which an event takes place that is potentially prejudicial or dangerous (a stressful or stressor event).

---

5 Kets de vries M., and Miller D. (1984) *The Neurotic Organization*. Jossey Bass S.F.
6 Lazarus R.S, Folkman S. (1984) *Stress, appraisal, and coping*. Springer, New York; see also: Monat A., and Lazarus R.S. (eds.) (1991) *Stress and Coping: An Anthology*. N.Y. Columbia university Press.

2. The event is "interpreted" as dangerous, prejudicial or threatening. The subject perceives and assesses it as such, independently of its objective characteristics.
3. The organism is activated in response to the threat.

There are two mental (and highly interrelated) processes which we use to make this appraisal:

1. **Primary Appraisal**: Individuals judge the meaning of a specific transaction with respect to their well-being – if it is "irrelevant", "benign – positive" or "stressful".
2. **Secondary Appraisal**: Individuals assess their resources and options (physical, social, psychological, and material) in order to confront the stressor.

The Cognitive and Multidisciplinary Perspective of Stress

The Dolan and Arsenault's Model

Photos provided by the authors and used with their permission.

Simon L. Dolan worked with Hans Selye in his laboratory at the University of Montreal from 1979 to 1982. Although Selye focused his work on tests with animals, Dolan was interested in developing a theoretical framework to apply to humans and, especially, within the workplace. In order to carry out this research, a multidisciplinary team was developed. From the 1980s onward, Dolan, a work psychologist, and Arsenault, a physician and statistician, have proposed a synthetic and more holistic model which allows for a diagnosis to be made which will serve to diminish the frequency of the irreversible, long-term consequences of stress. This model sets out to answer four questions:[7]

1. What are the sources of stress in the workplace?
2. Why are workers not affected the same way by stress?

---

[7] For example, see Dolan S.L., and Arsenault A. (1979) The Organizational and Individual Consequences of Stress at Work: A New Frontier to Human Resource Administration, in Veysey V.V., Hall G.A. Jr. (eds.), *The New World of Managing Human Resources*. Pasadina, California Institute of Technology. 4.01–4.22; Dolan S.L., and Arsenault A. (1980) Stress, santé et rendement au travail. Montréal. ÉRI, monographie n° 5, Université de Montréal; Rohan P., and Dolan S.L. (1980), The Management of Occupational Stress, *Stress*, 1(2), 13–18; Dolan S.L., and Arsenault A (1981) Occupational Stress. *Quality of Working Life*, Part I: 4 (1), 6–9; Part II: 4(2), 10–15. The model was validated by a dozen of empirical studies published at later consecutive years.

3. What are the individual consequences of stress from a physical and psychological point of view?
4. What are the consequences for the organization in terms of workers' performance (productivity, absenteeism, frequency of work-related accidents, etc.)?

The authors of this model maintain that the discordance between the individual and his/her work environment is what causes problems of adaptation. From the degree of concordance, the presence or absence of a variety of signs and symptoms of tension which make up the stress indicators can be observed.

The occupational/job stress model presented in Figure 2.6 identifies three principal components involved in the causes of stress at work:

- *Perception of job demands.* Employees' perception of a situation can influence how (and whether) they will experience stress. For example, a manager's request that two subordinates stay an extra hour to finish important work can be perceived as stressful by one employee and have no effect on the other. Stress can originate from a single stressor or from a combination of environmental job demands.
- *Individual differences.* There are a number of individual differences that play an important role in the ways in which employees experience and respond to stress. Individual differences in needs, values, attitudes, abilities, and, of course, personality traits are important in that they may increase or reduce the perception of the harmfulness of work demands. Thus, to understand whether job incumbents will be stressed, it is critical to understand their perception about their work and their organization; what one person may consider to be a major source of stress, another may hardly notice.
- *Social support.* Compensatory mechanisms (commonly referred to as "buffers" or "moderators") that may be present or absent during stressful periods are important mediators of responses to stress. One such buffer is social support. The support of others in one's social environment includes co-workers, superiors, family and friends. The availability of such support increases confidence and strengthens the ability to cope.

The essence of the model in Figure 2.6 has been validated in different organizations, and for a variety of occupations – including hospital employees, teachers, police officers, prosecutors, executives, middle-level managers, first line supervisors, programmers and secretaries, by researchers at the University of Montreal.[8] Notice that the consequences of job stress are labelled **strain** and are grouped along two categories: those that harm the individual's health and those that are detrimental to the health of the organization.

---

8 See, for example, Dolan, S.L. (1987) Job stress among college administrators: An empirical study. *The International Journal of Management,* 4 (4), 553–560; van Ameringen, M.R., Arsenault, A., & Dolan, S.L. (1988) Intrinsic job stress as predictor of diastolic blood pressure among female hospital workers. *Journal of Occupational Medicine,* 30(2), 93–97; Dolan, S.L., and Tziner, A. (1988) Implementing computer-based automation in the office: A comparative study of experienced stress. *Journal of Organizational Behavior,* 19, 183–187; Dolan, S.L. (1990) Case illustration of proneness to stress among hospital workers. In L.E. Miller & J. Seltzer (Eds.), *Innovations in research and teaching,* Proceedings of the 27th annual meeting of the Eastern Academy of Management. Philadelphia, EAM, 308–311; Dolan, S.L. (1995). Individual, organizational and social determinants of managerial burnout: Theoretical and empirical update. In P. Perrewe (Ed.), *Occupational stress: A handbook,* New York, Taylor & Francis, 223–238.

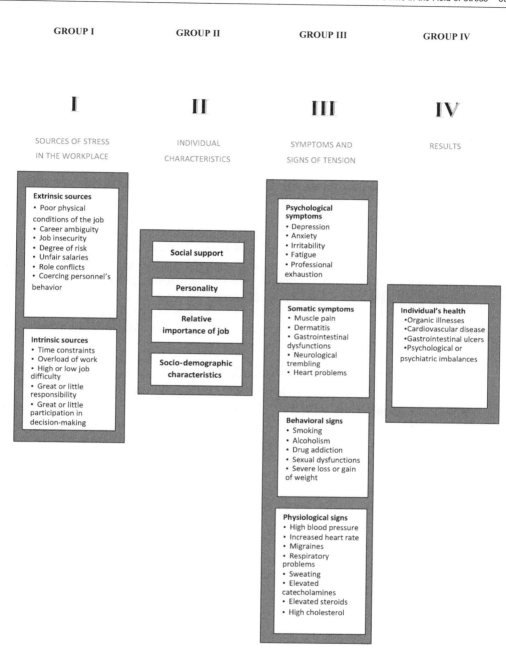

FIGURE 2.6 The Cognitive and conditional model of occupational stress of Dolan & Arsenault.

The Five Generic Models of Workplace Stress

Job stress is heavily associated with workplace environment. Because workplace stress is the result of many complex interactions between an individual and a large systematically operating organization, there are numerous theories propagated to explain the relation between both.

The models that explain workplace stress, can be classified into five generic categories:

- The Person Environment Fit Model
- The Job Characteristics model
- The Jobs-Demand-control and Resources Model
- The Effort-Reward Imbalance Model
- The Diathesis-Stress Model

The Person Environment Fit Model – According to this model, a person starts to feel stress in a job where his aptitude, skills, abilities and resources are not in-line with the necessities of their job. The job profile he/she is operating in should be in accordance to his/her needs, knowledge and skills-sets.

If these needs are not addressed, then it makes these employees "misfits" in that domain, which results in lagging behind in performances and not meeting management expectations. These employees end up with lower productivity, face isolation and resort to denial, as a defence mechanism. The latter are early signs of stress.

Note that research has gone beyond person-job fit, to include other types, levels and scopes of fits (or actually misfits). Researchers have studied consequences of the following:

- *Person-Organization misfit* (This implied implies a strong misfit with the culture and shared core values between the person and the organization).
- *Person-group/team misfit* – this is a relatively new topic with regard to person–environment fit. Since person–group fit is so new, limited research has been conducted to demonstrate how the psychological compatibility between coworkers influences individual outcomes in group situations. However, person–group fit is most strongly related to group-oriented outcomes like co-worker satisfaction and feelings of cohesion. When these are absent, stress starts to show.
- *Person–person misfit* – is conceptualized as the fit between an individual's culture preferences and those preferences of others. It corresponds to the similarity-attraction hypothesis which states people are drawn to similar others based on their values, attitudes and opinions. The most studied types are mentors and protégés, supervisors and subordinates, or even applicants and recruiters. Research has shown that person–supervisor fit is most strongly related to supervisor-oriented outcomes like supervisor satisfaction. And vice versa – when it results in misfit, symptoms of strain are showing.

The Job Characteristics model – This model proposes that for an employee to be successful in any job he/she needs to have some degree of autonomy and he/she should be able to give feedback which is heard. Such conditions result in job enrichment and employee loyalty. The absence of these factors can cause work disassociation and drops in productivity. This model also specifies that numerous talented professionals lose their attitude towards the same work that they had once been very interested in and were good at. These, again, are early signs of stress.

The Jobs-Demand-Control and Resources Model – This model is often called JDR and often associated with the name of its developer, Dr Karasek. His model

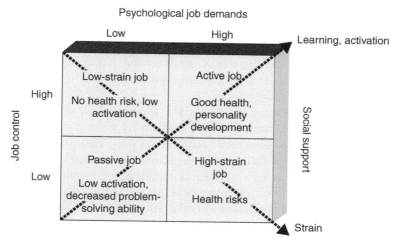

FIGURE 2.7 The Karasek Job Demands Model.

posits that workplace stress can be associated with the difference of job demands and resources. Experienced at managerial levels, it is caused when a bully management expects workers to deliver high results with low resources and limited control. In other words, there is a severely skewed ration between job demands and job resources. Even good employees cannot deal with these requirements of being a constant "superman" or "superwomen" and they end up stressed.

The Karasek JDR model goes even further and suggests that high demands plus low control contribute to strain, particularly when combined with home stress and the absence of social support.[9]

The Karasek's job demands–control model is one of the most widely studied models of occupational stress (see Figure 2.7). The key idea behind the job demands-control model is that control buffers the impact of job demands on strain and can help enhance employees' job satisfaction with the opportunity to engage in challenging tasks and learn new skills.

The Demand/Control/support model has stimulated much research during recent years. The model has helped to document more specifically the importance of social and psychological factors in the structure of current occupations as a risk factor for industrial society's most burdensome diseases and social conditions. Empirically, the model has been successful: a clear relationship between adverse job conditions (particularly low decision latitude) and coronary heart disease has been established.

The Effort-Reward Imbalance Model – is similar to the Karasek JDR but emphasizes that high effort/low reward conditions are associated with a variety of adverse health outcomes prominent among which are cardiovascular disease and mental health problems such as anxiety and depression. This model, as the name suggests, focuses on the relation between efforts and rewards. When employees put in hard work, they expect management to reward their efforts. In the absence of

---

[9] See for example: Karasek, R.A., Jr. (1979) Job demands, job decision latitude and mental strain: Implications for job redesign. *Administrative Science Quarterly*, 24, 285–308; Karasek, R.A., and Theorell T. (1990). *Healthy Work* . New York, Basic Books.

any such reward program, the employees get demotivated and underperform. It is not enough in today's world to expect good output from employees as "part of the job". Companies that think they are entitled to get good output from employees just because they pay them, need to realize that it is not paying, but compensating them for their time (i.e. the employees could have done something way more productive with the time they spend in the company).

In other words, the effort-reward imbalance is a theoretical model to identify a stressful psychosocial work environment which explains its adverse effects on stress-related health risks. It posits that failed reciprocity between high efforts spent at work and low rewards received in turn elicits strong negative emotions and stress reactions with adverse long-term effects on health. Rewards include salary, promotion prospects, job security and esteem, recognition. A stream of research explains the various sociological and social psychological basis of the model, its roots in human stress theory, and its consequences. Based on an extensive body of international research, it shows the elevated risks of depression, ischemic heart disease and other health outcomes among people exposed to this chronic stressor at work.[10]

The Diathesis-Stress Model – The diathesis–stress model, also known as the vulnerability–stress model, is a psychological theory that attempts to explain a disorder, or its trajectory, as the result of an interaction between a predisposition vulnerability, the diathesis and a stress caused by life experiences. The term diathesis derives from the Greek term (διάθεσις) for a predisposition, or sensibility.

The diathesis–stress model is used in many fields of psychology, specifically for studying the development of psychopathology. It is useful for the purposes of understanding the interplay of nature and nurture in the susceptibility to psychological disorders throughout the lifespan. Diathesis–stress models can also assist in determining who will develop a disorder and who will not. For example, in the context of depression, the diathesis–stress model can help explain why Person A may become depressed while Person B does not, even when exposed to the same stressors. More recently, the diathesis–stress model has been used to explain why some individuals are more at risk for developing a disorder than others.

A diathesis can take the form of genetic, psychological, biological, or situational factors. A large range of differences exists among individuals' vulnerabilities to the development of a disorder. This model makes a distinction between stressful job conditions and individual strains. Strains can be mental, physical, or emotional and most of the times, these strains change from person to person. A schematic presentation of the diathesis-stress model is presented in Figure 2.8

By contrast, protective factors, such as positive social networks or high self-esteem, can counteract the effects of stressors and prevent or curb the effects of disorder. Many psychological disorders have a window of vulnerability, during which time an individual is more likely to develop disorder than others. Diathesis–stress models are often conceptualized as multi-causal developmental models, which propose that

---

10 See for example: Bakker, A.B., Killmer, C.H., Siegrist, J., and Schaufeli, W.B. (2008) Effort–reward imbalance and burnout among nurses, *Journal of Advanced Nursing*, 31(4); Tsutsumi, A., Kayaba, K., Nagami, M., Miki, A., Kawano, Y., Ohya, Y., Odagiri, Y., and Shimomitsu T. (2003) The Effort-reward Imbalance Model: Experience in Japanese Working Population, *Journal of Occupational Health*, 44(6).

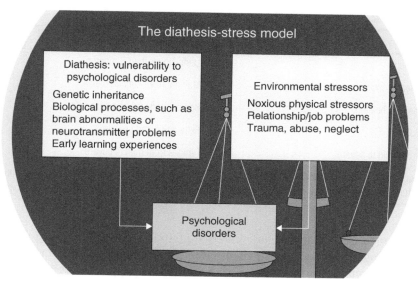

FIGURE 2.8 The diathesis–stress concept.

multiple risk factors over the course of development interact with stressors and protective factors contributing to normal development or psychopathology.[11]

The Principal Difference between Acute Stress and Chronic Stress Models

There are two main types of stress; acute stress and chronic stress, which are both a part of the body's natural stress response (see Table 2.2). When someone feels under threat, their body releases stress hormones. Both types of stress can lead to sleepless nights, lack of clarity, irritability and excessive worry. However, there are a couple of key differences between the two though:

- Acute stress is short-term stress whereas chronic stress is more long-term.
- Acute stress tends to be in response to a recognized threat, while chronic stress can linger occurring more days than not for at least six months. It can either by caused by multiple triggers or sometimes seem out of nowhere, as if nothing is triggering it.
- Acute stress results from specific events or situations that involve novelty, unpredictability, a threat to the ego, and leave us with a poor sense of control; Chronic stress results from repeated exposure to situations that lead to the release of stress hormones.

---

11 Source: Wikipedia. https://en.m.wikipedia.org/wiki/Diathesis%E2%80%93stress_model#:~:text=The%20diathesis%E2%80%93stress%20model,%20also%20known%20as%20the%20vulnerability%E2%80%93stress,from%20the%20Greek%20term%20(%CE%B4%CE%B9%CE%AC%CE%B8%CE%B5%CF%83%CE%B9%CF%82)%20for%20a

TABLE 2.2 Characteristics of acute vs chronic stress

ACUTE	CHRONIC
Short duration	Lasts longer than 3 months
Well-defined cause	May not have defined cause
Decreases with healing	Begins gradually and persists
Is reversible	Exhausting and useless
Ranges from mild to severe	Ranges from mild to severe
May be accompanied by restlessness and anxiety, decrease functionality bur recuperates after treatment	May be accompanied by depression, emotional fatigue, decreased functionality and very slow to recuperate

Examples of acute stressors include external lifestyle factors like having a job interview or getting a speeding ticket, which cause a temporary but natural rush in adrenalin. Often chronic stress isn't caused by anything that happens to you but stimulated by internal stressors like negative thoughts that pop into your head. Common internal stressors include fear of failure, lack of control and personal pressures put on yourself (i.e. career acceleration).

One thing is common to both acute and chronic stress: They both cause "wear and tear" to the body and/or the mind (soul). Yet, sometimes, experiencing and overcoming situations involving acute stress, is the path to develop resiliency.
Here are two simplified generalizations:

- Our body is reasonably good at handling acute episodes of stress. We are designed to recover quickly from short-term stress (disease, death in the family, other events). Some experts actually think that the quicker you recover or bounce back from an acute episode of stress, the more resilient you become. While experiencing acute stress, your blood pressure, heart rate, breathing rate and levels of muscle tension may skyrocket for a short while, but for most people, these markers of stress quickly revert back to their normal (pre-stressful event) levels.

- By contrast, the body ISN'T so good at handling chronic stress. Over time, chronic stress gradually increases our resting heart rate, blood pressure, breathing rate and levels of muscle tension so the body has to work even harder when it's at rest to keep us functioning normally. In other words, chronic stress creates a new normal inside your body. Dolan and Arsenault, in their studies refer to it as an escalating zero point. And this new normal can eventually lead to a host of health problems including heart disease, diabetes, chronic pain, high blood pressure and depression.

Determining Factors of Occupational Stress

During the last decade there has been increased interest in knowing about and better understanding the conditions which can make the workplace more humane and less harmful for people. It is virtually impossible, however, to provide a complete list of stressors and their consequences especially if we bear in mind that the stressor condition depends on the assessment each individual makes of a specific condition. Nevertheless, we can establish and identify a set of stressors at different levels: organizational stressors and extra-organizational stressors.

Individual and Extra-organizational Stressors Many authors have underscored the importance of individual factors, such as personal values, needs, skills, as well as personality and personal aspirations in determining each individual's susceptibility to stress. These individual factors encompass particular characteristics on the perceptual and cognitive levels which influence both the subjective interpretation of what is considered stress as well as the reaction to stress.

Many facets of personality have been the object of study regarding stress. Typical reactions to stress vary depending on personality traits, such as neurotic anxiety, introversion and extroversion, rigidity, flexibility, and ambition. A questionnaire is included in this chapter to identify a stressful person or a person with type A behaviour.

Extra-organizational stressors are those which arise beyond the work environment. They include family, political, social and economic factors, which have an impact on the individual. Though recent studies suggest that work-related stress factors outnumber family or spousal-related factors, we cannot fail to mention the existing interrelationship between the workplace and home or social relationships.

The inadequate home-workplace interconnection generates psychological conflicts and mental fatigue, a lack of motivation and a decrease in productivity, as well as deterioration in family relationships.

Undoubtedly, organizational or intra-organizational problems or stressors, that is, those that arise within the workplace, have an impact on the subject's personal life, provoking domestic problems which, as they increase are then fomented, generating further stress which is projected onto the workplace, creating more difficulties in job performance thereby producing a vicious cycle. Individuals spend a great deal of time at work, obtaining a substantial part of their identity and personal gratification from their tasks. However, these considerations are not always adequately assessed by companies or by the workers themselves.

Intra-organizational Stressors

In order to facilitate the study and understanding of these stressors, they are grouped into four types:

1. **Physical Stressors**: light, noise, vibrations and space.
2. **Individual Stressors**: work overload, conflict and ambiguity of roles, and discrepancy with career objectives.
3. **Group Stressors:** lack of cohesion, conflict, climate and group pressures.
4. **Organizational Stressors**: climate, size and management style, hierarchical structure, technology, and irrational deadlines.

1. **Physical Stressors:** These factors require double adaptation, both physical as well as psychological. In this section, we will briefly outline the main physical stressors in the workplace:

- ***Insufficient or excessive light*** – Inadequate lighting in the workplace can lead to negative consequences in terms of vision, headaches, fatigued vision, tension, and frustration as the job becomes bothersome and difficult.
- ***Noise*** – Working with noise has a negative influence on the degree of satisfaction, productivity and vulnerability to accidents, increasing the percentage of errors made. Additionally, cooperative behaviour is reduced, and negative attitudes are increased regarding others. Greater levels of hostility can be observed.
- ***Vibrations*** – Being constantly exposed to vibrations leads to an increase of catecholamines, spinal injuries and neurological alterations.
- ***Amount and layout of physical space in the workplace*** – A lack of physical space or poor layout increases the number of movements which need to be made with the resulting increase in effort and loss of time.

2. **Individual Stressors:** These factors include:
   - ***Work overload*** – An excessive amount of work, both quantitatively and qualitatively, is a common source of stress. This overload or stress due to overstimulation can be objective or subjective depending on the individual's assessment and characteristics. On the other hand, the lack of work can also be stressful due to a lack of stimulation. This is produced by a lack of normal and physiological stimulus and allows for little or no creativity and independent thought. This situation leads to distraction, a lack of attention and an increase in work-related accidents. An overload of work generates dissatisfaction, tension, a lack of self-esteem, a sense of threat, heart palpitations, high cholesterol, and the consumption of nicotine and other addictive substances to try to respond to the over-demand.
   - ***Conflict of roles*** – The conflict of roles can be objective or subjective. An objective conflict of roles arises when two or more people give conflicting orders. On the other hand, a subjective conflict of roles arises because of the contradiction between the formal orders received by the individual and the individual's own values and goals. Conflicts of roles generate a high degree of anxiety and dissatisfaction with respect to work, even more so the greater the authority of the person giving the contradictory orders. These situations lessen the individual's creativity since fear of failure provokes less satisfying job performance. On a personal level, the individual generally has high blood pressure and a high level of cholesterol.
   - ***Ambiguity of roles*** – This refers to a lack of clarity regarding the role of the individual, the objectives of the job itself and the scope of the individual's responsibilities. Typically, there is a drop in self-esteem because of a lack of satisfaction from the task being carried out, as well as work satisfaction, quality and participation in decision-making. Adequate information and communication reduce this type of conflict since they improve how work-related tasks are oriented.
   - ***Discrepancies with career goals*** – Discrepancies and doubts regarding the individual's career or profession arise due to a lack of job security, doubts regarding pay rises and legitimate, frustrated ambitions. Dissatisfaction in terms of discrepancies between an individual's hopes and achievements

creates anxiety and frustration, depression, and stress, especially among individuals in the 40–50 age group. As well as unsatisfactory job performance, it is common to find addictions to substances, such as alcohol, drugs, coffee, tobacco, etc.

3. **Group Stressors:** The quality of relationships is an important factor when determining their potential stress factor. A good relationship between members of the same team is a key factor for personal and organizational health. On the contrary, an untrusting relationship lacking in support and cooperation, and which is primarily destructive, can produce a high degree of tension and stress within the group or organization. The following stressful factors are included in the Group Stressors:
   - *Lack of cohesion* – Not having this bond is one of the characteristics which can be stressful for individuals.
   - *Group conflict* – A degree of conflict is always healthy in groups or teams. In fact, it is necessary in order to achieve optimal performance. However, continued, and non-constructive conflict between members of the same team can lead to emotional responses and stressful situations, such as frustration, tension, dissatisfaction, emotional exhaustion, somatic ailments, insomnia, etc.
   - *Group climate* – The climate within the team is another relevant stressor for its members. Several researchers among teams found that members in teams whose climate was characterized by imbalances (between the levels of support offered to the individuals and the orientation towards the goals, and respecting the rules and an innovative orientation) suffered greater degrees of role-related stress and work tension and greater dissatisfaction than members of teams with more balanced scores.
   - *Group pressure* – The pressures the groups exert on the individual members can lead to stress, especially if the object is to have the members assume values or beliefs which go against their own principles. These pressures cause various psychological and behavioural changes.

4. **Organizational Stressors:** The following are worth noting:
   - *Climate within the organization* – Every organization has its own personality, its own climate. This climate conditions the behavior of the individuals who make up the organization, though it is difficult to appraise since there are no scientifically valid tools available to measure it. The climate may or may not be tense, relaxed, cordial, etc. All this produces different levels of stress in the individuals depending on their susceptibility and vulnerability.
   - *Size and management style* – The most common source of stress arises from the combination of the organization's size and how formal its functioning is, in other words, bureaucracy. Many studies have shown that highly bureaucratic organizations try to mould individuals to conform to a stereotype.
   - *Hierarchical structure* – In all hierarchies where there is an unequal distribution of power, the higher the level, the greater the tendency of autocratic control of a few at the expense of others. Managers are in a good position to demand behaviours which exceed the ability of the individuals to tolerate such demands.

- **Technology** – The incorporation of new technologies has important implications for numerous work-related and organizational aspects. Changes develop in the tasks and job roles, in the supervision, in the structures and in the organizational style. These can make way for new stressors in the workplace, while eliminating others.[12]
- **Irrational deadlines** – Everyone knows the impact produced by the establishment of unreachable goals given the time allotted to complete them.

But, What Exactly is Occupational Stress?

Most would agree that occupational stress is the result of the interaction between the worker and the working conditions. However, opinions differ regarding the importance attributed to the *worker's characteristics* compared to the importance of the *working conditions* as the primary cause of stress.

These different opinions are important because they suggest different ways to avoid occupational stress.

According to one school of thought, the differences between personal characteristics, such as personality and how people cope with stress, are more important in predicting whether certain working conditions will result in stress. In other words, what is stressful for one person may not be stressful for someone else. This opinion leads to prevention strategies concentrated on workers and ways to help them cope with the demanding conditions of their work.

Although the importance of individual differences cannot be ignored, scientific evidence suggests that certain working conditions are stressful for the majority of people.

Occupational stress related hazards at work can be divided into work content (or intrinsic factors) and work context (or extrinsic factors):

- Work contents includes job content (monotony, under-stimulation, meaningless of tasks, lack of variety, etc); workload and work pace (too much or too little to do, work under time pressure, etc.); working hours (strict or inflexible, long, and unsocial, unpredictable, badly designed shift systems); and participation and control (lack of participation in decision-making, lack of control over work processes, pace, hours, methods and the work environment).
- Work context includes career development, status and pay (job insecurity, lack of promotion opportunities, under- or over-promotion, work of low social value, piece rate payment schemes, unclear or unfair performance evaluation systems, being over- or under-skilled for a job); the worker's role in the organization (unclear role, conflicting roles); interpersonal relationships (inadequate, inconsiderate or unsupportive supervision, poor relationships with colleagues, bullying/harassment and violence, isolated or solitary work, etc.); organizational culture (poor communication, poor leadership, lack of behavioural rule, lack of clarity about organizational objectives, structures and strategies); and work-life balance

(conflicting demands of work and home, lack of support for domestic problems at work, lack of support for work problems at home, lack of organizational rules and policies to support work-life balance).

Chapter Summary and Postscript

"Job stress results when the requirements of the job do not match the capabilities, resources or needs of the worker" (NIOSH).[12]

Stress is one of the factors directly responsible for the most common and most lethal psychological and physical illnesses affecting mankind, hence the importance of its study within organizations.

There is often confusion between pressure or challenge and stress and sometimes it is used to excuse bad management practice. Pressure at the workplace is unavoidable due to the demands of the contemporary work environment. Pressure perceived as acceptable by an individual, may even keep workers alert, motivated, able to work and learn, depending on the available resources and personal characteristics. However, when that pressure becomes excessive or otherwise unmanageable it leads to stress. Stress can damage workers' health and his or her business performance.

Stress results from a mismatch between the demands and pressures on the person, on the one hand, and their knowledge and abilities, on the other. It challenges their ability to cope with work. This includes not only situations where the pressures of work exceed the worker's ability to cope but also where the worker's knowledge and abilities are not sufficiently utilized and that is a problem for them. A healthy job is likely to be one where the pressures on employees are appropriate in relation to their abilities and resources, to the amount of control they have over their work, and to the support they receive from people who matter to them. As health is not merely the absence of disease or infirmity but a positive state of complete physical, mental and social well-being, a healthy working environment is one in which there is not only an absence of harmful conditions but an abundance of health promoting ones. These may include continuous assessment of risks to health, the provision of appropriate information and training on health issues and the availability of health promoting organizational support practices and structures. A healthy work environment is one in which staff have made health and health promotion a priority and part of their working lives.

There are different models used to explain stress, including models based on the physiological consequences of stress, those based on the psychological and behavioural consequences, and a multidisciplinary cognitive model which maintains that the discordance between the individual and his/her working environment gives rise to problems of adaptation.

---

12 Quote: STRESS...At Work (99–101) | NIOSH | CDC: www.cdc.gov/niosh/docs/99-101/default.html

ACTION: TEST YOUR STRESS LEVEL

How stressed are you?

The following questionnaire is designed to help you find out your stress level. Answer each question below. Use the following scale to give your answers:

NEVER　　　　　　　　　　　　SOMETIMES　　　　　　　　　　　　ALWAYS

0　1　2　3　4　5　6　7　8　9　10

*1. Are you known for seeing the positive side of life?

2. Do you feel that, in your case, you keep all your feelings locked up inside?

3. Do you ever get overwhelmed by the lack of time available to meet all of your obligations?

4. Do you ever have nothing to do?

*5. Do you know how to use humour in difficult situations?

6. Do you believe your job affects your relationship with the people you most love?

7. Do you need an increasingly frequent "dose" of work to feel stimulated?

8. Does it take you a while to get your day started?

*9. Do you feel you have real friends?

10. Do you ever feel "I can't take it anymore"?

11. Is it hard for you to find someone to talk to about your problems?

12. Do you want to be left alone?

13. Do you feel life is flying by?

*14. Do you think you're thought of as a friendly person?

*15. Do you know fun people?

How stressed are you?

16. Is it hard for you to disconnect from what's troubling you?

17. Do you have a difficult time falling asleep?

*18. Do you know how to encourage yourself?

19. Is it hard for you to disconnect after a long day at work?

*20. Do you know how to relax when you want to?

*21. Do you have time for yourself?

22. Do you think you're "addicted" to your work?

23. Do you need to take substances (coffee, nicotine, alcohol, or others) to "keep going"?

24. Do you think "if I spoke up it would only make things worse"?

25. Are you irritable or bad tempered when faced with insignificant problems?

26. Do you think you demand too much of yourself?

27. Do you have backaches, headaches, or pains in your jaws?

*28. Do you laugh easily?

Before calculating the total score, you need to reverse the scores for the following 9 questions: 1,5,9,14,15,18,20,21 and 28. Reversing means: 10 becomes 0, and 0 becomes 10. 9 becomes 1 and 1 becomes 9, and so on. only 5 does not change. Same with the remainder of the scores.

Total Score: _____

RESULTS AND INTERPRETATION OF THE TEST

Score	Meaning
0–90	Not at all stressed
91–180	A little stressed
181–280	Very stressed:

A high score indicates that:

1. You want to take on more than you really can.
2. You don't express your feelings or demand your rights.
3. You don't manage your time well.
4. You're abandoning your friends.
5. You're hurting yourself by thinking negatively.
6. You're not aware of what is going on around you and inside you.
7. You're a workaholic
8. Your situation is very troubling. **It seems that You are extremely "burnt out" and "exhausted".**

CHAPTER 3

Understanding Stress from an Individual Angle

The Key Role of Personality, Self-esteem and Other Personal Characteristics

Introduction

Regardless of the nature of stress (acute or chronic), individual differences affect our perceptions and interpretations of events around us. They contribute to our experience of stress (primary appraisal), and our decisions what to do to deal with the stressor – our choice of coping process (secondary appraisal). There are, however, vast individual differences in vulnerability to stress alter an individual's perception of a potential source of stress (direct effect), impact on the transformation of perceived stress into various consequences of stress (indirect effect) and ameliorate these stress consequences (direct effect).

Within the cognitive models of occupational stress there are a range of specific individual differences that have been studied over the years. Some explain what and why people amplify perceived threats (exaggerate the situation and contribute to the ethology of stress), while other can **filter** threats and buffer the process that leads to the ethology of stress. In this chapter we will review the principal individual differences that has been associated with workplace stress (See Table 3.1):

Your Personality: Does It Amplify or Filter Your Stress?

Personality matters for many aspects of the stress process, including stress exposure, appraisals, coping, affective and physiological reactivity to stress, long-term adaptation processes, and rather distal outcomes at longer timescales. One could conceptualize personality as a moderator in the various aspects of the stress process.

Because stress is not a simple, stimulus-response reaction, but it is the interaction between an individual and the environment, involving subjective perception and assessment of stressors, thus constituting a highly personalized process. Specific inherited characteristics, early experience in life, and, learned cognitive predispositions make individuals susceptible to the effects of stressors. While there are hundreds of

TABLE 3.1 Key individual differences attributed to variation in perceived stress and its respective consequences

Attribute	Specific factor	comments
Stress Prone Personality	• Type A/B/C • Locus of Control • The five big Personality (Extraversion, agreeableness, openness, conscientiousness, and neuroticism).	There are other personality types proposed by the literature, but in this section, we describe only the most researched and the most popular
Stress prone Traits	• Self-Esteem	There might be other traits, but the most important has been discussed in the context of self-esteem
Selected sociodemographic characteristics and stress	• Gender • Age • Education • Job status-hierarchical level	These are the most common variables that explain differences in stress perception and adaptation

inventories of personality assessment, in this chapter we have selected to focus on the ones that have been most studied in stress research. Numerous characteristics of personality, such as locus of control, self-efficacy, self-esteem, optimism, hostility (component of type A personality) and the dimensions of the big 5 personality traits are covered herein. To understand the relation between personality and stress, it is essential to recognize the impact of individual differences in the following four aspects: (1) choice or avoidance of environments that are associated with specific stressors, challenges or benefits; (2) way of interpreting a stressful situation and evaluating one's own abilities and capacities for proactive behaviour so as to confront or avoid it; (3) intensity of response to a stressor; and (4) coping strategies employed by the individual facing a stressful situation.

Type A/B/C Personality, Your Heart and Your Stress

While the factors causing stress may be the same, the way people react is linked to their degree of vulnerability and their psychological profile. As such, a person's behaviour is subject to their personality traits, attitudes, beliefs, manifest behaviour and a certain psycho-physiological activation.

Everybody is different and responses differently to stressors. What causes one person to stress out can be a relaxation aid for another. People are unique. Some years ago, two cardiologists (Drs. Friedman and Rosenman) discovered a pattern between personality types and their reactions to stress. Doubtless you have heard of these "types" of people – they relate how you deal with stress that comes into your life.[1]

---

1 See: Friedman, H.S., and Booth-Kewley, S. (1987) Personality, Type a behavior, and coronary heart disease: The role of emotional expression. *Journal of Personality and Social Psychology.* 53(4), 783–792. doi:10.1037/0022-3514.53.4.783. PMID 3681651. S2CID 25769007; Friedman, M. (1996) *Type A Behavior: Its Diagnosis and Treatment.* New York, Plenum Press (Kluwer Academic Press), 31 ff; .; Friedman, M. and Rosenman, R. (1959) Association of specific overt behaviour pattern with blood and cardiovascular findings. *Journal of the American Medical Association,* 169(12): 1286–1296. doi:10.1001/jama.1959.03000290012005. PMID 13630753.

People defined as Type A personalities have a psychological profile in which an excessive response predominates. They appear hyperactive, irritable, ambitious, aggressive, hostile, impulsive, chronically impatient, tense and competitive. Their interpersonal relationships are problematic, and they tend to be dominant. People with Type **A Pattern of Behaviour**, with an autonomous response to stress, have a greater predisposition to suffer cardiovascular pathologies due to the activation of catecholamines. At the same time, these people frequently have a high degree of LDL cholesterol and reduced HDL cholesterol, while accumulating other risk factors, such as obesity, high blood pressure and an addiction to nicotine.

People with **Type B Pattern of Behaviour** are generally calm, trusting and confidant, relaxed and open to their emotions, including hostile emotions. The role of adaptative mechanisms when coping with stress in the event of failure is clear, provoking and leading to neurotic and depressive processes.

Type C Pattern of Behaviour occurs in people who are introverted, obsessive, passive, resigned and placid, extremely cooperative, submissive and conformist, who interiorize their response to stress and always control their hostility, desiring social approval. Although the type C patterns were not discovered initially by Drs, Freidman and Rosenman, published research suggest that by and large people with Type C behaviour, are statistically more predisposed to rheumatism, infections, allergies and various dermatological ills, including cancer, the latter associated to the immuno-logical inhibition which these individuals suffer from.

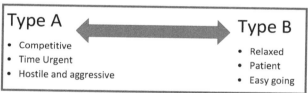

 SELF-ASSESSMENT EXERCISE

ASSESS YOUR TYPE A/B PERSONALITY

Answer YES or NO based on your immediate reaction to the following questions. That is to say, after reading each item, you need to respond instantly without spending too much time thinking about your response. If you do not follow this guideline, the validity of the assessment will not be as good.

____1. I talk fast and really stress the key words.
____2. I tend to walk, move and act fast.
____3. I always get impatient and angry with how most events take place because they don't go fast enough or they're too tiresome.
____4. I tend to steer conversations to topics and matters that are really important to me.
____5. I feel guilty when I'm resting or have free time.
____6. I tend not to notice new details that show up in my environment.
____7. I'm more concerned with what is worth *having* then what is worth *being*.

____ 8. I tend to increasingly plan more and more in less time.
____ 9. I feel I'm competing against people who are also under time deadlines and pressures.
____ 10. I have developed nervous tics or gestures, such as making fists or hitting the table while speaking.
____ 11. I think success is doing things faster than anyone else.
____ 12. I tend to perceive and evaluate my personal activities and those of others' in terms of numbers.

Note: *This test was inspired by the work of Friedman and Roseman (1974) but was adapted and validated by the author in numerous studies with diverse samples.*

RESULTS AND INTERPRETATION

If you answered YES to most of the questions, you have a Type A personality. Type A behaviour is understood as the "speed disease". People with this type of behaviour display the behaviours outlined in the questionnaire. In high-pressure jobs centered on success, Type A behaviour is admired – even unconsciously. By contrast, Type B personalities are relaxed and easy to deal with, and it is less likely that they will react in a hostile or aggressive manner.

Locus of Control and Your Stress

Control is one of the most important variables in coping with stressful situations. Having or perceiving control over stressor situations or events increases the degree of stress tolerance and reduces the severity of its negative effects.

People who perceive themselves as having a **low capacity for controlling their environments** tend to be more vulnerable when coping with stressor events. The concept developed by Rotter regarding the locus of control, referring to the causal attributions people make with specific results, is widely used to evaluate the variable of controlling their environment.[2] Julian Rotter observed people in therapy and noticed that:

- Different people, given identical conditions for learning, learn different things.
- Some people respond predictably to reinforcement, others less, and some respond unpredictably.
- Some people see a direct and strong connection between their behaviour and the rewards and punishments they receive.

---

2 Rotter, J. B. (1954). *Social learning and clinical psychology*; Rotter, J. B. (1966). Generalized expectancies for internal versus external control of reinforcement. *Psychological monographs: General and applied*, 80(1), 1.

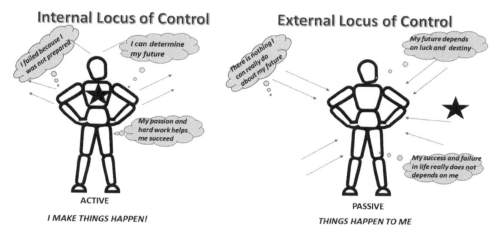

FIGURE 3.1 Internal vs external locus of control.

The core of his approach is called Expectancy Value Theory: the basic assumption is that your behaviour is determined not just by the presence or size of reinforcements, but by the beliefs about what the results of your behaviour are likely to be i.e., how likely you are to get the reinforcement. Those with an **external locus of control** attribute the results to external forces beyond their control. Those with an **internal locus of control** establish a direct connection between their behaviour and the reinforcements and results they obtain (see examples in Figure 3.1).

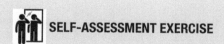 **SELF-ASSESSMENT EXERCISE**

ARE YOU IN CONTROL OF YOUR WORK?

Indicate how often the following situations occur at work. Use only one number value, from 1 to 4, for each situation.

1 = Always 2 = Often 3 = Rarely 4 = Never

1.	I can decide how I do my job.	
2.	I can decide what to do in my job.	
3.	I have a lot of say in the decisions made regarding my job.	
4.	Others make decisions about my job.	
5.	I can play a part in determining the speed of doing my job.	

6.	My time schedule can be flexible.
7.	I can decide when to take breaks.
8.	I can choose who I work with.
9.	At work, I can play a part in planning.
10.	I have to do different things.
11.	My job offers me a variety of interesting things to do.
12.	My job is fun.
13.	I can learn new things at work.
14.	My job requires a lot of skill and experience.
15.	My job requires me to take the initiative.

Results and Interpretation

Total score for the sum of questions 1–9 is: _____

Total score for the sum of questions 10–15 is: _____

Questions 1–9 evaluate the degree of authority one has in decision-making. A low score (**between 9 and 18 points**) indicates a high degree of authority in decision making at work, implying an internal locus of control. By contrast, a high score (**more than 27 points**) indicates a low degree of authority at work, in other words, an external locus of control.

Questions 10–15 measure the degree of professional competencies required for the job. A low score (**between 6 and 12 points**) indicates a more internal locus of control, in which the job requires personal skills and abilities in order to carry it out. By contrast, a high score (**more than 18 points**) indicates a more external locus of control, in which a job requires few personal skills.

How About Combining Type A/B Personality and Locus of Control? Does the Diagnosis of Stress is Less Blurred?

In the previous sections I have described the commonly used measures of personality in stress research. While investigating stress amongst hospital employees in Canada, a team of us working with huge ample discovered that combining the type A/B personality with the locus of control adds significant value in explaining how people perceive their work environment and how they to it. Using a median-split method, each personality scale was split in the 50% percentile and thus four categories of personality were detected. Labels were also attributed to personality types using the following arguments: Type A personality were labelled (**HOT** comes from the Hot temper or Hot

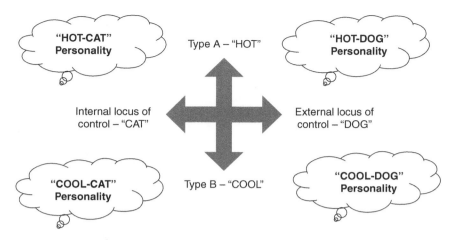

FIGURE 3.2 The Dolan & Arsenault personality classification.

reactors) while Type B personality was labelled **COOL** (i.e. named after Fonzy from the Happy days TV series in the 1980s... means a cool Dude... takes things easy). Animals were used to denominate the locus of control, where the internal locus of control was called **CAT** (if you own or know a CAT you know that cats are very independent); external personalities were labelled DOG (if you own a Dog, you know that DOGs are very dependent on external stimuli).[3] Figure 3.2 shows this typology. In combining the two dimensions, we get the following four categories of personalities which were described by Dolan and his colleagues as the following:

- The **HOT-CAT**s are competitive, preoccupied with control of their territory, must engage in immediate action and exert control over their emotional reactions. They see themselves as formal and authoritative leaders, they are the so-called dominant of the social structure. They strive in order to maintain control.

- The **HOT-DOG**s are hyperactive optimistic individuals who feel guided by external events. They are restless individuals who find satisfaction in the demonstration that they have kept themselves busy doing whatever has to be done: They are more devoted than faithful; and formal roles in an organized social structure does not interest them. They strive and don't always believe in control.

- The **COOL-CAT**s tend to be overwhelmed by their analytical mind. Being extremely critical, they have a tendency towards pessimism. It is difficult to determine if they are solitary by choice or if others avoid them because of their

---

3 Dolan S.L., and Arsenault A. (1984) Stress, Personality and Samples of Work Attitudes and Behavior: Analysis Beyond A Single Level of Aggregation. In Burke R. (Ed.), *Current Issues in Occupational Stress: Research and Intervention*. Toronto, University of Toronto Press, 53–78; . Van Ameringen, R., Arsenault, A., Dolan, S.L. (1988), Intrinsic Job Stress As Predictor of Diastolic Blood Pressure among Female Hospital Workers, *Journal of Occupational Medicine*, 30(2): 93–97; **Dolan** S.L., van Ameringen M.R., and Arsenault A. (1992) The Role of Personality and Social Support in the etiology of workers' Stress and Psychological Strain, *Industrial Relations* (Canada), 47(1).

The big five personality traits

FIGURE 3.3 The big five personality traits.
Source: The Stress Map. Used with permission of Gestion MDS Inc and its president Prof. Simon L. Dolan.

retreating behaviour. They like to feel unpredictable and do not like to be controlled or directed. They don't strive or compete but believe in control.

- **COOL-DOGs** never act hastily. Their domain is more of quiet reflection and slow-paced jobs. They are quite sensitive to all sorts of joys and mishaps, yet do not search and even prefer not to have control of such happenings. They appear more faithful than devoted. They neither strive nor believe in control.

Which of the Five Big Personality Traits Can Explain Your Stress

The "big five" are broad categories of personality traits. While there is a significant body of literature supporting this five-factor model of personality, researchers don't always agree on the exact labels for each dimension. Some refer to these dimensions in using the acronym OCEAN (openness, conscientiousness, extraversion, agreeableness and neuroticism) when trying to remember the big five traits. CANOE (for conscientiousness, agreeableness, neuroticism, openness and extraversion) is another commonly used acronym.

It is important to note that each of the five personality factors represents a range between two extremes. For example, extraversion represents a continuum between extreme extraversion and extreme introversion. In the real world, most people lie somewhere in between the two polar ends of each dimension.

Worth noting that research on the big five shows found that the traits are remarkably universal even across cultures. Many psychologists now believe that the five personality dimensions are routed and have biological origins. Psychologist David Buss even went to an extreme to suggest that these personality traits represent the most important qualities that shape our social landscape.[4]

---

4 The Big Five Personality Traits According to David Buss the Big Five | Course Hero

Openness – features characteristics such as imagination and insight. People who are high in this trait also tend to have a broad range of interests. They are curious about the world and other people and eager to learn new things and enjoy new experiences. People who are high in this trait also tend to be more adventurous and creative. People low in this trait are often much more traditional and may struggle with abstract thinking. So, based on the person-fit model, one can imagine that any polarization or perceived contrast between people that are high or low on this trait can brings about stress.

High on Openness

- Very creative
- Open to trying new things
- Focused on tackling new challenges
- Happy to think about abstract concepts

Low on Openness

- Dislikes change
- Does not enjoy new things
- Resists new ideas
- Not very imaginative
- Dislikes abstract or theoretical concepts

In sum: When someone scores higher in this category, they are more likely to be adaptable, accept change and appreciate innovative technology. They are intuitive and original, offering new ideas every day. Openness allows people to be vulnerable and honest, which can offer them emotional understanding and deep friendships. By contrast, when someone is lower in this trait, they tend to fear or dislike change. They usually prefer routine and tradition and generally think more logically and concretely. They have a more difficult time being honest about how they feel and may feel isolated at times.

Conscientiousness – Standard features of this dimension include high levels of thoughtfulness, good impulse control, and goal-directed behaviours. Highly conscientious people tend to be organized and mindful of details. They plan, think about how their behaviour affects others, and are mindful of deadlines.

High on Conscientiousness

- Spends time preparing
- Finishes important tasks right away
- Pays attention to detail
- Enjoys having a set schedule

Low on Conscientiousness

- Dislike's structure and schedules
- Makes messes and doesn't take care of things
- Fails to return things or put them back where they belong
- Procrastinates important tasks
- Fails to complete necessary or assigned tasks

By and large, research suggest that conscientiousness serves as a protective factor from stress through its influence on coping strategy selection.[5]

Extraversion (or extroversion) is characterized by excitability, sociability, talkativeness, assertiveness and high amounts of emotional expressiveness. People who are high in extraversion are outgoing and tend to gain energy in social situations. Being around other people helps them feel energized and excited.

People who are low in extraversion (or introverted) tend to be more reserved and have less energy to expend in social settings. Social events can feel draining, and introverts often require a period of solitude and quiet in order to "recharge".

High

- Enjoys being the centre of attention
- Likes to start conversations
- Enjoys meeting new people
- Has a wide social circle of friends and acquaintances

Low

- Prefers solitude
- Feels exhausted when having to socialize a lot
- Finds it difficult to start conversations
- Dislikes making small talk
- Carefully thinks things through

In sum, there exists a lay perception that extraversion confers benefits for coping with stress and promotes salubrious stress and health outcomes. Generally, research supports this assertion. It seems plausible that extraversion would affect stress outcomes through stressor appraisals, because extraverts are thought to be more likely to attend to the positive aspects of a stressor.

Agreeableness – is a personality dimension that includes attributes such as trust, altruism, kindness, affection, and other prosocial behaviours. People who are high in agreeableness tend to be more cooperative while those low in this trait tend to be more competitive and sometimes even manipulative.

---

5 See for example: Bartley, C.E.S., and Roesch, S. (2011) Coping with Daily Stress: The Role of Conscientiousness, *Personality and Individual Differences*, 50(1), 79–83.

High on Agreeableness

- Has a great deal of interest in other people
- Cares about others
- Feels empathy and concern for other people
- Enjoys helping and contributing to the happiness of other people
- Assists others who need help

Low on Agreeableness

- Takes little interest in others
- Doesn't care about how other people feel
- Has little interest in other people's problems
- Insults and belittles others
- Manipulates others to get what they want

In sum, scholars have mentioned that agreeableness is one of the factors negatively related to stress because agreeable individuals perceive daily activities as less stressful and report fewer fights with others. Despite a seemingly protective effect, high agreeableness also carries a risk: individuals who are high in this trait are more susceptible to peer-drinking influences. Apparently, in their concern for complying with others and their efforts to meet group expectations, more agreeable individuals tend to drink less around light drinking peers, but drink more around heavy drinking peers.

Neuroticism is a trait characterized by sadness, moodiness and emotional instability. Individuals who are high in this trait tend to experience mood swings, anxiety, irritability and sadness. Those low in this trait tend to be more stable and emotionally resilient.

High on Neuroticism

- Experiences a lot of stress
- Worries about many different things
- Gets upset easily
- Experiences dramatic shifts in mood
- Feels anxious
- Struggles to bounce back after stressful events

Low on Neuroticism

- Emotionally stable
- Deals well with stress
- Rarely feels sad or depressed
- Doesn't worry much
- Is very relaxed

In sum, neuroticism is a trait that primarily measures emotional stability. People high on this trait are more susceptible to experiencing emotional distress including feelings of fear, anger, anxiety, disgust, or guilt. These people might also cope poorly with stress. While neuroticism is not a measure of psychopathology, many people who score highly on this trait may be at risk for some psychiatric disorders or problems. People who score lower on this trait tend to be more relaxed, calm, and level-headed even when facing stressful situations.

The Key Role of Self-esteem in the Aetiology of Stress

Self-esteem is one of the most popularized psychological concepts of our times, probably due to its practical use in understanding a good part of our journey through life in search of happiness.

Intuitively, we know that "self/esteem" is something desirable and positive, especially if it is balanced and does not end up as self-hate or narcissism.

Self-esteem and Purpose

"Self-esteem" according to Webster's New Collegiate Dictionary (G. & C. Merriam-Webster) 2022 (Self-esteem Definition & Meaning – Merriam-Webster) is defined as 1) a confidence and satisfaction in one's own self: self-respect, and 2) self-conceit

At a deep, existential level we assess ourselves depending on where we see ourselves on our journey through life, or if we are on the right path (see Figure 3.4). The final destination on this road, what everyone is searching for throughout life, is to be happy. Happiness, the Hellenic *eudeimonia*, is to find the correct destiny and be

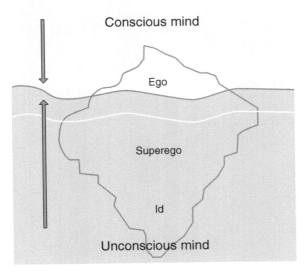

FIGURE 3.4 Self-esteem and the "ego" dimensions.

comfortable with it. Happiness consists of savoring one's freely chosen path in life. Self-esteem, then, is absolutely necessary to be happy.

Self-esteem is at the center of a loop: It depends on what each individual does with their life based on, and as a consequence, of their private appraisal of what life is. The real moral task is to become everything one can possibly be with what one is, as Aranguren says:

> "Human beings are blessed with an essential and originating self-esteem, which, little by little, is lost as they navigate the seas of mistrust and the desire to control variables beyond themselves, no matter how well the individual has learned to navigate through the Internet in the so-called era of knowledge and information".[6]

Human beings are blessed with an essential and originating self-esteem, which, little by little, is lost as they navigate the seas of mistrust and the desire to control variables beyond themselves, no matter how well the individual has learned to navigate through the Internet in the so-called era of knowledge and information.

Part of life's mission is to assume the responsibility for creating greater health, greater happiness, greater commitment, and greater endeavor in the world around us and in ourselves. When this occurs, we increase our real self-esteem .

Self-love is the source of self-conservation and survival as well as awareness of oneself and others. Personal dignity, our own honor, is the *axioprepia*; the final goal, *par excellence*, is making the right values fit together.

Loving oneself (self-love) has its biological foundation, based on our natural survival instinct and on our quest to constantly improve. Everyone must love himself or herself above or at least in equal measure to any other person or thing. From this stems that some might want their own failure as a dysfunctional form of self-affirmation. It would also explain the golden rule found in most religions, to "love others as you love yourself". The coincidence among different cultures and religions regarding this essential bit of wisdom, to treat and love others, as you would have them treat and love you, is nevertheless surprising.

Regardless, people see themselves as valid or non-valid, as "good" or "bad", they love themselves or not to a greater or lesser degree, and they have a higher or lower opinion of themselves depending on the positive or negative experiences and the way they react to the events in their lives. All this occurs with varying degrees of pathology, sobriety, arrogance and drama, depending on individual differences.

Apparent, Fantasized and Profound Self-esteem

One thing is apparent, self-esteem derives from the portrayal of a character more or less appreciated by oneself and others. Another matter is real self-esteem, the connection with the essential and authentic *ego*.

The first type is fragile and volatile, the second, solid and permanent, and allows many defense mechanisms against the anxiety caused by feeling fake or vulnerable to

---

6 Free translation from Spanish from: https://es.wikipedia.org/wiki/Jos%C3%A9_Luis_L%C3%B3pez_Aranguren (validated last at 13-2-2022)

be eliminated. One of these not so uncommon defense mechanisms is the obsessive, active and exhausting accumulation of professional and materialistic achievements.

There is also another dimension to self-esteem, which is based on our fantasies and desires about what we would like to do. We can identify three types of egos amongst managers and employees normally found in your average organization (see Figure 3.3):

1. The Ego Character – A pragmatic adaptive person who generates an "apparent" self-esteem;
2. The Wishful Ego – the hopeful, creative person who generates fantasized self-esteem (sometimes feels that acts in a dreamland); and
3. The Ego Conscience – a truly concerned individual, ethically oriented who generates the deepest and most fundamental self-esteem.

These characters, can be connected very well to the Freudian psychodynamic model, where the assumptions about human behavior are based on the following:

- The Id – contains a reservoir of unconscious psychic energy; strives to satisfy basic sexual and aggressive drives; and operates on the pleasure principle, demanding immediate gratification
- The Superego – the part of personality that presents internalized ideals; provides standards for judgment (the conscience) and for future aspirations
- The Ego – the largely conscious, "executive" part of personality; it mediates among the demands of the id, superego, and reality; operates on the reality principle, satisfying the id's desires in ways that will realistically bring pleasure rather than pain

Thus, extrapolating from Freud's view of the struggle between our conscious and unconscious mind, the internal struggle can be reflected in the type of ego adapted. **The Ego Character** or **Apparent Ego** is the character we play in our daily interactions with others, the conventional mask of our true wishes and human essence in our efforts to survive. It is associated to what is known as the sound judgement or practical reasoning. It is our mental identity, standardized, rational and prudent. Psycho-dynamic theory would easily identify it with the controlling super ego, formed basically by the interaction with authority figures in our childhood, namely our parents and teachers.[7]

This adaptative mask is superficially calming and is conventionally designed to interpret a socially accepted and reinforced role, approved by our groups of reference and the groups we belong to, those we would like to emulate, and, in those groups, we feel we are included. It conforms to a life script, which oftentimes limits real possibilities, whether practical, emotional, or ethical. When we talk about the utopian principle, that the person is the end in itself, we refer to the person in all their fullness.

---

7 Based on an essay by Vinney (2019): Psychodynamic Theory: Approaches and Proponents (www.thoughtco.com/psychodynamic-theory-4588302)

The **Wishful Ego** is the dimension of our being which responds to the "poetic" impulses of life (poiesis= generate, give birth to): creation, spontaneity, madness, pleasure, and Salvador Dali's "rauxa". In psycho-dynamic theory, it corresponds to the libidinous impulse which, as we shall see, is conventionally modulated, and even repressed during our conventional education. It corresponds to the "pre-conventional" phase in the evolution of moral consciousness according to Kohlberg's theory of Moral development.[8]

The Ego Conscience is the real, essential, and characteristic person. It is the home of the being, the deepest ethical instance of our moral character (ethos = abode and character). Its existence is especially serene, inspirational, and it is the generator of self-esteem well beyond conventionalisms. An excess of externalization and stimuli derived from the desire to control, and the fear of boredom and social rejection makes it difficult to access this essential asset and source of freedom, goodwill, and vital wisdom which we all have inside us.

And, on a more conventional basis, Freud's ego-defense mechanisms can be connected to self-esteem issues in the following manner:

- **COMPENSATION:** The process of masking perceived negative self-concepts, or of developing positive self-concepts, to make up for the perceived negative self-concepts. For example, if you think you are an idiot you may work at becoming physically more fit than others to make up for this shortcoming.
- **DENIAL:** This is the subconscious or conscious process of blinding yourself to negative self-concepts that you believe exist, but that you do not want to deal with. It is "closing your eyes" to the negative self-concepts about people, places, or things that you find too severe to deal with. For example, a family may pretend and act as if the father is only sick when it is obvious that he is an alcoholic.
- **DISPLACEMENT:** This is when you express feelings to a substitute target because you are unwilling to express them to the real target. And the feelings expressed to the substitute target are based on your negative self-concepts about the real target. "Crooked anger" or "dumping" on another are examples of displacement. In these examples, you let out your anger and frustration about the negative self-concepts you are feeling about someone else on a safer target: such as someone below you, someone dependent on you, or someone under your control.
- **IDENTIFICATION:** This is the identification of yourself with heroes, stars, organizations, causes, religions, groups, or whatever you perceive as good self-concepts. This is a way to think of yourself as good self-concepts. For example, you may identify with a crusade to help starving children so that you can incorporate into your ego some of the good self-concepts associated with that crusade.
- **INTROJECTION:** This is the acceptance of the standards of others to avoid being rated as negative self-concepts by their standards. For example, you may uncritically accept the standards of your government or religion in order to be accepted as good self-concepts by them.

---

8 McLeod, S. (2013) Kohlberg's Theory of Moral Development, (www.simplypsychology.org/kohlberg.html).

- **PROJECTION:** This is the attribution to others of your own negative self-concepts. This occurs when you want to avoid facing negative self-concepts about your behaviors or intentions and you do so by seeing them, instead, in other people. For example, you may be mad at your spouse and think, instead, that they are mad at you.
- **RATIONALIZATION:** This is the process of explaining why, this time, you do not have to be judged as negative self-concepts because of your behaviors or intentions. It is sometimes referred to as "sour grapes" when, for example, you rationalize that you do not want something that you did not get because "it was lousy anyway". Rationalization can also take the opposite tack, or what is sometimes referred to as the "sweet lemon". In this case, you justify, for example, an error in purchasing by extolling some of the insignificant good points of the product.
- **REACTION FORMATION:** This is the process of developing conscious positive self-concepts in order to cover and hide opposite, negative self-concepts. It is the making up for negative self-concepts by showing off their reverse. For example, you may hate your parents, but you go out of your way to show care and concern for them.
- **REGRESSION:** This is the returning to an earlier time in your life when you were not so threatened with becoming negative self-concepts. You return to thoughts, feelings, and-or behaviors of an earlier developmental stage in order to identify yourself as you used to back then. For example, you may be being criticized as an adult and feeling horrible about it. And to escape this, you revert back to acting like a little child because you did not own criticism then as meaning you were negative self-concepts.
- **REPRESSION:** This is the unconscious and seemingly involuntary removal from awareness of the negative self-concepts that your ego finds too painful to tolerate. For example, you may completely block out thoughts of killing a parent. This is not the same as suppression, which is also the removal from consciousness of intolerable negative self-concepts--but by conscious choice.
- **RITUAL AND UNDOING:** This is the process of trying to undo negative self-concept ratings of yourself by performing rituals or behaviors designed to offset the behaviors that the negative ratings of you were based on. For example, a millionaire might give to charities for the poor to make up for profiting from the poor. Or, a parent may buy their child a lot of gifts to make up for not spending time with them.
- **SUBLIMATION:** This is the process of diverting your feelings about the negative self-concepts that you have of yourself or others into more socially acceptable activities. For example, if you generally hate people, you might be an aggressive environmental activist, an aggressive political activist, or join a fighting army. This way you can get some approval for the feelings that you disapprove of.

THE PYTHAGORAS TRIANGLE

According to Brian Bacon, a global management consultant and author of numerous publications on Management and Leadership, Pythagoras theorized the existence of a wise, triangular relationship between self, others, and truth (Figure 3.5). Habitually,

Understanding Stress from an Individual Angle 69

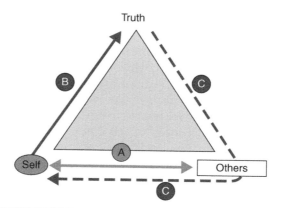

A: Normal exchanges and influences between self and others
B: Possible connections with the "real" truth
C: Consequences connected with relative truth in order to maintain relationships with others

FIGURE 3.5 The Pythagoras triangle of self-esteem, others, and the truth.
Source: Modified from Dolan S.L. Garcia S., Diez-Pinol M., "Autoestima, estrés y Trabajo". Madrid, McGraw Hill 2005 p.48. Used with permission.

we try to base our self-esteem on others giving us what we need in life: admiration, money, a job well done, support, affection, fun, etc. In fact, we spend life getting it one way or another, trying at the same time to be reciprocal.

However, there is another way for others to end up giving us what we need: not trying to get it directly, but by connecting our essential ego to a truth greater than ourselves, valid on its own. Like "magic" or something unexpected and without any logical cause and effect, life ends up giving us what we really need in order to achieve this truth or existential purpose, producing a full and deep construction of our self-esteem.

Self-effectiveness-efficacy, Self-concept, and "Hardiness"

Among the many psychological concepts related to self-esteem, the following are worth noting self-effectiveness or self-Efficacy, self-concept and hardiness".

Self-effectiveness or self-efficacy was defined by Bandura (1977) as the belief in one's own abilities to organize and execute the actions necessary to manage all possible situations; individuals are seen as products and producers of their own environments and social systems. According to Bandura, the first proponent of the concept, self-efficacy is the product of past experience, observation, persuasion, and emotion. Self-efficacy is linked to academic achievement and the ability to overcome phobias.[9] our ability to achieve a goal or complete a task depends on whether we think we can

---

[9] Bandura, A. (1977) Self-Efficacy: Toward a Unifying Theory of Behavioral Change. Psychological Review, 84(2), 191–215. http://psycnet.apa.org/record/1977-25733-001. See also: Hopper, E. (updated August 11, 2021) Understanding Self-Efficacy. What Is Self-Efficacy? Definition and Examples. (thoughtco.com)

do it (self-efficacy), and whether we think it will have good results (outcome expectancy). Self-efficacy has important effects on the amount of effort individuals apply to a given task. Someone with high levels of self-efficacy for a given task will be resilient and persistent in the face of setbacks, while someone with low levels of self-efficacy for that task may disengage or avoid the situation. For example, a student who has a lower level of self-efficacy for math might avoid signing up for challenging math classes. Importantly, our level of self-efficacy varies from one domain to the next. For example, you might have high levels of self-efficacy about your ability to navigate your hometown but have very low levels of self-efficacy about your ability to navigate a foreign city where you do not speak the language. Generally, an individual's level of self-efficacy for one task cannot be used to predict their self-efficacy for another task.

Self-concept is the sum of a series of attitudes individuals have about themselves and which can predict the actions individuals carry out to maintain this concept, whether the content is positive or negative, like a "self-fulfilling prophecy" (Burns, 1979[10]).

Hardiness – Hardiness is connected to resilience for which we will discuss separately in another chapter. But it is generally defined as the capacity for enduring or sustaining hardship, privation, etc.; it is the capability of surviving under unfavorable conditions. In the early days of research on hardiness, it was usually defined as a personality structure comprising the three related general dispositions of 1) commitment, 2) control and 3) challenge that functions as a resistance resource in encounters with stressful conditions. The commitment disposition was defined as a tendency to involve oneself in activities in life and as having a genuine interest in and curiosity about the surrounding world (activities, things, other people). The control disposition was defined as a tendency to believe and act as if one can influence the events taking place around oneself through one's own efforts. Finally, the challenge disposition was defined as the belief that change, rather than stability, is the normal mode of life and constitutes motivating opportunities for personal growth rather than threats to security.

Lately, researchers have characterized hardiness as a combination of three attitudes (commitment, control, and challenge) that together provide the courage and motivation needed to turn stressful circumstances from potential calamities into opportunities for personal growth. While acknowledging the importance of the three core dimensions, others consider hardiness as something more global than mere attitudes. Yet others, conceive hardiness as a broad personality style or generalized mode of functioning that includes cognitive, emotional, and behavioral qualities. This generalized style of functioning, which incorporates commitment, control, and challenge, is believed to affect how one views oneself and interacts with the world around. From historical perspective, the pioneer of the concept of hardiness is Susan Kobasa (1979) which has studied it in relation to protection against life stressors.[11]

---

10 Burns, R. B. (1979) *The Self-Concept: Theory, Measurement, Development and Behavior*. London and New York, Longman.
11 Kobasa, S. C. (1979) Stressful Life Events, Personality, and Health – Inquiry into Hardiness. *Journal of Personality and Social Psychology*, 37 (1), 1–11. doi:10.1037/0022-3514.37.1.1. PMID 458548.

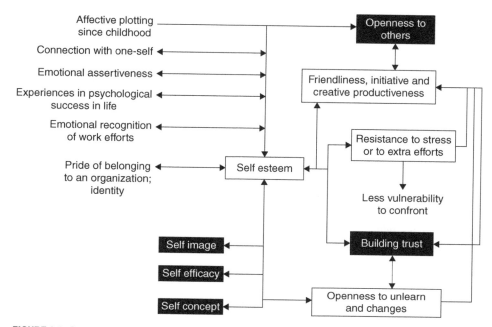

FIGURE 3.6 Some antecedents and consequences of self-esteem and occupational stress.
Source: Modified from Dolan S.L. Garcia S., Diez-Pinol M., "Autoestima, estrés y trabajo". Madrid, McGraw Hill 2005 p. 50. Used with permission.

Antecedent and Consequential Variables of Self-esteem

As we have seen, self-esteem is complex, the result of numerous, antecedent variables and the generator at the same time of diverse individual and organizational consequences. The complexity is shown in Figure 3.6.

Affective Plotting in Infancy and Adolescence – The parents' availability, accessibility, credibility, tenderness, stimulus, and reinforcement are essential for a child's self-esteem, the undeniable base on which the adult's self-esteem depends. Affective plotting or mapping consists of the early relationships of affection occurring within the home, other members of the family who more or less accept the child unconditionally, just by virtue of existing, while, at the same time, establishing limits as to what is correct or incorrect behavior. Feeling loved is essential to knowing how to love others and to be able to love oneself. It is very difficult for children to trust themselves if they haven't first trusted their parents. One of the best sources of self-esteem is having parents who exemplify good self-esteem.

Parents who generate self-esteem adopt a series of values and conducts with respect to their children:

- They raise them with love and respect.
- They allow them to feel a coherent and benevolent acceptance of themselves.
- They offer a support structure which includes reasonable rules and adequate expectations.
- They do not bombard their children with contradictions.

- They do not resort to ridicule, humiliation, or physical abuse to control them; and
- They demonstrate that they believe in their children's competence, goodwill, and responsible autonomy.

Autonomy and the Management of One's Own Self – Fernando Savater, a well-known Spanish author and philosopher, outlines in his book, *"La tarea del héroe (The Hero's mission)"* the following:

> *When man loses his creative autonomy, he begins to live himself from without, precisely because he has furnished his interior – his nothingness, his empty night – with the external, causal order. The technical ease of managing the world is accompanied by the unequivocal conviction experienced that he is no longer in charge: Theoretical king of this world, his familiarity with things has removed him from the throne. The price of forced normalisation with the trade of objects is compliance with death, in the least biological and more "spiritual" sense of the word.*[12]

This is based on the idea that the external world is not only dominated by technology and material objects, but that its dominion has also reached the very essence of human beings. Perhaps the technology and money that dominate the world are nothing more than the expression of our pre-existing levels of inner consciousness.

How many people control material fortunes yet do not control themselves, their emotions, their inner conscience, their being, or, simply, something as important as their health and continue smoking, for example? How many people go through life playing a part or reacting impulsively or more or less capriciously, without stopping to think first or decide for themselves, from within their very core?

Not being aware of what is going on around and inside you are tantamount to living your life alienated, out of control. Can you obtain a high degree of professional performance being aware of what is going on around and inside you? Of course. In fact, being incompetent in terms of self-management and being unaware of what is going on around and inside you are the source of mistakes, errors, oversights, accidents, and work-related conflict, all of which act as inhibitors of self-esteem at the same time. Being aware means feeling or thinking. It is contemplating from within what is valued: what is felt and thought and being able to freely choose another feeling or thought.

Self-esteem, Leadership, and the Success Syndrome

A great portion of contemporary management literature deals almost exclusively with success stories. A lot can be learned from them, naturally, but we must understand the root causes of that success in order to learn the right lessons.

Mark Twain once said that if a cat jumped on a hot stove, it would never jump on any stove again, hot, or cold. Success, then, can lead to conservatism, which, in a highly competitive and ever-changing environment, can lead to failure. Is this inevitable?

---

12 Free translation from: Fernando Savater (July 2005): La tarea del heroe / The Hero Mission. Destino.

Authors define the following series of causal relationships behind the "Success Syndrome": When companies become successful and dominate the market, they are convinced that they are right. This in turn makes them stop paying attention to the important changes taking place in the outside world. From this they deduce that they have nothing to fear or learn from their competitors. Besides, they reject any ideas or strategies not produced within the company.

For Kurt Lewin, one of the founders of social psychology, however, the most important success is the psychological one, the consequence of having established and recognized one's own adequate achievements, neither too difficult nor insufficiently challenging (www.brainyquote.com/quotes/kurt_lewin_178365).

As such, self-esteem can increase or decrease according to the values assigned to the numerator or the denominator in the equation above. Self-esteem is also described as "utilitarian pragmatism or efficiency-ism" by some scholars and is based on the results more than on the principles or the qualities of personal dignity. According to some observers, the person esteems or disesteems is based on what the individual obtains more than on how he acts. On the other hand, reality is always the perceived reality, and the potentialities perceived within oneself are always subjective and changing.

There is no doubt that this is an interesting approach to the phenomenon at hand. The esteem, recognition and admiration perceived from those relevant individuals we establish relationships with throughout our lives are the essential source of our perception of psychological success and self-esteem. That is why the emotional recognition for a job well done is so important in the work context, something that occurs less frequently than it should.

Self-esteem and the Triaxial Concept of Values

Dolan et al. has presented over the years a sophisticated model of values that can be reduced into 3 axes: ***Economical-Pragmatic***, ***Social-Ethical*** and ***Emotional***.[13] Accordingly, Self-esteem comes about as the result of the adequate configuration and combination of the core values considered important for the person to achieve psychological success: Example, humility (part of the social-ethical axis) in order to recognize one's own limits and avoid failures, and industriousness (part of the economic-pragmatic axis) to strive to reach goals and have successful experiences, or passion (part of the emotional axis) which states that regardless of economic success one needs to sustain passion and keep on struggling. When a person does not know the hierarchy and configuration of his/her values, these results and low self-esteem and incongruence and stress is on the rise.[14]

While research on value congruence and stress is scant, the limited studies amongst clinicians working in intensive care units often exposed to numerous stressors (i.e.,

---

[13] See for example: Dolan, S.L. (2020) *The Secrets of Coaching and Managing by Values*. Routledge; or, Dolan, Garcia and Richley (2006) *Managing by Values: The Corporate Guide to Living, Being Alive and Making a Living in the 21st Century*. Palgrave MacMillan.

[14] Dolan, and Garcia (2020) Covid-19, Stress, Self-Esteem, Values, and Psychological Well-being: How to Assess Risks of Becoming Depressed, Anxious, or Suicidal?, *The European Business Review*, May 13. (www.europeanbusinessreview.com/covid-19-stress-self-esteem-values-and-psychological-well-being-how-to-assess-risks-of-becoming-depressed-anxious-or-suicidal/)

the risk of being infected by the Corona virus, for example), shows that it affects their mental state and health. Among them, those who clearly understood their values, report less symptoms of depression and had much more vigor to assume their responsibilities.

An interesting manner to pose a diagnosis is to assess the combined classification of Self-Esteem and values. This can help map the probability of developing depression, anxiety and even suicides based on the quadrant that the person is being placed. Figure 3.7 proposes our classification:

Keys for Developing Individual Self-esteem and Avoiding Stress

While there are no universal "turn-key" recipes to boost self-esteem and lower stress, an amalgamation of advice taken from different sources, can perhaps include the following:

- **Centre yourself, calmly learn to be aware of what is going on within**. *The habitual practice of contemplative meditation allows us to be in touch with the never-changing essence of ourselves, with the best we have, with the purest, essential instance of our nature. It is an experience of serenity and essential centering to build true self-esteem, security and confidence in ourselves and others. It is especially important for those people who have influence over others, such as parents, manager s, political leaders, judges, doctors, or teachers. The aim is to reflect on oneself, looking in from the outside in order to truly see our inner self and contemplate our feelings, ideas and actions. Being aware of what we think, feel and do is very important in order to adopt the position of neutral observer with respect to our self-esteem, thereby changing it rationally and effectively for our own happiness and that of those around us.*

  Who you are is what you do? First comes being, and then comes doing. The things a person does gives added value to their being . From this idea comes Aristotle's concept of habit. The good person is one who transmits goodwill to the things they habitually work on.

  Interiorization is essential for true knowledge and awareness of one's own reality. Without knowing who you are, it is very difficult to love yourself. Nobody can love what he or she does not know. At the same time, by meditative reflection, reflecting on oneself, it is easier to redesign the real values and life purposes that will help appreciate oneself better, beyond the iconic or representative ego. You have to try to be interesting to yourself; if not, others won't find you interesting. If someone stops being interested in their own self, they cannot appreciate themselves and it will be difficult for others to appreciate them. Most likely, others won't be interesting to them either. Being able to have fun with yourself is fundamental to avoid being jealous. The effervescence inside has to be creative and fun for a deep and long-lasting self-esteem to be experienced.

- **Remember and rebuild as much as possible the love and trust with parents in childhood and adolescence.** *A person's life is worth what their love is worth. Especially, we could add, a person's life is worth what their love is worth, just as they perceive, remember, and rebuild it.*

  It is clear that affective plotting in childhood and adolescence is constructed more or less objectively. However, at times there are cognitive filters, which minimize or negatively distort our memories of having been loved and accepted by our parents and others in the first stages of our lives. It is very important, in this sense, for our self-esteem to try and rationalize to

Understanding Stress from an Individual Angle   75

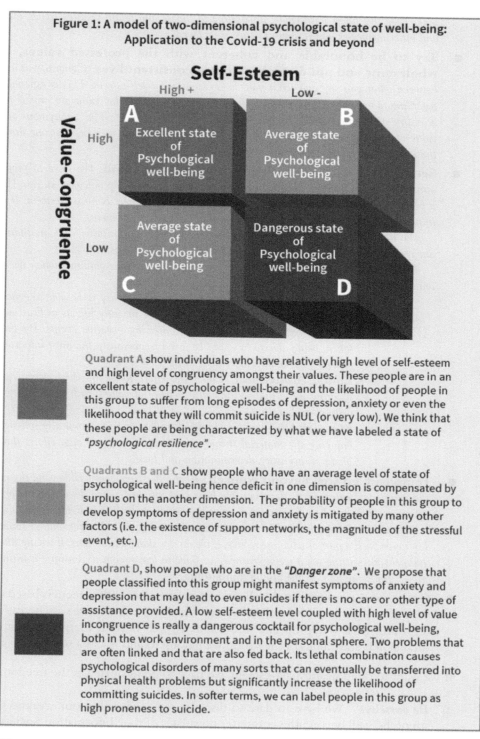

Figure 1: A model of two-dimensional psychological state of well-being: Application to the Covid-19 crisis and beyond

Quadrant A show individuals who have relatively high level of self-esteem and high level of congruency amongst their values. These people are in an excellent state of psychological well-being and the likelihood of people in this group to suffer from long episodes of depression, anxiety or even the likelihood that they will commit suicide is NUL (or very low). We think that these people are being characterized by what we have labeled a state of *"psychological resilience"*.

Quadrants B and C show people who have an average level of state of psychological well-being hence deficit in one dimension is compensated by surplus on the another dimension. The probability of people in this group to develop symptoms of depression and anxiety is mitigated by many other factors (i.e. the existence of support networks, the magnitude of the stressful event, etc.)

Quadrant D, show people who are in the *"Danger zone"*. We propose that people classified into this group might manifest symptoms of anxiety and depression that may lead to even suicides if there is no care or other type of assistance provided. A low self-esteem level coupled with high level of value incongruence is really a dangerous cocktail for psychological well-being, both in the work environment and in the personal sphere. Two problems that are often linked and that are also fed back. Its lethal combination causes psychological disorders of many sorts that can eventually be transferred into physical health problems but significantly increase the likelihood of committing suicides. In softer terms, we can label people in this group as high proneness to suicide.

FIGURE 3.7 A two-dimensional model of self-esteem and values.
Source: Dolan & Garcia (2020) The European Business Review, Used with authors permission.

make cognitive filters positive, by attempting to choose and retain positive scenes, dialogues and other memories which remind us we were loved.

- **Try to be honorable and coherent with the professed values, living wholesome and not dissociated nor inconsistent lives.** *Congruity or integrity between what you say and what you do is essential for self-esteem. This is especially true regarding moral values. The problem often lies in the fact that the values we profess to hold, according to Maturana51, are relegated to mere "lip service". The anonymous negative value of integrity is corruption. It is very difficult for someone corrupt, someone broken on the inside, to experience authentic self-esteem.*

- **Set projects with psychological successes in mind.** *We have to project our aims with perseverance and determination until we achieve psychological success. Without a project and without celebrating the results of the project there is no self-esteem. It is very important to celebrate both quantitative and qualitative achievements.*

    We must reward ourselves based on real events, both quantitative and qualitative, but always based on truth. It is impossible to lie to one's deeper-most inner-self.

    It is important not to forget that true psychological success is obtained when we incorporate and balance material, emotional and ethical achievements.

    a) **Emotional Achievement**: *Make the effort to try to be able to generate on your own positive thoughts and emotions in daily life, as well as modulate your reactive emotions when confronted by negative events. By the same token, being able to love and be loved is, obviously, the most important and general emotional achievement in life.*

    b) **Ethical Achievement**: *Make the effort to be the best person possible, savoring the actual putting into practice of values, such as integrity, generosity or authenticity.*

    c) **Material Achievement**: *Make the effort to be economically self-sufficient, enjoying the material things you obtain from your own efforts through a blend of ingenuity, determination and luck.*

- **Transcend, go well beyond yourself.** *Real self-esteem goes well beyond the material and emotional achievements that everyone has. As mentioned, when discussing the origins of self-esteem, it is based on the perception of utility for others, beyond individual utilitarianism.*

    It is also very improbable that we will reach elevated goals, either personal or social, if we don't give back a part of what we receive, if we do not share with others. If we are like a TV channel transmitting what we've learned, we have to leave room to continue learning to be alive. "Trans-mission" is the aim of transmitting.

- **Go beyond conventional beliefs and values.** *Real self-esteem is based on the adoption of judgements and behaviors which arise from one's own conscience regarding what is appropriate to do and say, well beyond the predominant cultural beliefs and values in the group we belong to and use as a reference.*

If we want to build healthy self-esteem, we have to grant ourselves the freedom to:

a) ***Be ourselves*** – We have to dare to discover our own reality, our weaknesses and strengths, well beyond the computer postulates of the "Information Society".

b) ***Come out of the emotional closet*** – We have to express ourselves, be spontaneous, show our feelings, pains and joys, as well as our own principles and criteria: aesthetic, ethical, political, etc. But especially, we have to be able to give ourselves the freedom for an adequate expression of these emotions and rights. We have to overcome the fear of making a fool of ourselves and adopt an expressive style which is neither passive nor aggressive, which allows us to express ourselves politely and at the right time let others have the opportunity to participate and help us build our own reasoning (basic emotional rights of self-esteem).

c) ***Really achieve what we visualize*** by maintaining our intention over time and transferring energy where we project it.

d) ***Enjoy learning*** about everything from everyone.

e) ***Savor*** what life offers every single moment.

f) ***Accept our own body and self-image*** – The body manifests the *ego* to the world. For example, one of the best indicators of self-esteem and mental health is to elegantly accept those little extra kilos.

 INTERESTING TO KNOW

The basic emotional rights of self-esteem, which should be assertively expressed and executed, are:

- *The right to say "no";*
- *The right to say "I don't know";*
- *The right to not do anything or have time for yourself, regardless of work-related, family, or other type of obligations.*
- *The right to take risks and make mistakes (whether that's cooking, shopping or playing your favorite sport);*
- *he right to change your opinion or criteria about people and things.*
- *The right to change your appearance or even lifestyle.*
- *The right to ask for help when you think you need it;*
- *The right to not have to put up with meaningless commitments or relationships*
- *The right to interrupt to ask a question or ask for clarification.*
- *The right to not always have to be witty and funny.*
- *The right to be sad when you're not happy.*
- *The right to have a job well done formally recognized.*
- *The right to look for new roads in life.*
- *The right to not accept advice (including, of course, the advice mentioned in this chapter).*

In sum, Study after study has found that increasing someone's self-esteem will reduce the relative amount of stress they experience, especially in work settings. The jury is still out, however, about whether increasing someone's job chronic stress (without giving them time to relax and recharge) will reduce their self-esteem levels. There is anecdotal evidence that, if a person starts with high self-esteem, stress does not seem to affect it. If, however, the person self-esteem levels start out low, stress will often reduce them even further. The question then becomes, if we know that raising our self-esteem is going to help us manage our stress, what do we do to boost it? How do we go about building our self-esteem to the level that we are in the optimum state possible to manage all those work stressors before they affect our health? As with every complex topic, there are many theories – some were reviewed in this chapter; some may seem more logical to you than others. There seem not to be a quick fix.

And finally, you need to remember that gauging the value of self-esteem requires, first of all, a sensible way to measure it. Most investigators just ask people what they think of themselves. Naturally enough, the answers are often colored by the common tendency to want to make oneself look good. Unfortunately, psychologists lack any better method to assess the phenomenon of self-esteem.

Key Demographic Factors Connecting to Stress

Perceived stress and respective adaptation have been also studied for years as a function of some key sociodemographic characteristics. There is a range of stressors at work and in personal life to which individuals are exposed. Not every stressor affects all individuals the same. Also, the relative impact of stress on individuals can change by the context (sector, industry, type of organization, type of leadership, etc.). However, some generic factors are emerging from research and the COVID-19 pandemic was an excellent opportunity for researchers to isolate those who have been more stressed than others. At the risk of overgeneralizing, a few observations are proposed herein.

Gender and Stress

While both men and women recognize the impact stress can have on physical health, men appear to be somewhat more reluctant to believe that it's having an impact on their own health. Likewise, men put less emphasis on the need to manage their stress than women do. Men see psychologists as less helpful and are less likely to employ strategies to make lifestyle and behavior changes. Yet men are more likely than women to report being diagnosed with the types of chronic physical illnesses that are often linked to high stress levels and unhealthy lifestyles and behaviors, signalling that there may be some important gender differences when it comes to stress management.[15]

---

15 Source: APA, stress and Gender (www.apa.org/news/press/releases/stress/2011/gender.pdf#:~:text=%E2%80%A2%20Historically%2C%20women%20report%20higher%20levels%20of%20stress,and%2010%20is%20a%20great%20deal%20of%20stress%29.)

Here are some several additional observations:

- Historically, women report higher levels of stress than men; men reports 5.4 and women 4.8 respectively on a scale of 1 to 10 where 1 is little or no stress and 10 is a great deal of stress.
- Not only do men and women manage stress differently, but they also place a different level of importance on doing so. Men report being less concerned about managing stress and are more likely to say they are doing enough in this area, whereas women place more emphasis on the need to do so but feel they are not doing well enough. Only 52 percent of men say it is very/extremely important to manage stress, compared to 68 percent of women. And 63 percent of men say they're doing enough to manage their stress, compared to 51 percent of women
- Only 52 percent of men say it is very/extremely important to manage stress, compared to 68 percent of women. And 63 percent of men say they're doing enough to manage their stress, compared to 51 percent of women
- Men are more likely to report relying on playing sports as a stress management technique (14 percent vs. 4 percent).
- Women are substantially more likely than men (70 percent vs. 50 percent) to say they have tried to reduce stress over the past 5 years

Figure 3.8 shows that in so far as to impact on physical health, men are more likely to report relying on playing sports as a stress management technique (14 percent) vs. (4 percent) for women. Men are less likely than women to report that stress has a very strong/strong impact on a person's health (78 percent vs. 88 percent). Furthermore, they are more likely than women to report that their own stress has slight or no impact on their physical (36 percent vs. 26 percent) or mental health (40 percent vs. 32 percent)

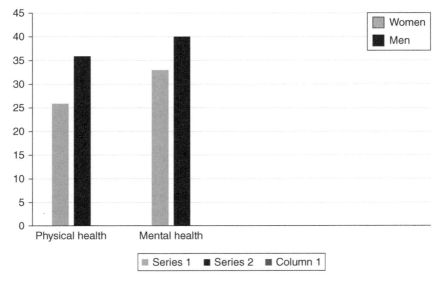

FIGURE 3.8 Effect of stress on physical and mental health of men and women.
Source: inspired by: www.stressinamerica.org

Age and Stress – Stress and Premature Aging

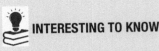

> **INTERESTING TO KNOW**
>
> *The idea of stress and aging was born many years ago while I was a junior researcher working with the team of Dr. Hans Selye at the University of Montreal. I joined the team in 1978 and stayed and worked with Hans Selye until his unexpected death in 1982. The team had several periodic meetings where new discoveries by members of the team were shared, and substantial time was also devoted to new ideas for setting a future research agenda. This was the first time that we heard Hans Selye and his close friend Dr. Paul Rohan propose a redefinition of stress as a concept of accelerated aging (or premature aging). But we did not really set up a program to study it.*

Most of us believe that stress comes only after certain years of lifespan. But it's not true. At any stage, stress can be a part of our life. Whether we are young or old, we must face difficult situations. In a later chapter we may suggest that facing stressful situations at younger age and being able to overcome it, is part of the formula of developing hardiness or resilient skills. Where young people find it difficult in finding jobs or building up careers, older people on the other hand face difficulties of declining health and financial security and their knowledge becomes obsolete. The common wisdom suggest that experience (that comes with age) helps us appraise the situation differently, so what was perceived a threat at an early age, is no longer viewed so in later age and thus consequences are less marked.

While we cannot conclude that stress comes and goes away at a certain age, there is an emerging argument proposing that an exposure to long term chronic stress or having significant episodes of acute stress can cause premature aging.

Stress and Premature Aging[16]

Simply stated, aging in humans represents the accumulation of changes in a human being over time and can encompass physical, psychological, and social changes. Reaction time, for example, may slow with age, while memories and general knowledge typically increase. Ageing increases the risk of human diseases: of the roughly 150,000 people who die each day across the globe, about two-thirds die from age-related causes. More than 70% of people over 65 have two or more chronic conditions such as arthritis, diabetes, cancer, heart disease and stroke. Studies of diet, genes, and drugs indicate that delaying one age-related disease probably staves off others. At least

---

16 This section is based on a recent paper by Dolan, S.L., and Raich, M. (2021) A Voyage into Premature Aging: The Role of Chronic Stress and Its Principal Correlates. *The European Business Review*.

FIGURE 3.9 Chronic stress, its correlates, and derivatives, which accelerate premature ageing.
Source: Illustration by Sebastian Fernandez – ZINQUO (Used with permission).

a dozen molecular pathways seem to set the pace of physiological ageing. The factors affecting premature aging are depicted in Figure 3.9.

Biologically, ageing results from the impact of the accumulation of a wide range of molecular and cellular damage over time. Thus, this leads to a gradual decline in physical and mental capacity, a growing risk of diseases, and ultimately, death. These changes are usually consistent, and they are associated with a person's age in years. While some people aged 70 years may be strong and enjoy good health, others who are 70 years old may be weak and require others to help them. The real question about aging is whether the chronological age and the biological age are identical. There is growing evidence that this might not be the case. Hence, some people reach premature aging, and others benefit from postmature (delayed) aging. The real question is: Why is it happening? Why do some people look older in their 20s, while others look like they'll stay young forever? In recent years, there have been some interesting studies that have found all kinds of factors that influence the process and may shed more light on one of the most important questions of mankind.

The underlying hypothesis proposed by Dolan and Raich in their paper, includes the following:

- Stress, being acute or chronic, damages cells, and eventually leading to early (or premature) aging.
- Chronic stress ages the brain.

- Chronic stress leads to vision and hearing loss.
- Chronic Stress contributes to an unhealthy lifestyle.

Level of Education and Stress

The common wisdom suggests that those with more education live longer, healthier lives than those with fewer years of schooling. The question is: why does education matter so much to health? The links are complex and tied closely to income and to the skills and opportunities that people have to lead healthy lives in their communities.

In today's knowledge economy, a person with more education is more likely to be employed and land a job that provides health-promoting benefits such as health insurance, paid leave, and retirement. Conversely, people with less education are more likely to work in high-risk occupations with few benefits.

People with more education – and thus higher incomes – are often spared the health-harming stresses that accompany prolonged social and economic hardship. Those with less education often have fewer resources (e.g., social support, sense of control over life, and high self-esteem) to buffer the effects of stress.

In addition, education in school and other learning opportunities outside the classroom build skills and foster traits that are important throughout life and may be important to health, such as conscientiousness, perseverance, a sense of personal control, flexibility, the capacity for negotiation, and the ability to form relationships and establish social networks. These skills can help with a variety of life's challenges – from work to family life – and with managing one's stress including navigating the health care system.

Educated people tend to have larger social networks – and these connections bring access to financial, psychological, and emotional resources that may help reduce hardship and stress and improve health

Obviously, all the above are generalizations, but all in all having higher level of education helps to perceived more accurate perception of reality and engage in a range of adaptation behavior that can help alleviate stress.

Job Status-hierarchical Level and Stress

There are hundreds of pieces of research that shows that in a typical organization, high-status managers are theorized to reduce stress compared with subordinate roles, albeit the fact that higher rank is not always stress-free. True that high status inhibits stress responses and improves performance during complex task accomplishment, but high-status boosts stress responses and carries no performance advantage in an unstable hierarchy. Feeling in control seems to be the real asset for any employee at any level to reduce stress.

Moreover, high social (hierarchical) status reduces stress responses in numerous species, but the stress-buffering effect of status may dissipate or even reverse during times of hierarchical instability. Social status is robustly linked with health outcomes in most human societies. Individuals with higher socioeconomic status live longer, experience increased well-being, and have lower rates of stress-related diseases such as cardiovascular conditions and type 2 diabetes. These health benefits may be explained in part by the stress-buffering effects of status. High status inhibits responses to acute stressors which reduces physiological wear and tear and the likelihood of developing stress-linked diseases. In further support of the hypothesis that status buffers stress, attaining high rank in a hierarchy, such as a leadership position, is related to reduced concentrations of basal cortisol, a hormone released as part of the hypothalamic–pituitary–adrenal axis in response to psychological stress.

Despite a growing scientific consensus that high status is related to lower stress in humans, this previous research has focused primarily on stable hierarchies. During times of hierarchical instability, when status could change, it was found that high status might boost, not buffer, stress responses. After all, the threat of losing a powerful, high-ranking position and the need to defend it may be stressful.[17]

Chapter Summary and Postscript

In this chapter we described the relationship between some individual characteristics and stress especially through the angles of personality, self-esteem, and some key sociodemographic characteristics. However, regardless of the latter, there is an issue that has been under studied over the years and has to do with the connections between values and stress.

The relationship between incongruence amongst core values and stress tends to become stronger when a value is ranked as more important, but people do not live coherently with it. Our own studies show that there is considerable evidence that not knowing or not living congruently with our core values leads to stress. If it persists, it leads to all the negative "wear and tear" consequences. A host of studies connect values – especially the notion of value incongruence – with the social-psychological construct of "dissonance" or more specifically "cognitive dissonance". The latter refers to a situation involving conflicting attitudes, beliefs, values, or behaviors. The theory proposes that this is not sustainable as it produces abnormal behavior or even diseases and thus this feeling of discomfort eventually leads a person to alter some of his/her attitudes, beliefs, or behaviors in order to restore balance.

One thing is certain: a prolonged state of value incongruence leads to stress, and stress is a condition that debilitates the body and the soul. I am convinced that the latter negatively affects our physical and mental health.

Interestingly, though, the medical and biological literature has started to borrow concepts from psychology and sociology to explain the mutation of cells (or diseases). Traditional medical textbooks classify diseases by the affected organ or system, and frequently by the agent involved, for example, viral and bacterial diseases. But increasingly, mental, and physical diseases are appearing that cannot be explained sufficiently in this manner – among them the process of aging. The models of diseases have changed, and the new paradigm includes the social phenomenon involved in the

---

17 Knight, E.L., and Mehta, P.H. (2017) Hierarchy Stability Moderates the Effect of Status on Stress and Performance in Humans, *PNAS* January 3, 2017, 114(1), 78–83; first published December 19, 2016; https://doi.org/10.1073/pnas.1609811114

etiology of a disease. One of the social factors that has been identified in this context is value incongruence

When an individual experiences chronic value incongruence, the likelihood of health-related problems increases dramatically. In our own research, our colleagues found out that nurses who felt trapped in their jobs (they wanted out because of value incongruence) but were forced to stay in their positions because of economic needs, experience a higher level of job burnout and also have an incidence of metabolic syndrome higher than expected given their age.[18] Metabolic syndrome is a key predictor of heart disease and type 2 diabetes. Burnout – an unpleasant and dysfunctional condition that both individuals and organizations would like to avoid – has been established as a stress phenomenon. It presents a pattern of health correlates one would expect to find with the following conditions: headaches, gastrointestinal disorders, muscle tension, hypertension, cold/flu episodes, and sleep disturbances, among others. Stress phenomenon is also a form of mental distress characterized by (a) a predominance of dysphoric symptoms such as emotional exhaustion; (b) a predominance of mental and behavioral symptoms; and (c) decreased work performance resulting from negative attitudes and behaviors.

The scientific evidence for the negative outcomes of chronic value incongruence for both organizations (e.g., productivity loss, or incapacity to retain talent) and individuals (e.g., likelihood of mental and physical diseases) is overwhelming. Mind you, we are not talking about a form of temporary or transitory incongruence; we are talking about a permanent feeling or perception.

Despite the obvious connections, the relationships between values, cognition, stress, and illnesses are complex and not fully understood. But science is advancing our understanding of psychological experiences. We now know that these experiences in some ways both arise from (or are manifestations of) and affect brain chemistry and biology. It appears that cognitions leading to stress influence biology (i.e., ageing).

 ACTION

A QUICK QUIZ TO ASSESS YOUR SELF ESTEEM AND YOUR VALUE CONGRUENCE:

For each of the questions describing your feelings, emotions, and actions, simply mark the "yes" or "no" option. Sometimes, answering will not be easy. However, you still need to elect if it is more a "yes" or more a "no".

---

18 Bao, Y., Vedina, R., Moodie, S., and Dolan, S. The Relationship between Value Incongruence and Individual and Organizational Well-being Outcomes: An Exploratory Study among Catalan Nurses, *Journal of Advanced Nursing* 69(3), 631–641.

A. SELF-ESTEEM

Question	Yes (or strongly agree)	No (or strongly disagree)
1. I feel that I am a person of worth; I am as good as anybody else		
2. I feel that there are a lot of good things about me		
3. I feel that I fail a lot		
4. I can do most things as well as most other people		
5. I do not have much to be proud of		
6. I wish I had more respect for myself		
7. I feel useless at times		
8. Sometimes I think I am no good at all		
9. I like myself		
10. I am happy with myself		

Reverse the score for questions 3,5,6,7,8 (if you answered yes – place an X in the No column, and if you marked No – place an X in the Yes column.

INTERPRETATION

The scale ranges from 1 to 10. If you have accumulated a total of 6 and more "no", it suggests low self-esteem.

B. VALUE CONGRUENCE

Question	Yes (or strongly agree)	No (or strongly disagree)
1. From the hundreds of values that are important to you, can you identify clearly your 5 core values?		
2. Are you able to clearly place 5 core values in a hierarchy from the most important to the relatively least important?		
3. Do you feel ambiguous about your core values?		
4. When there is a conflict between some of your core values, are you able to solve it quickly?		
5. All in all, do you feel that your daily conduct and behaviour (work and home) is aligned with your values?		
6. Do your core values serve you the same way at home and at work?		
7. Is your behaviour during crisis (like the Corona pandemic) guided by your core values?		
8. Do you keep changing your core values to satisfy your surroundings (your partner, family and relatives)?		
9. Do you keep changing your core values to satisfy your bosses and colleagues in work settings?		
10. Would you agree that your core values and corresponding conduct are meaningful and give essence to your life?		

Reverse the score for questions 3, 8, 9 (if you answered "yes" – place an X in the "No" column, and if you marked "No" – place an X in the "Yes" column)

INTERPRETATION

Note: the scale ranges from 1 to 10. If you have accumulated a total of 6 and more "no", it suggests a relatively high level of value-incongruence

Once completed the two short quizzes, place it on the template herein, and then go back for the explanation provided in Figure 3.7 for the interpretation

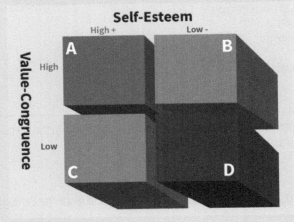

FIGURE 3.10 Self-esteem.

* The self-esteem scale was modified from Rosenberg 1965. www.socialworkerstoolbox.com/rosenberg-self-esteem-scale/. Free tools. used with permission.

CHAPTER 4

Stress, Coping, and Consequences

Individual and Organizational

Introduction: Stress as a Difficulty in Adapting to the Environment

Stress is a normal part of our daily lives. It is generally associated with a negative state or detrimental experience, which must be eliminated at all costs. But this isn't always the case. Stress becomes negative when this experience becomes *excessive, uncontrolled,* or *uncontrollable*. In the workplace, an insufficient amount of work as well as an overload of work can lead to the worker feeling inhibited, with the resulting physical and mental consequences.

Depending on the type of job and the organizational and cultural characteristics of the job, work-related stress can take many forms. From this perspective, stress, in general, means an *effort to adapt*. Faced with an excess of environmental demands (*over-stimulation*) related to the person's very source of satisfaction, the person feels unable to resolve them. However, there can also be a lack of environmental stimulation (*under-stimulation*), which produces boredom and fatigue within the individual. Both in over and under-stimulation the action necessary to cope with the situation is inhibited. Thus, the traditional Performance-Stress Relationship Curve, looks like an inverted "U" (see Figure 4.1), At zero arousal, the person has zero performance—which means that he/she is either sleeping or inactive. At maximum arousal, the person *also* has zero performance—here, being overwhelmed incapacitates the person. Curiously enough, the only way to have any performance is to have *some* level of arousal. At the same time, specific areas of the brain are activated producing an inhibition of the body's defence mechanisms, along with reduced mobility and a lack of exploratory behaviours. This leads to greater vulnerability to disease and infection. Only with a level of moderate activity do behaviors such as friendliness, creativity and professional commitment arise.

In order to find out if someone adapts well to the stress in an environment, researchers have developed a tool called "Stressful Life Events". Any change in the routine of our lives – even welcome changes – can be stressful, both in terms of the way in we perceive them and in terms of the increased incidence of physical illness and death that occur during the 12 months following the changes. The Holmes-Rahe

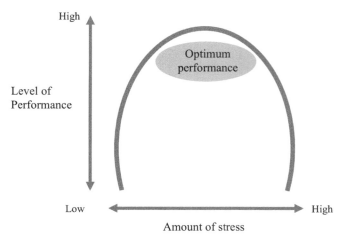

FIGURE 4.1 Stress & performance: The Inverted U Stress Curve.

Scale assigns values (based upon the sample being told that marriage represents 50 points) attributed by a sample of 394 individuals to the life events concerned.[1]

 SELF-ASSESSMENT EXERCISE

ASSESS YOUR LIFE STRESS AND ADAPTATION

This is a list of stressful events in your life which have different number values to show the pressure that it ads to your life. Sit back, take a moment, and review your life over the past one to two years. Go through the following list. Place a check mark on the box of those stressful events that have happened or are taking place in your life. When you are done calculate your total score and see the general interpretation. Note that in life additional events can generate stress. However, the following is based on the original work of Holmes and Rahe.

1. Death of spouse	100	23. Child leaving home	29
2. Divorce	73	24. Trouble with in-laws	29
3. Marital separation	65	25. Outstanding personal achievement	28
4. Prison sentence	63	26. Spouse starts or stops work	26
5. Death of an immediate family member	63	27. Starting or ending school	26
6. Personal injury or illness	53	28. Change in living conditions	25
7. Getting married	50	29. Revision of personal habits	24
8. Dismissed from job	47	30. Trouble with boss	23
9. Marital reconciliation	45	31. Change in working hours or conditions	20
10. Retirement	45	32. Change in residence	20
11. Change in health of family member	44	33. Change in schools	20

---

1 Holmes, and Rahe (1967) Holmes-Rahe Life Changes Scale. *Journal of Psychosomatic Research*, 11, 213–218.

12. Pregnancy	40	34. Change in recreation	19
13. Sexual difficulties	39	35. Change in church activities	19
14. Gaining a new family member	39	36. Change in social activities	18
15. Business readjustment	39	37. Minor mortgage or loan	17
16. Change in financial state	38	38. Change in sleeping habits	16
17. Death of a dear friend	37	39. Change in number of family reunions	15
18. Change to a different line of work	36	40. Change in eating habits	15
19. Change in frequency of arguments	35	41. Trips	13
20. Major mortgage	32	42. Major holiday	12
21. Foreclosure of mortgage or loan	30	43. Minor violation of law	11
22. Change in responsibilities at work	29		

Your overall Stress Score is:_____

Result and Interpretation of the scores

0–149 –   *Relatively low susceptibility to stress-related illness.*

150–299 –   *Medium susceptibility to stress-related illness (you need to learn and practice stress management skills and adaptation techniques in order to pursue a healthy lifestyle).*

300 and over –   *High susceptibility to stress-related illness (Daily practice of stress management skills are called for. It is very important for your wellness. Take care of it now before a serious illness erupts or an affliction becomes worse.*

Some notes and observations about this Holmes and Rahe scale:

Note 1: *Some critics have suggested that the Holmes and Rahe Stress Scale is weak in certain areas. For example, some believe that different cultural groups react differently to different life events. For example, one study compared American and Malaysian participants. Interestingly, the Malaysians' attitudes toward breaking the law and toward relationships were different overall from those of the Americans studied, meaning that their experience of stress was different, even though they had the same score. So, keep cultural differences in mind as you score your own life events.*

Note 2: *While it's useful to know about this idea so that you can act, don't dwell on it, and don't let this knowledge negatively affect your mood.* Think positively!

In the workplace, **occupational stress** consists of the *imbalance between the individuals' aspirations and the realities of the person's work conditions*. It is the perceived difference between the professional demands and the person's ability to carry out the demands. As such, the perception of a lack of control over the situation and a feeling of over-exertion beyond the individual's resources leads to feeling run down due to excessive activation. This wear and tear has consequences at different levels: it generates a state of irritability, a feeling of adaptative failure in controlling the situation, and an initiation of biological processes which favour the appearance of illnesses (mood, cardiovascular and immunological disorders primarily).

Specialized literature offers many theoretical models to explain and understand work related stress. The model proposed by us (Dolan and Arsenault, 1980), for example, allows for a diagnosis to be made so that the long-term, irreversible consequences of stress can be reduced. The authors maintain that problems of adaptation are produced by the discordance between the person and the person's work environment. Depending on the degree of discordance, a variety of signs and symptoms of strain (i.e. the stress indicators) will appear. The relationship established between the individual and the person's work environment evolves depending on the adaptation cycle. This is subject to variation depending on time-related issues and changes either in the organization or in the individual. A general description of this model was described earlier in Chapter 2 of this book, however there are six blocks of relevant variables in studies regarding occupational stress.

- **Environmental Variables (stressors and resources)** – Environmental variables are basically conceived as a discrepancy or as an imbalance between the environmental demands and the available resources (personal and environmental). It has been demonstrated that control, decision-making ability and social support can work as moderators or shock-absorbers affecting the results and consequences.
- **Personal Characteristics** – Various stress models (as presented in the previous chapter) have emphasized the importance of individual characteristics and their differences regarding the processes of stress. The Type A personality, the resistant personality, neuroticism, cognitive styles, self-efficacy, the locus of control, values, and other more or less stable characteristics play a modulating role over the different influences which appear during the stress process (stressor-appraisal, appraisal-confrontation, appraisal-results-consequences, appraisal-coping). We will elaborate these concepts later in presenting the chapter on the stress map (Chapter 7).
- **The Subjective Experience** – This block distinguishes between the appraisal and the coping processes. Some scientists distinguish between primary appraisal (the evaluation of an event as benign, irrelevant or negative) and a secondary appraisal (the evaluation of the necessary resources once the event has been categorized as negative). Coping refers to the cognitive and behavioural efforts to control, reduce or eliminate the effects of the situation perceived to be negative.
- **Individual Responses: Coping Strategies** – This is directly related to the previous block and takes into consideration the individual's coping strategies and the appraisal regarding whether or not these strategies have been successful.
- **The Result of Stress** – This block defines the physiological, cognitive and behavioural reactions, which take place when an individual faces stressing stimulus.

Antecedents of Stress

The first studies on stress were aimed at finding a single definition, either focusing on physical factors or on psychological and/or social factors. However, I share the current school of thought that stress is an illness with various and diverse causes (it is a multifactorial and dynamic concept) including individual characteristics, psycho-social working characteristics, organizational characteristics, and social and cultural aspects, among others.

It is virtually impossible to provide a single and complete list of stressors and their consequences, especially if we bear in mind that the definition of stressor depends on the individual appraising a specific situation as such. However, we can establish and identify a series of stressors based on their source

Intrinsic Sources, and Extrinsic Sources

What is truly interesting is that these two sources of stress are related differently to the negative consequences of stress. **Extrinsic sources** of stress, for example, are *related linearly* (i.e., directly) in that these sources accumulate (see Figure 4.2). Extrinsic means that these sources of stress have a common denominator – they are related to the work context (for example, salary, timetable, company policies, benefits, etc.). On the contrary, **intrinsic sources of stress are** related to the specific job content (responsibilities, decision making, etc.), and they have an *inverted U relationship* with the negative consequences generated by stress, as can be seen in Figure 4.2.

Some Typical Intrinsic Antecedents in Work Settings

Opportunity to control – A characteristic that can produce stress or, on the contrary, psychological wellbeing is the *degree to which a work environment allows the individual to control the tasks at hand*. This characteristic can be described as: autonomy, participation in decision-making, influence, power, etc. First, it is important to distinguish between intrinsic and extrinsic control. Intrinsic control has a clear relationship with work satisfaction when it neutralizes other factors (pay, security, etc.). A lack of intrinsic control implies a series of negative psychological and somatic consequences (insomnia, headaches, anxiety, exhaustion, coronary disease, etc.). Excessive control

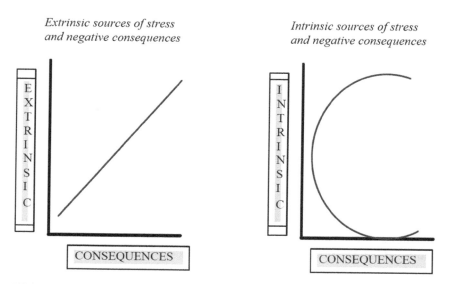

FIGURE 4.2 Extrinsic, intrinsic sources of stress and respective consequences.

also implies negative consequences. Extrinsic control seems much less related to mental health as it is often in the hands of unions and company representatives.

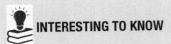 **INTERESTING TO KNOW**

Some jobs are more stressful than others. A great deal of stress is found in jobs with changing shifts, those with a demanding pace and those with little or no control over one's job. However, both the executive under pressure to meet short term goals and financial results as well as the worker who has to carry out a great deal of work at low pay are at risk of suffering stress due to work.

The University of Manchester Institute of Science and Technology (U.K.) carried out a study analyzing stress levels in different jobs, using a scale of 1 to 10. The results indicated a higher degree of stress among professionals within the mining, construction, and service sectors (police, journalists, dentists, doctors, etc.) than that found in management positions:

- *Miners 8.3*
- *Police 7.7*
- *Construction workers 7.5*
- *Journalists 7.5*
- *Dentists 7.3*
- *Doctors 6.8*
- *Nurses 6.5*
- *Ambulance drivers 6.3*
- *Teachers 6.2*
- *Personnel Managers 6.0*

The changes, which take place in companies, are a widely recognized, general source of stress. If these changes imply technological change or moving offices, they can be a very important source of stress, especially when there are doubts or little participation in terms of these changes.

Source: The University of Manchester Institute of Science and Technology (U.K.)

Opportunity to use one's skills – Another important characteristic of psychological wellbeing is the opportunity the job provides for us to use and develop our skills. It seems that the higher the position within the organization, the greater the opportunity to use skills at work. As with other characteristics, it seems that intermediate levels are the most adequate since little or very elevated opportunities produce stress. There have been problems reported with anxiety, insomnia, and indigestion, among others.

Variety of tasks – This characteristic refers to novelty and change within a specific job or work environment. As such, it is important to distinguish between the intrinsic and extrinsic variety of tasks. The intrinsic variety can be defined as the degree to which the job requires different activities in order to be carried out, implying the worker's use of different skills and talents. The extrinsic variety refers to the aspects not related to the task as such, but rather to the work environment (music, lighting, windows, etc.).

Feedback – The feedback received on an employee's actions and results is, up to a point, a valued aspect. It has been demonstrated that workers whose job has this characteristic are more motivated and enjoy greater job satisfaction.

Some Typical Extrinsic Antecedents in Work Settings

The environment in which people live influences their health and their physical, psychological and social wellbeing. Their environment can be a source of problems, restrictions and discomforts, putting to the test their capacity to adapt. An individual's expectations and needs regarding the characteristics of their work environment (location, size, etc.) are basically similar to those regarding where they live. In terms of work, the possibility of choosing a company that meets their expectations is often very limited. However, the need or desire for the company to fulfil certain characteristics (pleasant setting, close to home, positive social image, pleasant workplace, etc.) does not diminish.

The lack of these characteristics can turn into additional pressures to the demands of the job, thereby aggravating the psycho-social problems the individual already has. The stressors originating in the workplace affect the individual's personal and professional life, creating problems within the family on both the personal and professional levels. This turns into a vicious cycle, the stressful work situation affecting the worker personally, and the personal situation affecting work. We spend a great deal of our time at work and a large part of our identity stems from the jobs we do. For this reason, professional-work stressors are very important.

The Most Stressful Jobs during the COVID-19 Pandemic

There were many classifications and numerous studies offering to identify the most stressful jobs during the COVID-19 pandemic. Here is a quick summary of some of these suggestions.

Data from LifeWorks Mental Health Index – September 2021 & September 2020 shows the following differences for various sectors (Table 4.1).

The most stressful jobs in 2021 are those that are still the most directly affected by the COVID-19 pandemic. The most stressful jobs are found in the "Arts, Entertainment and Recreation" sector, which has experienced necessary restrictions and reduced government support longer than most other sectors.

Workers in the "Health Care and Social Assistance" sector are the second most stressed, after more

than nearly two years of dealing firsthand with the devastating COVID-19 pandemic while often putting their own health at risk. Employees in the "Wholesale Trade and Education Services" sector also report high levels of stress, linked to global supply issues and the difficulty of adapting initially to virtual learning and then to altered in-person learning environments.

TABLE 4.1 The most stressful jobs and changes between 2020 and 2021

Industry	2021 %	2020 %	CHANGE %
Arts, Entertainment and Recreation	63.4	57.9	+5.5
Health Care and Social Assistance	60.7	58.0	+2.7
Wholesale Trade	59.5	58.8	+0.7
Information and Cultural Industries	58.9	57.5	+1.4
Educational Services	58.9	60.3	-1.4
Automotive Industry	58.5	56.1	+2.4
Mining and Oil and Gas Extraction	57.4	52.0	+5.4
Accommodation and Food Services	57.4	60.7	-3.3
Retail Trade	56.8	56.6	+0.2
Manufacturing	56.5	55.8	+0.7
Construction	56.4	55.1	+1.3
Public Administration	56.3	56.6	-0.3
Full-time student	56.1	61.3	-5.2
Real Estate, Rental and Leasing	56.1	54.0	+2.1
Management of Companies and Enterprises	55.9	60.7	-4.8
Finance and Insurance	55.2	58.8	-3.6
Utilities	54.8	61.4	-6.6
Professional, Scientific and Technical Services	54.6	55.1	-0.5
Transportation and Warehousing	54.1	59.1	-5.0
Agriculture, Forestry, Fishing and Hunting	53.8	54.0	-0.2
Other	51.7	51.3	+0.4
Other services except public administration	51.1	56.0	-4.9

Source. The Most Stressful Jobs in 2021: Jobillico.com

Consequences of Occupational Stress

What consequences does stress have for workers? And for organizations? In today's world, organizations have to be able to give quick and effective responses to change, this pressure is passed on to the workers and creates a stressful situation at both the organizational and personal levels. A stressed organization is an organization where there is an imbalance between its objectives and its internal and external realities (Corporate strategy, technology, human resources, culture, values, economic results, competitors, etc.).

At the same time, the stressed worker suffers from an imbalance, in this case between his or her expectations and professional interest and the reality of his or her individual work conditions (responsibilities, autonomy and control, incentive programs, career plans and professional development, etc.).

Excess stress can manifest itself in a variety of emotional, behavioural, and even physical signs and symptoms. Some people distinguish the signs from the symptoms. The signs are data that can be collected objectively (photos, x-rays, blood or urine analysis) while symptoms are more subjective. The latter vary enormously among different individuals.

Personal Physical Consequences

Not everyone feels the same degree of stress nor shows similar reactions to a specific type of stress factor. Obviously, the previous section, which describes different types

TABLE 4.2 Borysennko dichotomy of connecting stress and disease

Autonomic Dysregulation (Over responsive autonomic nervous system)	Immune Dysregulation
migraines	infection
peptic ulcers	(virus)
irritable bowel	allergies
syndrome	AIDS
hypertension	cancer
coronary heart	lupus
disease asthma	arthritis

of personalities suggest that some people are more prone to stress than others. If, for example, the demand is matched by the person's abilities, knowledge, health and personality, stress will tend to diminish, and there will be positive, stimulating signals which will let the person advance in the professional arena while achieving greater achievements in terms of personal, spiritual and material gratification. Depression, anxiety, irritability and somatic problems are the more typical manifestations of stress, as well as various forms of addictions (i.e. to nicotine, alcoholism, drugs and others).

In terms of the physiological consequences of stress, researchers have detected an increase in the secretion of catecholamines (adrenaline and noradrenaline) and steroids, as well as an increase in blood pressure, all symptoms appear prior to the development of stomach ulcers and cardiovascular disease.

The symptomatology produced by occupational stress is, in great measure, psychosomatic and related to: migraines, gastrointestinal problems, virus-related processes, sleep disorders, dermatological problems, etc. This leads to the problem being treated more often than not as a common illness and not as a work-related pathology.

Although science has not been able to demonstrate a concrete connection between stress and disease in humans, this section presents various scientific views and explanations of hypothesized relationships between stress and disease. Taking together the thousands of papers and scientific articles published in various journals, disciplines, and geographical locations, one can conclude that 70 to 80 percent of health-related problems may be precipitated or aggravated by stress. Stress and illness in general have been studied with a focus on three subsystems: Endocrine sub system, immune sub system, and the nervous subsystem.

Borysenko has developed an interesting framework to connect stress and diseases.[2] A summary of the continuum proposed by Borysenko is exhibited in Table 4.2.

A word of caution: In order to understand the stress-disease/mind-body phenomenon, we need to consider individuals as greater than the sum of its physiological part.

In the workplace, the physical problems suffered by workers are easier to quantify than psychological effects, although both are equally important. Table 4.3 describes some of the pathologies, which may be produced by stress.

So, what we can observe is that stress, when accumulated and experienced over time, can cause serious physical diseases. Some research even suggests that stress can trigger cell mutations and produce cancer. Although cancer is multifactorial (genetic,

---

[2] Borysenko, J. (1988) *Minding the Body, Mending the Mind by Joan Borysenko* New York, Random House, Inc.

TABLE 4.3 Most frequent physical pathologies derived from stress

GASTROINTESTINAL DISORDERS	Peptic ulcer Functional dyspepsia Irritable bowel syndrome Ulcerous colitis Aerophagia Slow digestion
CARDIOVASCULAR DISORDERS	High blood pressure Coronary disease (angina, myocardium) Arrhythmia
RESPIRATORY DISORDERS	Asthma Hyperventilation Dyspnoea Feeling pressure in the thorax
ENDOCRINAL DISORDERS	Hypoglycaemia Diabetes Hyperthyroidism Hypothyroidism Cushing Syndrome
SEXUAL DISORDERS	Impotence Premature ejaculation Vaginism Painful intercourse Alterations in the libido
DERMATOLOGICAL DISORDERS	Itches Atypical dermatitis Excessive sweating Alopecia Trichotillomania
MUSCULAR DISORDERS	Tics and spasms Rigidity Muscle pain Alterations in muscular reflexes (hyperreflexia, hyporreflexia).
OTHERS	Migraines Chronic pain Insomnia Immunological disorders (flu, herpes,...) Loss of appetite Rheumatoid arthritis

eating habits, sedentary life, etc.) the impact of the psychological factors is non-negligible. In a similar manner to the exposure of certain chemicals causing cancer, so is the chronic exposure to the psychological work environment.

Moreover, stress is also causing sleep deprivation that is known to reduce our immune function and expose us to a variety of disease contaminations. Figure 4.3 shows the relationships between stress and the immune system.

Studies also show that negative mood (anxiety, depression, hostility), which are a characteristic of some people during acute stress, lead to fewer cytotoxic & suppressor T cells, and thus leads to more outbreaks of all forms of the herpes.

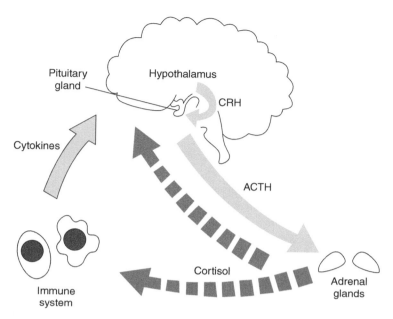

FIGURE 4.3 Stress and the immune system at the molecular level.
Source: The figure was borrowed from www.nih.gov/news/WordonHealth/oct2000/stressfigure.htm which is no longer available. The figure was used with permission in the former edition of this book.

FIGURE 4.4 Potential effects in healthy individuals.

Stress and ulcers is another recent discovery. Research suggests that 66 percent of people under stress eat MORE than usual (hyperphagic) and eat fast. During prolonged stress digestion shuts down. There is decreased acid release, decreased mucus, which protects the stomach and decreased thickness of stomach living.

But obviously not every person has the same proneness to develop certain diseases during stress. The importance of coping capacity is detrimental, this is demonstrated in Figures 4.4 and 4.5.

Personal Mental Consequences

A large number of emotional disorders dealt with primary healthcare centres masking cases of occupational stress. People suffering from stress habitually consult their healthcare centre more often than those who do not show this type of problem.

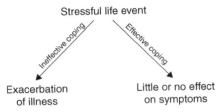

FIGURE 4.5 Potential effects in symptomatic individuals.

These people are normally treated therapeutically for the disorders but not for the underlying stress. This situation, without a doubt, leads to short-term remission of some of the stress related symptoms, though in the mid and/or long term, the individual will either feel the same or worse than before.

Below is a list of some of the mental and emotional consequences of stress:

- *Irritability:* Being in a bad mood, irascible, and the person feeling like "snapping at the slightest provocation" may be the consequence of a case of chronic stress.
- *Emotional exhaustion:* The person feels exhausted, without the vital energy necessary to carry out daily activities, especially those outside of the office and related to the family (partner, children) and friends, among others.
- *Forgetting important things:* There are frequent lapses in memory, especially with important life events (wedding anniversary) or those related with people we are very close to (meeting with a child's teacher, calling a friend, etc.).
- *Wanting to radically change our lives:* A stressed person tends to have polarized and inflexible thoughts, limiting the ability to see things relatively. This makes the person tend to overexert himself to adapt to work or life in general. Feeling stressed implies wanting a radical change in life, partner, and profession, among other things. Stressful thoughts, such as *"This can't go on"* or *"I need to separate"*, are common.
- *Repeatedly postponing planned actions:* A stressed individual tends to postpone the actions and tasks considered important. For example: *"one of these days I'll give up smoking"* or *"I need to make more time to be with my kids"*. However, getting round to finding those days and making more time never materializes.
- *Sense of a lack of time:* People suffering from stress tend to feel that there isn't enough time to take on the tasks and objectives before them. This feeling makes them uncomfortable and unhappy with themselves. They may have a low appreciation of what they do as they focus more on what they haven't been able to finish rather than on what they've accomplished.
- *Cynicism and mistrust:* The stressed individual tends to be pessimistic, frustrated and suspicious towards others. This type of behaviour is generally a consequence of repressed aggression within the individual.

Organizational Consequences

The effects of stress can be found not only on the personal level, but also within the organization. A prolonged situation of negative stress leads to a deterioration in the work environment, fewer and poorer interpersonal relationships, as well as a loss in productivity and job performance.

There are tens of different algorithms that were developed over the years by researchers, executives, consultant and accounting companies in an attempt to estimate the cost of stress to organizations. Some of these are obvious and make sense, others are more creative. As an example, in one case it is argued that the results of being stressed, or feeling underappreciated, is low engagement. And the latter is translated to a cost that is estimated at 9 percent of the payroll. That's a lot of lost profit, not to mention lost opportunity, and this is measured in so called normal times. In unusually, or prolonged, stressful times the risks of employee engagement impact clearly increase. I found the following presentation different from the more linear algorithms and thought that it will be interesting to present it (Table 4.4.). The left side of the cost matrix represents the average impact of engagement on earned versus paid compensation per 100k of employee cost. This leads to a theoretical cost of low engagement. The right side of the matrix represents the average percentage of employees at each of the engagement levels. This leads to a much more accurate cost of low engagement.

On a more traditional tone, job stress is estimated to cost American companies more than $300 billion a year in health costs, absenteeism and poor performance. Here are some relevant statistics:

TABLE 4.4 Stress, engagement, and impact on profits

Stress is a primary cause of Low Engagement

Summary	9% of table employee salary & benefits costs are lost to low engagement in the average organization				
Sources	Google search "employee engagement cost" will result in a long list of studies and data supporting this summary				
	Average % of contribution versus cost	Profit/Loss dollars per 100 k	Theoretical Profit/Loss of low engagement per 100 k	Actual % of employee engagement levels	Actual Profit/Loss of low engagement per 100 k of salary and benefits
Fully Engaged	120%	100 k x 120 % = 120 k	20 k PROFIT	12%	20 k profit x 12% of employees = 2.4 k PROFIT
Engaged	100%	100k x 100 % = 100 k	0 k P/L	40%	0 k profit x 40% of employees = 0 k P/L
Somewhat Engaged	80%	100 k x 80 % = 80 k	20 k LOSS	39%	20 k loss x 39 % of employees = 7.8 k LOSS
Disengaged	60%	100 k x 60 % = 60 k	40 k LOSS	9%	40 k loss x 9 % of employees = 3.6 k LOSS
			Theoretical loss **40,000.00** per 100 k of & Salary.		Actual loss **9,000.00** per 100 k of &Salary

Source: What is the COST OF STRESS to your organization? – BUILDING A HEALTHY COMMUNICATION CULTURE (jameslauber.com)

- 40% of job turnover is due to stress.
- Healthcare expenditures are nearly 50% greater for workers who report high levels of stress.
- Job stress is the source of more health complaints than financial or family problems.
- Replacing an average employee costs 120–200% of the salary of the position affected.
- The average cost of absenteeism in a large company is more than $3.6 million/year.
- Depression is the largest single predictor of absenteeism and work-related performance.
- Depressive illness, a common side effect of job stress, in employees is associated with nearly 10 annual sick days (this study included one large firm).
- For every 47 cents spent on treating depression, another 53 cents is indirectly spent on absenteeism, presenteeism and disability.
- Insurance data indicates insurance claims for stress related industrial accidents cost nearly twice as much as non stress related industrial accidents.

Source: Compiled by the University of Massachusetts – Lowel (www.uml.edu/Research/CPH-NEW/Worker/stress-at-work/financial-costs.aspx)

In 2002, the European Commission calculated the costs of work-related stress in the EU-15 at €20 billion a year. This figure was based on an EU-OSHA (1999) survey that found that the total cost to the EU-15 countries of work-related illness was between €185 and 289 billion a year. Using estimates derived from other researchers indicating that 10 percent of work-related illness is stress related, this percentage was applied to a conservative estimate of the total cost of work-related illness (€200 billion) to obtain the figure of €20 billion for the cost of work-related stress for this group of countries. In a more recent EU-funded project), the cost to Europe of work-related depression was estimated to be €617 billion annually. The total was made up of costs to employers resulting from absenteeism and presenteeism (€272 billion), loss of productivity (€242 billion), health care costs of €63 billion and social welfare costs in the form of disability benefit payments (€39 billion).[3]

Although the precision of the above figures is subject to debate, the message is very clear: the cost of stress in the workplace is enormous, and, if opportune measures are not taken, there is no doubt that this cost will steadily rise. This is why any program focused on stress with the aim of reducing the costs of stress will be extremely beneficial for the company.

Chapter Summary and Postscript

In this chapter, we have summarized the main causes of work-related stress and their consequences and effects at the personal and organizational levels. Without a doubt,

---

3 Source: Calculating the cost of work-related stress and psychosocial risks European Risk Observatory Literature Review, European Agency for Safety and Health at Work (2014) cost-of-work-related-stress.pdf

the consequences to both are enormous. When the working environment fosters an optimal level of activation, it helps promote healthy culture and all benefit (individuals, teams and organizations). But, when stress levels are high, it becomes toxic . Every possible attempt should be made to manage it. Thus, we will dedicate an entire chapter (Chapter 8) to focus on strategies of individual and organizational stress management techniques and interventions. We will also include in Chapter 9 our predictions about work stress in the future.

Work is a central part of human life. It is the expression of the basic need to accomplish, to create, to feel satisfaction, and to feel meaningful. Rewarding work is an important and positive part of our lives. However, when work denies people an opportunity to utilize their creativity, intelligence and decision-making ability, it causes stress.

The traditional response of management has been to "blame the victim", defining stress as an individual or "personal" problem that workers bring from home to work. In contrast in this chapter and the ensuing chapters, we will see that this approach that blames people for their inability to fit into a job or an organization is by far more complex. At time workers are subject to an inhumane work environment, or to be managed by toxic leaders or simply to be mismanaged. Stress is an interactive term, it is cognitive, but it is always recommended to analyze the structure of the job requirements, the nature of the social relationships at work and other factors in addition to individual traits and personality.

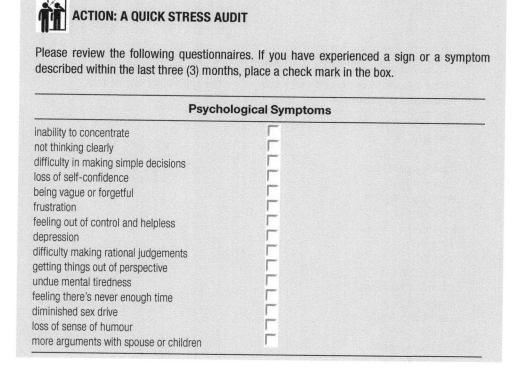

ACTION: A QUICK STRESS AUDIT

Please review the following questionnaires. If you have experienced a sign or a symptom described within the last three (3) months, place a check mark in the box.

Psychological Symptoms	
inability to concentrate	☐
not thinking clearly	☐
difficulty in making simple decisions	☐
loss of self-confidence	☐
being vague or forgetful	☐
frustration	☐
feeling out of control and helpless	☐
depression	☐
difficulty making rational judgements	☐
getting things out of perspective	☐
undue mental tiredness	☐
feeling there's never enough time	☐
diminished sex drive	☐
loss of sense of humour	☐
more arguments with spouse or children	☐

Emotional Symptoms

feelings of anxiety or worry	☐
irritability	☐
angry outbursts	☐
feelings of guilt	☐
feelings of hostility	☐
defensive and over-sensitive to criticism	☐
feeling isolated from colleagues and friends	☐
fear of rejection	☐
feelings of anxiety or worry	☐
irritability	☐
angry outbursts	☐
feelings of guilt	☐
feelings of hostility	☐
defensive and over-sensitive to criticism	☐
feeling isolated from colleagues and friends	☐
fear of rejection	☐
fear of failure	☐
fear of success or promotion	☐
panicky feelings or panic attacks	☐
nightmares or disturbing dreams	☐
feelings of impending doom	☐
feelings of worthlessness	☐
feelings of hopelessness	☐
feel lonely or sad	☐

Physical signs

Place a mark in the box if you experience the following symptoms frequently or severely

sweaty, clammy hands	☐
shaking hands	☐
knot in the stomach	☐
butterflies in the stomach	☐
hyperventilation	☐
erratic breathing	☐
palpitations	☐
rapid pulse	☐
dizziness	☐
faintness	☐
ringing in the ears	☐
difficulty in swallowing	☐
lump in the throat	☐
sore throat or hoarseness	☐
enlarged glands in the neck	☐
high-pitched voice	☐
talking faster than usual	☐
jelly legs	☐

cramps ☐
restless leg syndrome ☐
physical tiredness ☐
feeling of being drained ☐
insomnia ☐
waking up in the middle of the night or too early ☐
still tired after a night's sleep ☐
headache ☐
dry mouth ☐
muscle tension ☐
tight neck or shoulders ☐
teeth grinding ☐
sexual difficulties ☐
stiff jaw ☐
constipation ☐
diarrhea ☐
nausea ☐
abdominal pain or indigestion ☐
loss of appetite ☐
excess hunger ☐
high or low blood pressure ☐
frequent urination ☐

Women only:
Difficult menstruation ☐
Premenstrual syndrome ☐
Menopausal or pre-menopausal difficulties ☐

Men only:
Weak or slow urine stream ☐
Prostate trouble ☐
Trouble with erections ☐

Behavioural Signs
Smoke more than usual ☐
Drink more alcohol than is generally accepted is good for health ☐
Eat more sweets, chocolate, or pastries than usual ☐
Take antidepressants, tranquilizers, sleeping pills, narcotics, pain relievers, marijuana, or other street drugs ☐
Eat less than usual ☐
Eat more than usual ☐
Bingeing on foods or alcohol ☐
Taking laxatives or purging to control weight ☐
Becoming a workaholic with no time for relaxation or pleasurable activities ☐
Absenteeism from work ☐
Avoidance of certain people or places ☐
Withdrawal from social gatherings ☐

Obsessive or compulsive behaviour; for example, checking and re-checking you have locked the doors, switched the lights off, washing your hands over and over again, etc.

pulling your hair out (e.g., hair on head, eyebrows, arms, etc.).

RESULTS AND INTERPRETATION

A. PSYCHOLOGICAL MANIFESTATIONS

If you marked more than eight symptoms in this category, you are likely to suffer from significant stress and you manifest it psychologically. If you marked between five and seven you are experiencing medium-high stress, and below four is more or less normal.

B. EMOTIONAL SYMPTOMS

If you marked more than eight symptoms in this category, you are likely to suffer from significant stress and you manifest it emotionally. If you marked between five and seven you are experiencing medium-high stress, and below four is more or less normal.

C. PHYSICAL SIGNS

If you marked more than nine signs in this category, you are likely to suffer from significant stress and you show physical signs of it. Between five and eight marks medium-high stress, and below four is more or less normal.

D. BEHAVIOURAL SIGNS

If you marked more than nine signs in this category, you are likely to suffer from significant stress and you show physical signs of it. Between five and eight marks is medium-high stress, and below four is more or less normal.

Note: *Although this test is based on my accumulated research, it has not been empirically validated. We had used it again and again in our hundred's workshops to managers and executives, and the reaction was very favorable.*

A suggestion: *Repeat the same audit at two points of time in about 6 months interval. If the patterns of your responses are similar it means that you are suffering from chronic stress and if you marked many categories, it indicates your incapacity to manage the stress in your work/life. It also means that you might be better off to consult a health professional who may help you manage your stress and reduce your chances of serious health problems.*

CHAPTER 5

Understanding Stress from an Organizational Leadership Angle

Introduction

Stress has been implicated as an important determinant of leadership functioning. Conversely, the behaviour of leaders has long been argued to be a major factor in determining the stress levels of the followers. Yet despite the widespread acknowledgement that stress and leadership are linked, there has been limited systematic attempt to organize and summarize the knowledge in this area. Recently a comprehensive meta-analytic review shed more precision on the relationship between leadership style, stress and burnout.[1] We build on these results to suggest new frameworks to help develop leaders that on the one hand will be less stressed, less toxic to their followers and, on the other hand, build a stressless culture.

Being a leader often includes handling stressful situations, taking decisions and actions which could have implications for the leaders themselves, for their followers and in many cases to the entire organization. A recent survey by Gallup found that great leaders who avoid generating stress in the organization seem to have the following talents:

1. In addition to fostering trust and open communication, they offer complete transparency.
2. Not politics, but productivity drives their decisions.
3. With a compelling mission and vision, they motivate and engage all of their employees.
4. A culture of clear accountability is fostered by them.
5. They are capable of driving outcomes, overcoming adversity and overcoming resistance.

---

1 Harms P.D., Crede, M., Tynan,,M., Leon, M., and Jeung, W. (2017) Leadership and Stress: A Meta-analytic Review, *The Leadership Quarterly*, 28(1), 178–194.

The fundamental goal for a business leader is the achievement of success in the long term. In order to succeed, there are numerous leadership skills that need to be developed. The latter are not only important when building a company but maintaining and nurturing a healthy and productive workforce.

Nonetheless, almost 60% of leaders reported feeling worn out at the end of each day, which can be an indication of burnout. One recent survey found that 44% of leaders who feel worn out and used up planned to move to a new company in order to advance their careers.

Stress in leadership can have a negative effect on a company's bottom line. In fact, a recent survey of 2000 professionals found that 76% report that work stress **has negatively impacted** their relationships and **66%** report losing sleep because of work stress. A small but significant number, 16%, say they've had to quit a job due to stress.[2]

Leaders and Stress

Working in today's corporate environment tends to attract individuals who are comfortable with pressure. Private sector firms in most industries and sectors have distinct patterns of intense activity and are temporary endeavours, requiring the participants to "move on" and adapt to constant change. Corporate leaders expect a certain degree of stress and challenge and thrive on this, but there is a "mean tolerance threshold" and it is not sustainable to exceed this for long periods. Leaders are expected to be confident, but sometimes there is confusion around those who exhibit a high degree of self-assurance. Occasionally overconfidence is mistaken for great leadership.

One needs to realize that leaders are frequently solitary individuals with a "trailing spouse" who has followed them to some far-flung location and is struggling to adapt to cultural differences, often adding personal stress to the equation. In most innovative project environments, collaboration across the supplier eco-system is seen as a good approach to reduce transactional stress.

In their book "***Work Without Stress***", **Roger** and **Petrie** correctly point out that leaders in today's workplace are under ever-increasing pressure. These are among what they characterize as "BOCA conditions" in the workplace culture:[3]

- **Blurred boundaries** where new technologies mean that fork has penetrated all times and locations.
- **Overload** from the volume of work exceeding the ability to keep pace with it.
- **Complexity** of problems becoming more systemic and more difficult to solve.
- **Addictive**, meaning that many leaders with high-achieving personalities are addicted to the stimulation of work.

---

2 Source: 25 SURPRISING LEADERSHIP STATISTICS TO TAKE NOTE OF (2022), 25 Surprising Leadership Statistics To Take Note Of (2022) (apollotechnical.com)
3 Roger, D., and Petrie, N. (2017) *Work without stress: Building a Resilient Mindset for Lasting Success*, McGraw-Hill Education.

The Concept of Rumination

So how do we avoid stress? The key according to Roger and Patrie, based on three decades of research is that stress is not an inherent part of life. Pressure, on the other hand, is a part of life. Pressure according to them is the "demand to perform", and this may be intense but there is no inherent stress in it. The way to deal with this pressure is to have *resilience* – the ability to be cope with the challenges life throws at us. Pressure only brings on stress when we add another ingredient "**rumination**" – focusing on past regrets and anxieties about the future: "I should have done this", or "What if this happens?". Applying this formula to leaders Roger and Petrie propose the following interesting algorithm:

Pressure + Rumination = Stress.

And, fortunately, we are not genetically programmed to ruminate. It is a habit and, as neuroscience research has shown, the brain has the capacity to adapt and move away from bad habits.

Rumination is not the same as "reflection", which is the process of thinking over a problem to arrive at a solution, saying for example "What if we tried this approach? What else could we try?" Reflection is important and an essential leadership tool. But effective reflection can be hindered or shut down by rumination when we say for example "What if we fail? What if I end up losing my job?"

To be resilient means monitoring how we react to events. The ubiquitous phrase *"Shit happens!"* is unfinished say the authors. It should be *"Shit happens; misery is optional"*. Resilience is about reacting to unfolding events without adding emotional judgement or negativity and without adding the misery of stress.

Across the spectrum of mental health, stress may not seem the most acute problem, but it is a widespread one that causes personal misery and leads to organizational under-performance. Recently a few business leaders, such as Virgin Money CEO Jayne-Anne Gadhia, have spoken openly about mental health – the problems they have faced and the challenge of dealing with mental health issues that still make many uncomfortable. The mental well-being of employees is a leadership issue and helping people learn to work without stress is an important starting point.

Prevalence of Stress and Mental Health Issues among Leaders

Because leadership is hard work that requires immense sacrifice, many times CEOs are treated like heroes to celebrate or gods to worship. This mode of thinking perpetuates the pressures put on CEOs to be superhuman, and conceal their vulnerabilities and challenges behind closed doors, with sometimes fatal consequences. But when the cameras aren't rolling, the immense pressures of the job and the psychological extremes needed to get there start to reveal themselves.

It seems that leaders are not excluded from having high stress and eventually developing mental illnesses. In fact, some scholars conclude that they might be at a greater risk of developing mental health issues. In a recent review, Barnard reports that "Science shows that the pressures of leading at the top exhibit themselves in recurring pathologies in CEOs – narcissism, over-optimism, fear, anxiety, anger, obsessive compulsive disorder and depression". Barnard points out that some studies have shown that in fact CEOs may be depressed at more than double the rate of the general public.[4]

According to a study by Davidson and his colleagues at Duke University Medical Center, 50% (half) of the presidents of the US between 1776 and 1974, had been afflicted by mental illness – and 27% met those criteria while in office.[5]

Psychologist Michael Freeman and his colleagues have researched extensively mental health conditions among entrepreneurs. They report that of the 242 entrepreneurs surveyed, 49% reported struggling with a mental health condition. Depression ranked as the #1 reported condition and was present in 30% of participants. (Compare that to the U.S. population in general, where only 7% report themselves as depressed).[6]

And in a survey conducted by Vistage (an international organization for CEOs), 100% of 2,400 participating CEOs are suffering stress; CEO stress, according to this study comes namely from the need to operate in a VUCA world (external sources where U= uncertain economy).[7]

Remember that in many cases, mental health disorders and addiction often go hand-in-hand, but their prevalence amongst executives may be particularly high due to the unique path co-occurrence takes for this population. Unfortunately, executives may also be especially likely to avoid treatment by hiding behind their success, keeping them from getting the help they need. The medical establishment recognizes that substance abuse often arises as a form of self-medication. The problem is that in the long run it only makes mental health issues worse. Although there are no studies yet specifically focused on the prevalence of executives with mental illness and co-occurring addiction, clinicians believe that executives as a group may be particularly prone to psychological distress and self-medication for both lifestyle and personality reasons.

The diagnostic criteria of mental illnesses all share one thing in common: they cause distress and loss of normal function. And many executives cope with that distress by turning to drugs or alcohol, resulting in co-occurring disorders that push you deeper into danger. At the most basic level, a busy work schedule with poor work-life balance can leave little room for basic self-care activities such as exercise, good nutrition, forging meaningful personal relationships and simply relaxing. The lack of self-care in turn can compound pre-existing emotional distress and leave you vulnerable to substance abuse. Taking a pill, having a drink, snorting a line is fast and easy, much more so than carving out meaningful space for self-care.

There is also a more deeply rooted and less easily solved reason for the high rate of co-occurrence: Many CEOs fall into the personality type that we labelled in a

---

4 Barnard (2008), J.W. *Narcissism, Over-Optimism, Fear, Anger, and Depression: The Interior Lives of Corporate Leaders*, College of William & Mary Law School William & Mary Law School Scholarship Repository (Narcissism, Over-Optimism, Fear, Anger, and Depression: The Interior Lives of Corporate Leaders (wm.edu)

5 Jonathan, R.T., Kathryn, M.D., Connor Swartz, M. (2006) *Mental Illness in U.S. Presidents between 1776 and 1974: A Review of Biographical Sources.* | PubFacts

6 Freeman, M.A. Johnson, S.L., Staudenmaier, P.G., and Zisser, M.R. (2015) Are Entrepreneurs "Touched with Fire"? Pre-publication manuscript (Copy of Are entrepreneurs touched with fire 12/14.docx (michaelafreemanmd.com)

7 www.vistage.com/?s=stress

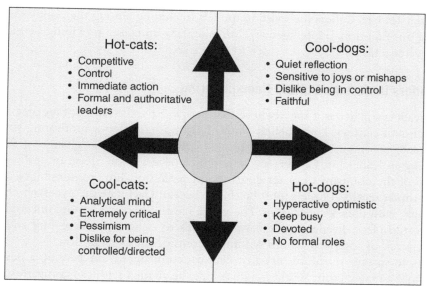

FIGURE 5.1 Dolan and Arsenault personality classification and stress.

former chapter "HOT-CAT". That means that they like to be involved in "Aggressive Action" (Type A behaviour) and in control (Rotter's Internal Locus).[8] Rather than turn to outside sources of help, such as psychiatrists, therapists, or even family and friends, they believe that they can manage their emotional and behavioural turbulence. After all, managing is what they think they do best.[9] The classification in Figure 5.1 complements with more information.

In sum, it is difficult for leaders to be stress-less. Nonetheless, their competences, personality and other factors can help them detect the acute as well as long term effect on the "wear and tear" of their body and soul, and undertake preventive measures to manage their stress and by doing so, not only that they can promote their own wellness, but also create a healthy and productive work environment and add value to their organizations. We will review and present the range of stress management techniques and strategies in Chapter 8.

Competences and Skills of a Leader Enabling Resilience and Better Stress Management

In today's work environment, there are numerous competency models floating around. Some organizations develop their own competency models and use it to

---

8 See also: Dolan S.L., van Amaringen M.R., and Arsenault A. (1983) Personality, Social Support and Workers' Stress. *Relations Industrielles / Industrial Relations,* 47(1) (Winter 1992), 125–139.

9 This is one of the reasons that we have developed the stress map, attempting to help hurries executives that they think they are not stresses, diagnose their condition but in a relaxing and gamification manner, so they are at easy. A full description of the tool is provided in Chapter 7.

train their leaders. Others use existing models (including among the popular models training in Emotional Intelligence Competencies and also providing services in executive coaching).[10]

Helping Leaders Undertake Culture Reengineering

Many leaders still act as if they believe that people have the same values they had in the twentieth century. These beliefs are no longer as effective at motivating staff and only create a context of misfit (i.e. stress). In the world, a clear change of focus is occurring in leadership. Leaders are required to have a higher level of performance because of the company's greater demands on professionalism, responsibility, quality and customer service. Leaders must be able to lead and facilitate the necessary changes to comply with these expectations. The world has also become a more uncertain and complicated place. Leaders must have the skills to cope with increasing and continuous levels of complexity both within and outside the organization.

Thus, to survive in the twenty-first century, companies must develop a new way of acting – a new culture. Workers' values must be aligned with the company's vision and mission. In this sense, the concept developed by Dolan et al. "**Managing by values**" (hereafter MBV) and "**Coaching by values**" (hereafter CBV), can serve as the framework for reengineering the culture of the company, which eventually will foster congruence and better fit (i.e. less stress).[11]

In other words, MBV is a philosophy that combines personal challenges and priorities with those of the surrounding environment, while core values are the primary element for understanding success in business life and in the life of business. Essentially, coaching for values in the context of leadership is a flexible framework (or approach) for the continuous renewal of corporate culture, and it is essential to inspire a collective commitment to the organization and its achievements.

Changing an entrenched culture is the hardest task a leader faces. To do this, he/she must gain the trust of the people they work with and act with cunning and persuasion. In their book "The Blue Ocean Strategy: creating new market spaces where competition is irrelevant", Kim and Mauborgne mention four obstacles that a leader has to overcome by trying to instill values, in a broad sense, in a company.[12]

- The first is cognitive, as people must have a certain understanding of why a new strategy is needed.
- The second is limiting resources. Inevitably, changes in the culture of a company require the movement of teams in certain areas.
- The third difficulty is to get the motivation of the workforce.
- The last step has to do with institutional policies.

---

10 For emotional intelligence see: Goleman, D., Boyatzis, R.E., and McKee, A. (2002). *Primal Leadership: Realizing the Value of Emotional Intelligence,* Boston: Harvard Business School Press. For executive coaching, see: Dolan, S.L. (2020) *The Secrets of Coaching and Leading by Values,* Routledge.

11 Dolan, S.L., Garcia, S., and Richely B. (2006) *Managing by Values,* Palgrave MacMillan; Dolan, S.L., (2020) *The Secrets of Coaching and Leading by Values,* Routledge.

12 Kim, W.C., and Mauborgne, R.A. (2015) *Blue Ocean Strategy: How to Create Uncontested Market Space and Make the Competition Irrelevant.* Harvard Business Review Press.

To overcome these limitations, they and many other experts suggest a "tipping point" approach and, from there, manage all other departments:

- First, the leader must recognize that it will not be able to introduce all the changes at the same time. They can start with people who are very influential in the company and get their commitment. Once they are involved, the others will receive the message and accept it more easily.
- Secondly, to generate sensitivity to the necessary change (speeches charged with emotions but complemented with data always helps) and look for ways where people are aware of the situation and thus can see the needed change.
- Finally, it is necessary to have clear methodology and simple tools to advance the changes. In this way, it will be easier to build coalitions and design the strategy towards the new direction of the organization.

All leaders run the risk of losing contact with what is actually happening in the lower positions, but if they can pre-plan benchmarks and be informed by the "Task Force", or by an internal or external consultant, it will help the leader go through the motions, adjust if needed and focus on the solution.

Helping Leaders Develop New Competences

In an increasingly globalized, chaotic and changing world, the principal role of leaders is to demonstrate that they have the skills to lead. There is ample research that shows that leaders who think that their current skills have become obsolete, are by far more stressed. To speak of a leadership implies much more than just having knowledge of an area, it has to do with the influence that is exerted on the followers and an awareness of the virtues and the shortcomings, that one possesses. Remember leadership is all about followership.

In the course of history, leadership has evolved and been approached from different angles. However, as of the beginning of this century, it is common to hear about skills and competencies. Nonetheless, it is difficult to agree on the basic skills and competences that a good leader needs to possess. Therefore, in this section, we will focus on four groups of main competencies: the competence to agglutinate followers around some core values including spiritual values; digital leadership; the critical soft skills of a leader connected with some personality traits; and finally, the leader capacity to overcome situations of stress, conflicts and other threats.

Competences of Digital Leadership

Digital leadership is an approach focused on the competences of the leader to harness the company's digital assets, including emails, digital documents, audible content, images, movies and other content stored on digital devices. Digital leadership has to do with digital commitment, collaboration and accountability.

Digital leaders ensure that the assets of those responsible have a maximum value. The digital leadership ensures that the system can be understood and used by all others in the firm as they depend on the reliability and speed of the digital/technological system.

To exercise the digital leadership for the quality and functional value of a company's information, the business has to rely on the people in charge of the digital assets and the information they provide. When a company needs to spend time validating sources and vetoing the digital information provided by the CEO or another self-proclaimed digital leader, this is time-consuming. When digital leadership is properly managed, organizations can move faster and create a competitive advantage.

Broadly speaking, the following observations regarding leaders in the digital age make sense:

1) They need a faster plan as speed matters in today's world.

2) They need to quickly utilize culture and relationships to further advance the organization (not themselves).

In short, in case leaders do not possess these digital skills, they need to get consultants that will help them become more successful in the digital age by increasing their ability to adapt quickly to changing technologies and contexts. Leaders must recognize that their behaviour and their interpersonal skills are increasingly public and open to the opinions or reactions of a wider range of stakeholders than in the past. They should be aware that simply not participating in online activities does not inoculate them from the effect that digital technologies have on themselves as well as on their organizations.

The Emerging Leadership Competencies: Enhance Resilience and Combat Stress

At this point, I wish to propose a set of leadership competence that we have developed over the years. It has a triaxial structure and includes nine competencies classified into three categories (see Figure 5.2):

- the first group of competencies are connected to the leader in generating "**Results**";
- the second group of competences are connected to the leader's ethical conduct and "**Integrity**";
- the third group of competencies are connected to the leader's personal traits and attitudes which we labeled "**Personal Mastery**".

A leader Has to Generate Results

The leader has to manage **the performance**. Obtaining the results desired by the organizations depends on being able to align and integrate the work of the collaborators with the strategy previously defined. In order to do this, performance management processes, which are the foundation of individual and collective compliance in any organization, must be incorporated.

Nonetheless, in order to generate results, the competence of **perseverance** stands out. Perseverance is what the sea uses to dissolve the rocks on the coast; perseverance is what the wind uses to turn the highest mountains into plains; perseverance implies

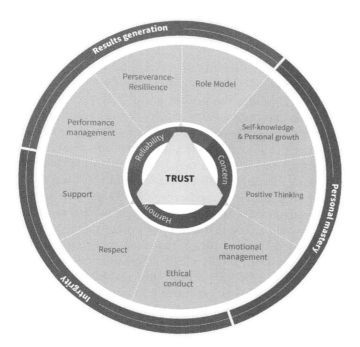

FIGURE 5.2 The triaxial PIR model of leader competences.
Note: the ideas and the competences were developed by me, based on my years of research and writings on leadership competences. However, the labels and the illustrations were co-developed by my associates in ZINQUO, namely by David Alonso and Sebastian Fernandez (www.zinquo.com).

a whole series of qualities such as discipline, constancy or repetition, will, patience and others.

> There is a story about Winston Churchill when he was already in an advanced age. He was supposed to deliver a lecture at a university. He appeared before a large audience, calmly approached the microphone, looked into the room, and after a while he exclaimed, "You should never surrender". Everyone was expecting what he would say next, but he kept quiet. He kept the silence for a long time and again approached the microphone and exclaimed, "You should never surrender", the room burst into applause until again there was silence. He went back to the microphone and again said, "You never surrender" after this, left the room.

Another important characteristic of a leader that produces results is his/her **role model** follow. After all, we have mentioned before that leadership is all about followership. So, followers wish to have a role model to follow; follow a leader who influences our working life in a positive way. Followers want to follow a leader they can point to as an example in almost all the things they do. Good leaders set the pace of their followers for their lifestyle, behaviour and actions. Followers will become a fanatic of the leader who becomes a mirror through which they see themselves and make adjustments to live a dignified and better life.

A leader Has to Be Integral – Integrity Includes Three Competencies: Respect, Support and Ethical Conduct

Respect – respect is mutual. The leader has to respect his followers, but the followers have to develop a respect for their leader. There are many ways to measure the respect of a follower towards a leader, although the greater proof of respect is given when a leader makes a big change in the organization and his respect remains intact. The reasons why people accept the changes of their leaders can be very diverse, but one of these reasons is that they are people who make a difference and want to be part of the vision of the organization. Another reason may be that the leader has invested a lot of time and energy in his relationships with people and added value to their lives.

Support – imagine that your father or mother is your leader. Can you imagine living without knowing if your parents support you? The same is true of a leader's relationship with his team. I'm not saying that you must instantly support everything that happens, you have to know that if the rules of the game are being followed, your team can always have the support from you as a leader. Scientific research shows that employees' perceptions of team leaders' support are more positive when the leader gets involved in four types of behaviours: (1) effectively monitor work (giving timely feedback and reacting to problems at work with an understanding and help); (2) provide emotional support (to show support for actions or decisions of a team member) and help to alleviate stressful situations for subordinates; (3) recognize good work in a private and public way; and (4) consult the subordinates about the work (asking for their ideas and opinions and acts on the ideas or desires of the subordinates).

Ethical behaviour – a leader with high ethical standards conveys a commitment to equity, inculcating the confidence that both they and their employees will honour the rules of the game. Similarly, when leaders clearly communicate their expectations, they prevent people from armouring and ensure that everyone is on the same page. In a safe environment, employees can relax, invoking the brain's greater capacity for social commitment, innovation, creativity and ambition. In the field of neuroscience, this point has been corroborated: when the amygdala registers a threat to our safety, the arteries harden and thicken to handle an increase in demands and even stress. This competition is about behaving in a way that is consistent with their values. If you find yourself making decisions that feel at odds with your principles or justifying actions despite an annoying feeling of discomfort, you probably need to reconnect with your core values.[13]

A Leader Must Apply Competences of Personal Mastery in His/Her Conduct

Self-knowledge and personal development – when the leader is willing to grow, the entire team grows because this attitude nurtures growth. All living organisms have an

---

13 I recommend that you read a paper that we have published recently on what happens when integrity and ethics symbolize only empty words in the company. It is a sarcastic way to show that talking about values and integrity without practicing them can only lead to deception and demise. Liran A., and Dolan S.L., "Values, values on the wall, just do business and forget them all: Wells Fargo, Volkswagen and others in the hall", published in the Business Times, September 2016 and also in the European Business Review in 2006. Can be download at: http://itemsweb.esade.edu/research/fwc/news/Liran&Dolan.pdf.

innate need to leave imprint of their genes. Those at the receiving end feel a sense of gratitude and loyalty. Think of the people you are most thankful for: parents, teachers, friends and mentors. Most likely, they have taken care of you or taught you something important. When leaders show a commitment to our growth, the same primary emotions are exploited.

Positive thinking – having a positive thinking helps to give followers a sense of optimism. A show of openness to new ideas encourages learning for all. To encourage employee learning, leaders must first ensure that they are open to learning (and changing course of action) themselves.

Managing emotions – leaders who lack emotional control will not remain in a leadership position for a long time. There has been no shortage of published articles on the subject of emotional intelligence in recent years. After all, being in touch with your emotions as well as being in tune with each other's emotions is an important trait for any leader to possess. Emotional control is a skill that most leaders need to be successful in managing their employees. Workers often look at leaders to see examples of how to behave, especially during times of agitation and change.

Therefore, leaders must be prepared to present a serene and rational front. When leaders are highly controlled in expressing emotions, they are seen as more sympathetic, ethical and working in the interest of the organization.

Is a Trustworthy Leader Less Stressed?

Leadership and Trust – the Value of Values

I have been studying TRUST in organizations for over 25 years (with colleagues such as Shay Tzafrir, Yehuda Baruch, Ben Capell, Merce Mach and Hila Chalutz). We have studied this important construct in different sectors, companies and contexts. It is not a surprise to see that we have labeled TRUST as the mother of all values, the "**Value of Values**". Hence without trust, a leader is powerless to influence the followers. We build our lives on the basis of trust relationships.

The "teams" of which we are members, be it organizational, social, political, families and couples define their qualities based on the trust of their individuals. We trust others to obey basic rules of behaviour. We trust that businesses accept our credit cards. Indeed, all aspects of a labour relationship – our organizational cultures – are based on the trust of and towards others.

Much of the conflicts in organizations arise because leaders do not have the capacity to generate and/or sustain trust. How can a leader have followers if he or she doesn't trust him? Unfortunately, research suggests that in more and more companies (families included if we use it as a metaphor for an organization), it seems that people have lost trust in their leaders and their peers. We note this breach of trust in business, government agencies, education and even in our churches (you only have to listen to the scandals that are published on the corrupt behaviour of the priests).

This general distrust by our leaders points to a cultural breakdown. The problem is not a lack of leaders, but a lack of a climate of trust, where leadership is possible and without which, it is impossible. Unless followers feel confident in fairness and reliability in their leaders, they will not continue to follow them. Trust can significantly alter individual and organizational effectiveness. It is trust, more than power and hierarchy that really makes an organization work effectively.

So, if we know that trust is a pre-requisite for any attempt by the leader to change the organizational culture, and to sustain the reliability, motivation and behaviour of the followers, why don't we help leaders to improve trust. In my opinion, people use the word trust too often in making a generic reference and therefore until we have a clear definition and a simple metric to measure it, we will continue to operate without a compass. The consequence will be simple: the more a leader uses the word trust (without precision), the more the followers and companions will lose interest in listening to him/her and it will naturally lead to disappointments and stress to all involved.

For this reason, at the beginning of the 2000s, I began to study trust in a work setting, in a rigorous and systematic way. In 2004, we published for the first time an article where we have identified the three key dimensions of the concept of trust (**RCH**), as we have refined the tools to measure it. The three dimensions that have emerged from the numerous scientific studies are:

Reliability, **C**oncern and **H**armony

- **Reliability** is a leader's competence that shows that he is true to his words, makes him/her do what they say, and does it consistently. This dimension is connected to the efficiency of performance and related to the economic-pragmatic axis of the triaxial value model (**red colour** in the original "value of the values" card game and light grey in Fig. 5.3).
- **Concern** is equated with the interest that the leader really displayed in interacting with his/her subordinates. The leader is affectively and emotionally involved in the relationship, shares common and complementary goals. It also shows that the leader is concerned and manifests interest in problems that his/her followers and companions might have and shares values such as empathy or sympathy. This dimension is connected to the emotional axis of the triaxial value model (**green colour** in the original "value of the values" card game and grey colour in Figure 5.3).
- **Harmony** occurs when there is an ethical-social bond between the leader and his follower. This means that there are elements such as integrity, respect and other ethical-social facets (**blue colour** in the original "value of the values" card game and dark grey in Figure 5.3).

Today, an executive coach can measure and categorize the three dimensions of trust and translate it into the template such as the triaxial RCH model. With this model, we can identify the percentage of trust that the collaborators have in their leader and detect which of the dimensions dominate (it means good level of trust) and which one has to improve. To help executive coaches and consultants do a better job in diagnosing low levels of trust and also in designing training or coaching sessions for improving the problematic dimensions, we have developed an online platform that produces analysis at 360° instantaneously (see: www.leadershipbyvalues.com).

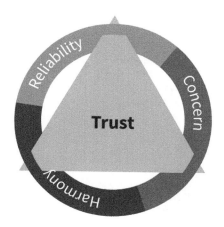

FIGURE 5.3 Tzafrir and Dolan's RCH model of Trust.
Note: This model was published for the first time in 2004 but was studied in other contexts many times by Tzafrir and Dolan and our collaborators. Within the scientific research of trust in the workplace, there are other definitions and other models, but this one has become the most popular and most cited. See: Tzafrir S., Dolan S.L. (2004) Trust Me: A Scale for Measuring Manager-Employee Trust, Management Research: Journal of the Iberoamerican Academy of Management, Vol. 2 Issue: 2, pp.115–132, https://doi.org/10.1108/153654 30480000505; Dolan, S.L., Tzafrir S., Baruch Y. (2005) Testing the causal relationships between procedural justice, trust and organizational citizenship behavior, Revue de gestion de ressources humanies; Mach, M., Dolan S.L., Tzafrir S. (2010) The differential effect of team members' trust on team performance: The mediation role of team cohesion, Journal of Occupational and Organizational Psychology, Vol 83(3):771–794 (https:// doi. org/10.1348/096317909X473903); Chaluz H., Tzafrir S., Dolan S.L. (2015) Actionable trust in service organizations: A multi-dimensional perspective, Journal of Work and Organizational Psychology 31–39; Capell B., Tzafrir S., Enosh G., Dolan, S.L. (2018) Explaining sexual minorities' disclosure: The role of trust embedded in organizational practices, Organization Studies, Vol 39 (7) 947–973 https://journals.sagepub. com/doi/full/ 10.1177/0170840617708000.

What about the Toxic Leader? The So Called "Stress Generator"

On the other hand, there are these leaders who, albeit the fact that they, themselves, are not stressed, their attitudes and behaviour have toxic effects on the followers. They are characterized by diametrically opposite traits and behaviours of the trustworthy leaders. This type of leader impacts the mental state of the subordinates (see for example Figure 5.4).

None of us are born toxic leaders, but anyone can easily become one. Toxic leaders at the workplace have made life unbearable for employees, and these employees repeat this behaviour when they get themselves to the position of authority, creating a never-ending cycle in the firm. The impact, though, on the followers can be traumatic and lead to severe physical or mental illnesses.

So, if you are in a leadership position, you probably wish to know if you are toxic? Here are a couple of hints

- ☐ Do you constantly compare yourself to others?
- ☐ Do you consider your self-esteem (or self-worth) driven by your latest results?

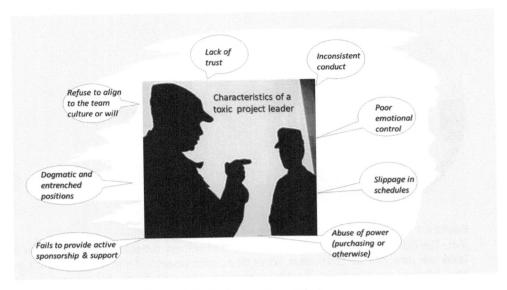

FIGURE 5.4 What happens when a toxic leader is managing a project.

- ☐ Do you suffer when you celebrate someone else's success; Does it makes you jealous and/or angry because you feel you deserve that celebration?
- ☐ Do you constantly live with the fear of looking out for people who are your competition (your enemies), and you find out ways to overtake them even if that way is unjust?
- ☐ Do you often take credit for others' people work?

Interpretation

If you ticked only one of the five options, you are still ok but, on the way, to becoming a toxic leader.
If you ticked two to three of the five options, you are a moderately toxic leader.
If you ticked four of the options, most likely you fall into the category of a real toxic leader.

In sum, toxic leadership occurs when an individual in a leadership role abuses his/her authority by violating the leader/follower relationship of trust through unfair practices. A toxic leader is selfish and self-destructive; destroying corporate structures for personal gains or to satisfy his/her ego (in a former chapter we labelled this person of having narcissist trait). The term "toxic leader" was coined and is often associated with various dysfunctional styles of leadership.

Chapter Summary and Postscript

Leadership can make or break an organization. An effective leader will bring out the best in their team and inspire them to do more than they even thought possible. Effective leaders allow employees to reach their full potential, and keep them highly motivated, committed to the team and the organization, and productive.

On the other hand, ineffective leaders can make a team feel like they don't care about them. That feeling of not being important or valued shuts down creativity, innovation, productivity and slowly demotivates a team. Ineffective leaders create stress and lead to low employee morale, lesser engagement, overall employee dissatisfaction and ultimately unpredictable business performance as the effect of low morale slowly seeps further and further into the organization.

TABLE 5.1 Comparing your attitudes and behaviour under stress-less leader vs toxic leader

Working under stress-less leader	Working under toxic leader
The organization can be a happy and fun place to which you look forward to returning every morning and to which you willingly want to give extra hours at the end of the day. Such organizations create an overriding sense of job engagement and satisfaction.	Each day, each moment is difficult to pass with this impossible leader(boss) breathing menacingly down the employee's neck; and wicked set of colleagues rubbing their hands in malicious glee every time they pull the employee down like the proverbial crab.
The organization is healthy, conducive to work with unsurpassed functionality and highly ethical work practices. Responsibilities and recognition, exemplary output and rewards go hand in hand in such places.	The organization is sick, divisive, undermining and demoralizing. What might get you ahead is hoodwinking and proximity to the influential people like the bosses or the boss' right hand man; even if such easily ill-gotten prizes are short-lived and open to scrutiny.
The organization is a place that allows you to blossom as a star worker with positive strokes that help germinate your skills and talent into wonderful fruits of productivity.	It can also be a place where there is so much of negative energy that all that can flower there is more bad blood splattered about by parasitic employees who eat into the climate.
The organization is a place where workers breathe in fresh air, enjoy positive influences, are allowed space to make mistakes and grow, have access to information, become a two way process in clear communication and are given learning opportunities.	The organization lives in the dark zone of fear, punishment, connivance and control. Leaders operate like secret missions where unnecessary stuff is hidden and kept out of reach of the employees thereby acting as major impediment in the processes and execution of duty.
A healthy and buzzing organizations that promote good work practices, innovation and creativity and encourage everybody to take ownership of their actions.	A flattery, manipulative, bad performances, terrible attitudes, and overall downward slope in almost all areas rule the roost.

ACTION

ASSESSING THE LEVEL OF TRUST YOU PLACE IN YOUR LEADER (BOSS) (OR ANY OTHER FOCAL PERSON IN YOUR SURROUNDING THAT YOU WISH TO ASSESS)

Here are 21 statements that demonstrate dimensions of actionable trust that you have in a focal person (perhaps your boss or your leader). This tool is based on a similar one that has been validated in a "work context" and was labelled: "TRUST-ME" (Tzafrir and Dolan, 2004).

Indicate the degree to which you agree with each statement/behaviour by using the following scale.

1	2	3	4	5
Disagree strongly	Disagree	neither agree nor disagree	Agree	strongly Agree

Think about yourself and the person in your surrounding that you wish to assess. This can be a colleague, a family member, a friend, a leader at work or anyone else. For each statement, place the number that best describes how much you agree or disagree with each statement/behaviour.

Item #	Statement	Score (1–5)
1	Based on the person's behavior, I conclude that his/her pragmatic needs and desires are very common to both of us	
2	Based on the person's behavior, I conclude that I can count on the person help when I experience difficulties	
3	Based on the person's behavior, I conclude that he/she is open, up front, and transparent with me	
4	Based on the person's behavior, I observe that people around me succeed because he/she do not let conflicts to arise (he/she don't let people step on each other)	
5	Based on the person's behavior, I conclude that he/she will keep the promises they made	
6	Based on the person's behavior, I conclude that he/she looks out for me to ensure that I get what I deserve	
7	Based on the person's behavior I realize that he/she has lot of knowledge about the situation that we are in together (they know what needs to be done).	
8	Based on the person's behavior I conclude that he/she is successful in the things they attempt to accomplish	
9	Based on the person's behavior I noticed that when I make a mistake, he/she will "forgive and forget"	
10	Based on the person's behavior, I noticed that his/her behavior and actions add harmony to the relationships	
11	Based on the person's behavior, I conclude that he/she take actions that are consistent with their words (they walk the talk)	
12	Based on the person's behavior I feel very comfortable in sharing personal or intimate information with him/her	
13	Based on the person's behavior I noticed that there is a lot of warmth and caring in the relationships between us	

Item #	Statement	Score (1–5)
14	Based on the person's behavior I conclude that he/she makes personal sacrifices for me in order to maintain the relationships	
15	Based on the person's behavior, I noticed that he/she expresses their true feelings about important issues that concerned us	
16	Based on the person's behavior, I observe that he/she brings the best of who they are to our relationships	
17	Based on the person's behavior, I noticed that he/she really shows concern to my needs and qualities	
18	Based on the person's behavior, I conclude that he/she is a reliable person	
19	Based on the person's behavior, I noticed that he/she operate as the message, not the messenger, with an alignment between their words and actions.	
20	Based on the person's behavior I observed that he/she often attempt to collaborate and cooperate with me	
21	Based on the person's behavior, I noticed that he/she makes an extra effort to show genuine respect to me	

Interpreting the results

Calculate your total score by adding the following items.

Actionable Trust Dimensions	Items	Total score
Reliability	1, 5, 7,8,11,18,19	
Harmony	2,4,10,12, 14,20,21	
Concern	3, 6,9, 13,15,16,17	

CALCULATING AND VISUALIZING YOUR ACTIONABLE TRUST ZONE WITH THE FOCAL PERSON

- Please retake the scores obtained before and place them respectively for each dimension in column 2.
- Take your score and divide it by 7 and then multiply each by 2, and place each of them in Column 3 respectively. This will generate a final score on a scale range from 1–10 to be used in the template.

1	2	3
Trust Dimension	Score obtained before	Final calculated score on a scale of 1–10 to be placed on the template
Reliability		
Harmony		
Concern		

- Now, mark your final score on each of the corresponding dimension in the triaxial ACTIONABLE TRUST template (Figure 5.5). Once marked, connect the dots with a straight line. Please shade the area. This is your perceived TRUST zone with the person that you are assessing.

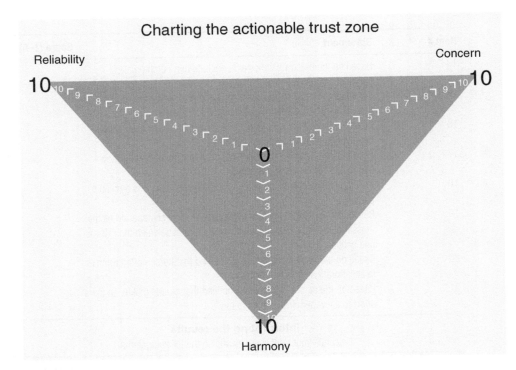

FIGURE 5.5 Charting the Actionable Trust Zone.

CHAPTER 6

Work and Family Triangle Synchronization as Resilience to Stressful Work–Family Conflict

*Garti Anat and Tzafrir Shay**

Introduction

The relationships between work and family have been studied in three different contexts: in a **spillover context** (which seems to be about 70% of all cases) and has been modeled in this chapter, **a segmentation effect context** for which everything that happens in each sphere of life is independent from the other, and in a **compensation effect context** all of which suggests that stress and dissatisfaction in one sphere of life will drive the person to compensate in the other sphere of life.[1]

The term work-family spillover is often used in a general way to refer to the effects that paid employment has on family relationships (and vice versa). Initial research focused on maternal employment, based on the idea that a mother's work outside

---

* This chapter was written by two experts in the interface of Work–Family relationships and resilience.

Dr Anat Garti is a social psychologist, couple and family therapist, management consultant, and a coach. She is also the chief psychologist and coach of the Israel Value Center (Anatgarti@gmail.com).

Prof. Shay Tzafrir is the Dean of teaching and learning at the University of Haifa (Israel). He is a prolific author with tens of research publications in scholarly journals. Known for his research on trust and other themes connected to people management (stzafrir@univ.haifa.ac.il)

1 Lambert, S.J. (1990) *Processes Linking Work and Family: A Critical Review and Research Agenda*, Human Relations, March (https://doi.org/10.1177%2F001872679004300303); Repetti, R.L., and Wang, S.-W. (2018) *Work-Family Spillover*, Entry for Encyclopedia of Human Relationships (http://shuwen.haverford.edu/wp-content/uploads/2018/09/RepettiWang-2009-Encyclopedia-of-Human-Relationships.pdf), Dolan, S.L., and Gosselin, E. (2000) OB Satisfaction and Life Satisfaction: Analysis of a Reciprocal Model with Social Demographic Moderators, Research paper # 81, ERI, University of Montreal (www.semanticscholar.org/paper/Job-satisfaction-and-life-satisfaction%3A-Analysis-of-Dolan-Gosselin/eae076c3483f7271bc9d1e1f2a3b9c4cc4ffef9e)

DOI: 10.4324/9781003217626-7

of the home might adversely affect her children and family. We now know that this assumption was incorrect and painted a far too simplistic picture of work and family life; rather, the specific characteristics and experiences of jobs – not merely employment itself – have both positive and negative consequences for the family.

Studies of job conditions and job characteristics now commonly include subjective appraisals of work and longitudinal research designs, in which participants are followed over time, to understand how individuals' experiences or views of their jobs might bring about changes in family dynamics. Job satisfaction is one of the chief features of work life that is studied. In general, parents who are more satisfied with their careers show greater warmth and responsiveness to their children, and also report greater marital satisfaction. Workers who experience more autonomy and complexity on the job also display more positive parenting and less harsh and restrictive parenting. Thus, jobs can serve as an arena outside the household where workers may experience achievement and fulfillment that can carry over into the family with positive implications for those relationships.

On the flip side of job satisfaction is job stress. Research consistently indicates that chronic job stress affects family relationships through an impact on individual well-being. For example, the subjective experience of job stress has been associated with self-reports of distress, such as depression, that have then been linked to poorer marital and parent-child relations. In the absence of individual distress as an intervening link, however, there is no connection between chronic job stressors and family outcomes. One facet of job stress is the social climate or the quality of social relationships at work. Parents who experience a non-cohesive or conflictive work atmosphere seem to have more negative interactions with their children (e.g., they are less affectionate, angrier), with longitudinal studies suggesting that these effects can hold up over the course of months. Similarly, couples who report negative and unsupportive relationships at work also experience more marital tension and arguments. While investigators have tended to focus on the impact of a negative work atmosphere, social support in the workplace has been linked with greater individual health and well-being; these links are thought to have positive implications for family life.

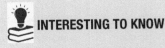 **INTERESTING TO KNOW**

CAUSES OF WORK-FAMILY CONFLICT IN THE NORTH AMERICAN WORKFORCE

Work-family conflict exists in all segments of society. Only the very wealthy don't report it as having a real impact on their lives. There are many possible causes behind work-family conflict including:

- *Changes in the structure of the American family: 70 percent of children live in households where both parents work compared to only 20 percent in the 1960s.*
- *Many families have extended family care responsibilities: on a daily basis, 1 in 4 Americans is caring for an elderly family member or someone who is ill.*

> - *The current economy is requiring organizations to do more with less: this translates into workers becoming multifaceted and taking on more roles and responsibilities than ever before. In turn, people are working more days and longer hours.*
> - *Career advancement requires a proven work ethic: professionals who want to advance their career are required to show their loyalty to employers by going above and beyond the call of duty, often at the expense of their personal family lives.*
>
> Source: (https://study.com/academy/lesson/work-family-conflict-definition-types-examples.html

Another aspect of job stress is time pressure and work overload which can lead to parents feeling overwhelmed by and conflicted about their work and family roles. Similar to the association between the social atmosphere at work and family relations, studies reliably show that overloaded parents have poorer relations with their children (e.g., more conflict, less acceptance). In addition, more time pressure at work has been connected to reduced parental monitoring, meaning less knowledge about children's activities and whereabouts, and less allocation of time to parenting. For couples, time pressure and work overload are associated with greater marital tension and poorer marital adjustment. The subjective appraisal of job demands as being stressful or overwhelming seems to have a greater influence on family interactions and relationships than the objective job conditions.

One such objective measure of job conditions is the length of the workday, or the number of hours spent on the job. Initially, it was assumed that long hours at work would be associated with poorer family outcomes. However, research indicates that long work hours are not a predictor of individual or family functioning, with the majority of studies reporting no reliable linkages between time on the job and lower marital quality or poorer home environments for children. This is probably because of the host of benefits (income, access to health care, social support) that typically increase with more hours of employment. However, the distribution of parents' work hours over the day (e.g., amount of overlap with spouse's work schedule and child's school day) and the subjective appraisal of those work hours (e.g., do work hours fit one's needs) do influence family relationships. In particular, among dual earner families in which one parent works a non-standard shift (e.g., at night), there is often a disruption of family routines and increased rates of marital dissatisfaction have also been observed. In single parent households, shift work can place an extreme burden on the family.

Researchers have also turned their attention to experiences that occur in transit between work and home. Although commuter stress is associated with negative individual health outcomes, such as high blood pressure, there does not appear to be a substantive link between commuting and family relations and functioning. Studies have implicated the length, unpredictability and uncontrollability of commuting as characteristics that help explain commuter stress via their associations with employee's Work-Family Spillover – greater negative mood, and decreased frustration tolerance and task motivation. However, there is no conclusive evidence that these effects contribute to increased tension in the home.

How is it that a high stress day at work comes to affect behaviour in the family? Psychologists believe that job stressors leave a cognitive, affective and physiological residue, such that the employee's thoughts, feelings and biology are changed, at least in the short-term, by his/her experiences at work. Those repercussions can be felt in the home. This is the more technical and narrow meaning of the term "spillover": the experience of negative mood or physiological arousal in one setting that was generated in a different setting. Negative mood and physiological arousal due to stressors experienced at work sometimes do persist when the employed person returns home and evidence suggests that those spillover effects account for some of the increase in anger and conflict that were described above.

The social withdrawal response to job stress consists of short-term decreases in the employed individual's usual level of social engagement at home. Coming home after a stressful day at work, he or she might speak less, express less positive and less negative emotion, and be less interested and less involved in social interaction. For instance, a parent may be less likely to help with homework or to discipline a child. The second type Work-Family Spillover of response is quite different. After more difficult or stressful days, the employed family member may express more anger and be more critical than usual. For example, researchers have found that a one-day increase in stress at work is associated with increases in marital arguments and use of disciplinary tactics with children later that day.

There is, of course, an alternative to simply experiencing and directly expressing the residue of job stress at home; employees can attempt to change their physical and psychological state, perhaps by relaxing, or distracting themselves from thoughts about a difficult day, or engaging in any one of a number of coping tactics. The social withdrawal response to job stress may be one such coping strategy. In other words, rather than discuss job-related worries or problems at home, the employee may avoid social interaction, perhaps to reduce the chances that negative mood or irritability will lead to arguments and to facilitate a process of relaxation and unwinding.

Whether the residue of stress at work directly affects the employed family member's social behaviour through spillover processes or indirectly affects his or her behaviour through a coping response, the impact is felt by the partner in the social interaction. Researchers are beginning to investigate processes of emotion transmission, whereby emotions are transferred from one member of a dyad to another through their social interactions. Likewise, there is some evidence that stress hormone levels in couples are linked when couples are at home together. We are thus beginning to see how stress at work can ultimately affect the psychological and biological functioning of other family members. However, it should be remembered that spouses and children are active participants in the daily social life of families. They also contribute to the dynamics of the employed family member's reactions at home to stress at work. For example, studies have uncovered different ways that other family members can either encourage or disrupt an employee's attempts at social withdrawal.

In conclusion, while many employed adults say they worry that time spent at work may harm their families, on the whole, employment benefits the family environment. Jobs typically bring income, health care, social support and a sense of accomplishment that contribute to the well-being of employees and their families. It is only under certain circumstances (e.g., high job stress, mismatch of work shift with family schedule) that employment can also bring negative consequences for the family.

After years of consulting with couples and organizations coping with the stress of WFC, we concluded that a new approach for managing the conflict is essential.

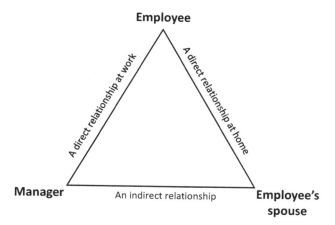

FIGURE 6.1 Work–family triangle relationship.

We developed an innovative model that is a concept, methodology and tool for developing resilience to the daily conflict in which we all find ourselves. We named the model **work–family triangle synchronization (WFTS)**. The model is fully presented in the book *Work–Family Triangle Synchronization*[2] and summarized in this chapter. It addresses the three players who face WFC daily – manager, employee, and employee's spouse – and their triangle relationship. In the WFTS vision, these three stakeholders, through a trustful relationship, make a joint effort to synchronize work and family needs with clever use of work and family knowledge, skills and abilities.

The work–family triangle relationship consists of a triangle of dyads: the direct dyads of manager–employee and the couple, and the indirect dyad of the manager–employee's spouse. Figure 6.1 demonstrates this tripartite relationship. Dual-earner families have four work–family system stakeholders: Partner A, Partner B, Partner A's manager, and Partner B's manager.[3] These four stakeholders are best represented as two adjacent triangles, as depicted in Figure 6.2.

The dyads and triangles are managed through psychological contracts. Psychological contracts are subjective, and each party believes that the others share their interpretation of the contract. Researchers studying these psychological contracts have examined the implications of violating a psychological contract. They found that when a contract is violated, it generates distrust, dissatisfaction and possibly the dissolution of the relationship. These outcomes cause stress.[4]

---

2 Garti, A., and Tzafrir, S., (2022) *Work–Family Triangle Synchronization*. Berlin, Germany: De Gruyter.
3 In 2022, different types of family structure exist, such as those involving people who are divorced, gay, lesbian, and single parents. The two triangles system can be applied to married, divorced, heterosexual, and homosexual families.
4 Baruch, Y., and Rousseau, D.M. (2019) Integrating Psychological Contracts and Ecosystems in Career Studies and Management. *Academy of Management Annals*, 13(1), 84–111; Robinson, S.L., and Rousseau, D.M., (1994) Violating the Psychological Contract: Not the Exception but the Norm. *Journal of Organizational Behavior*, 15(3), 245–259; Rousseau, D.M. (1989) Psychological and Implied Contracts in Organizations. *Employee Responsibilities and Rights Journal*, 2(2), 121–139; Turnley, W.H., and Feldman, D.C., (2000) Re-examining the Effects of Psychological Contract Violations: Unmet Expectations and Job Dissatisfaction as Mediators. *Journal of Organizational Behavior*, 21(1), 25–42.

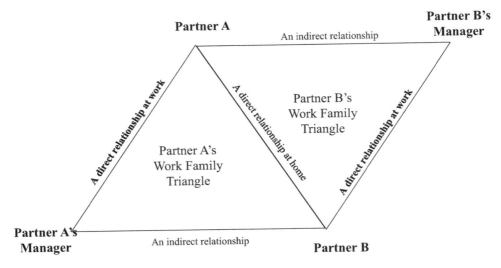

FIGURE 6.2 Dual-earner work–family triangles relationship.

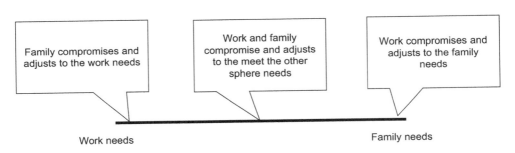

FIGURE 6.3 Continuum of work–family hierarchy.

Themes That Stimulates Work–Family Stress

We found two themes – that when the psychological contract was not synchronized, WFC generated the highest tension among the work–family triangles: work–family hierarchy and work–family mixture. Work–family hierarchy deals with the challenging questions: "*Which sphere makes the rules and which sphere needs to adjust*"? "*Which sphere has to help the other do its job*"? "*Does family have to compromise and fit itself to work demands and enable employees to do their job, or does work have to compromise and adjust to family needs to make it possible for employees to manage their family*"? Figure 6.3 demonstrates the continuum of work–family hierarchy.

The case of Alice demonstrates how work–family hierarchy affects the triangle relationship. Anna, a manager in a biotech company, offered Alice, her employee, a promotion. Alice's spouse, Gregory, did not want her to take the promotion. He wanted her to perceive the family as higher in the hierarchy, in a place that manages the work so it will suit the family. A year earlier, she had been offered another promotion and declined it because of Gregory's influence. This time, Anna did not yield. She was angry with Gregory for preventing his wife's advancement. She offered to speak with him, but Alice asked her not to do so, saying that it would only make matters worse. The unsynchronized perception about work–family hierarchy between Anna and Gregory created considerable tension in all three dyads: Anna and Gregory, Alice and Gregory, and Anna and Alice. In this case, they didn't try to synchronize things, and the tension affected life at both work and home.

Some work and family adjustments occur at a high level, such as place of residence. We found that some families decided to move residences and live close to one or both parents' workplaces, whereas other families decided to stay in their place of residence, and the employee drove long distances every day to work or sometimes saw the family only on weekends or even less (when the workplace was farther away or abroad). In the same way, some employees chose their workplace according to the family's place of residence. Other adjustments involved regular situations, wherein work and family needs were in daily conflict. For example, Levi and Sarah intended to go out with friends in the evening, but there was a problem at work and the manager asked Sarah to stay and handle the situation. In their triangle work–family hierarchy, the work adjusts to the family, and Sarah apologized and told the manager about the family obligation and did not stay. The manager and Sarah were synchronized regarding the work–family hierarchy, and no tension was generated. In a similar case of Owen and Lydia, whose triangle work–family hierarchy mandates that the family adjusts to work, Lydia called Owen and apologized for canceling their plans. Again, no tension was generated. The situation was different in the triangle of Nora (manager), Aiden (employee) and Zoey (Aiden's spouse). The work–family hierarchy was not synchronized. Nora and Aiden thought that work manages the family, whereas Zoey thought otherwise. Every time Aiden canceled a family plan because of work, there was a big fight at home. In one case, Aiden wanted to delay going on vacation for a day due to work constraints, and his wife angrily informed him that she was going to the hotel with the kids, and he was welcome to join them when he was available.

An important point to clarify is that even when the triangle work–family hierarchy contract is one in which the work comes first and the family has to adjust to work demands, there is a red line, after which the contract is overturned. When there is a significant event in the family – happy or sad, such as a wedding or hospitalization of a relative – all stakeholders agreed that the contract changes and the work should adapt itself as much as possible to the needs of the family.

Partner A's work–family hierarchy was found to be interdependent with Partner B's work–family hierarchy, creating a work–family triangle system hierarchy – a hierarchy between Partner A's work sphere, Partner B's work sphere, and the family's sphere, as depicted in Figure 6.4.

An example is the case of Wyatt and Rylee. Wyatt is a doctor and Rylee a consultant. Rylee agreed to the work–family triangles system hierarchy contract that Wyatt's work comes before the family and her work. When Wyatt was with the children and required at the hospital, Rylee would return home from work or the activity in which she was engaged. In one case, Rylee was at the beginning of an important meeting when Wyatt called. He was required for a complicated surgery. She apologized to the client and returned home. "*I knew that was the deal the day I met him. It's tough, and some friends and colleagues don't understand me. But that was the deal, and I accept it*".

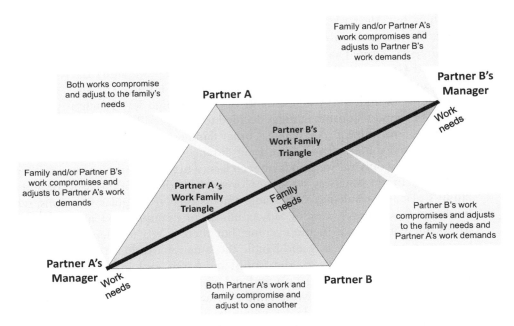

FIGURE 6.4 Continuum of work–family triangle system hierarchy.

In some work–family triangle systems, the family has to adjust to both partners' work needs. This is the case of the triangle system of Jack and Natalia. Both parents are officers with a work–family hierarchy in which the work manages the family. The family adjusts to both work needs. The main family need that was not fulfilled and had to adjust was the need of the children for a parent as the caregiver. Jack and Natalia acknowledged the price their family pays for their choices:

> We know that the children pay the price of our professional decisions. The work of both of us dictate the tone, and the family has to adjust itself. It is exceedingly difficult. We find ourselves compensating the children and not putting enough boundaries because we feel we have no right to demand. This is not an easy situation to live with.

Beyond the work–family triangle system hierarchy's general contract, the stakeholders manage the hierarchy depending on the case. Some work–family triangle systems have a rigid hierarchy contract and others have a more flexible contract, but all have a basic work–family triangle system hierarchy that guides the decisions.

The second theme that created tension between stakeholders is **work–family mixture**. Work–family mixture deals with the extent and intensity with which the two spheres interrelate. The spheres interrelated in three main areas: (a) the extent to and intensity with which the employee handles family or work matters when at work or home; (b) the extent to and intensity with which the employee talks about his family or work with his manager or spouse; and (c) the extent to and intensity with which the employee is occupied and not fully focused with family or work matters when at work or home, respectively.

When we analysed the extent and the intensity of these areas, we found that the work–family mixture was on a continuum from work–family separation through work–family interaction to work–family integration. Work–family separation means that the stakeholders separated work from the family and vice versa. When the employee was at work, the employee was only at work and not occupied with family matters, and vice versa. This included not talking about family when at work and not talking about work when with family. The employee perceived the two spheres as separate and that one should not interfere with the other. The new Apple TV series *Severance* is an extreme example of work–family separation. In *Severance*, Mark leads a team of office workers whose memories have been surgically divided between their work and personal lives.

On the other end of the continuum, work–family integration is the state of mind that the best way to manage two roles is to occupy them together, as one employee told us:

> *I am the mother of all my children at the same time. I love them and take care of them together. It is the same with work and family. I handle family and work together. I work from home and answer work calls while I prepare lunch for my kids. I write emails when I breastfeed my little baby. Work and family today are blended, and many people struggle with it. I think we should embrace it. This is the new era.*

Work–family interaction is between these two ends of the continuum; that is, there is interaction between the spheres, but they are not entirely blended. At any given time, one sphere is in the foreground and the other is in the background. When the employee is at work, the main task is to be involved in work matters. Sometimes, when needed, the employee will take care of a family matter. The same applies when the employee is at home with family. The main sphere is the family. Sometimes, the employee answers work calls and handles work matters. Figure 6.5 depicts this continuum.

As in work–family hierarchy, when the stakeholders were not synchronized regarding the work–family mixture, we witnessed stress. In one case, the employee believed that there should be complete separation between work and family. He did not bring his wife to company events and did not talk about her at work. The manager saw this as a loyalty issue, thinking the work–family mixture should be interaction

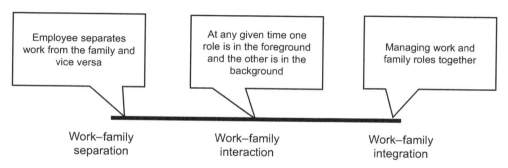

FIGURE 6.5 Continuum of work–family mixture.

and not separation. He did not understand how work is not a significant part of his family life.

Managing Triangle Disagreements

We found two forms of managing triangle disagreements: competition and co-opetition. In **competition**, conflict management is like a "tug-of-war". When the tug-of-war is between the manager and the employee or between members of a couple, conflict management is through direct interaction between the two parties. When the tug-of-war is between the manager and the employee's spouse, conflict management is through indirect interaction. In the direct tug-of-war management form, the third player can be passive or active. If this player is active, a coalition is often created, as in cases where the couple pulls together as a coalition in the tug-of-war against a manager who demanded high-level availability.

We refer to the indirect tug-of-war management between the manager and employee's spouse as being "between a rock and a hard place". In this management form, the employee manages the tug-of-war between the manager and the spouse, as a messenger. In these cases, we hear conversations such as: "*Tell your boss that …*" or "*My wife will kill me if I miss another kindergarten show*". The employee does not take a stand and says what he thinks is right, such as telling the manager that he wants to attend his child's show or telling his wife that he cannot attend. We found that in these cases, the employee hid behind the spouse or manager and avoided the confrontation, sometimes for good reasons, understanding that confrontation will not be effective because the triangle is not a co-opetition triangle.

An example of a competition triangle involved Roy (employee), Amber (spouse), and Randy (manager). Roy is a senior manager in a demanding firm. He comes home late and has many business trips abroad. Amber works from 08:00 to 16:00. They have three children, aged 3–10 years. Amber and Roy are not synchronized regarding Roy's involvement as a father. Moreover, Amber does not believe Roy's statements, such as "I will get home on time today and help him with his homework", "This is an important trip that I can't miss", and so on. Amber is sure that Randy does not care about her or her children, his only interest is the business, and he perceives the work–family hierarchy as work managing the family. Amber does not feel she is in a co-opetition relationship but rather a competition relationship, and if she does not fight hard, she will lose. Amber and Roy manage the work–family hierarchy in a tug-of-war management style, and Roy manages the work–family hierarchy with his manager as being between a rock and a hard place, consistently complaining that his wife will give him a hard time if he does not comply with her request.

In the case of a **co-opetition relationship**, each stakeholder considers the needs of all stakeholders when managing WFC. The term "co-opetition" is a portmanteau of cooperation and competition. We borrowed the term from the business literature, which refers to competitors working together to open new markets. Managing WFC with co-opetition means acknowledging the competitive elements of work and family spheres and managing them in cooperation. The co-opetition management style was described as effective for satisfying needs and reducing tension.

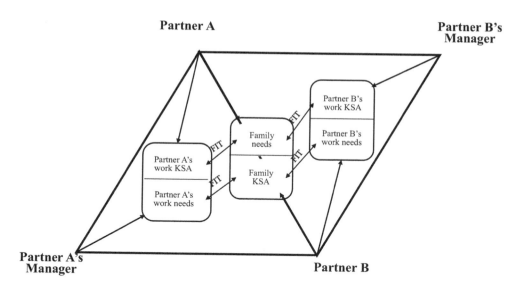

FIGURE 6.6 Dual-earner work–family triangle synchronization.

We found that the process in which the three stakeholders synchronize their preferences in co-opetition created resilience to WFC stress. WFTS is a trustful process in which all stakeholders are mutually available, respectful and openly monitor these interactions: (a) openly speak and reveal the needs and abilities of all stakeholders; (b) accept and acknowledge that the goal is to find a way to meet, in the best possible way, these needs and abilities; and (c) mutually decide to reach this synchronization by managing the conflict with co-opetition and not a tug-of-war. Figure 6.6 presents the synchronization of the needs and abilities.

The Employee's Spouse as a Valued Stakeholder

We found that many managers didn't understand the effect of the employee's spouse on the work dyad. Furthermore, they didn't recognize the employee's spouse's needs and abilities and did not consider them when deciding to regard or affect the employee. The spouse, on the other hand, was always aware of the manager and the manager's impact on family life.

The relationship between the manager and the employee's spouse can be direct or indirect. By direct, we mean that the manager and the employee's spouse know each other directly and speak to each other. For example, when army families live on an army base, it is common for the manager (commander) to know, meet and routinely speak to the spouses of his officers. Direct dyads were also found wherein the manager and employee worked together for years, the manager met the spouse at various events, and in cases where the manager thought it important to meet and know the spouse, held get-togethers.

A unique case was that of Robert, a manager who routinely invited each employee and the employee's spouse to a restaurant with his wife (the manager's spouse), creating an out-of-office situation that enabled an open conversation. The manager told us he learns much from these events and recommended to some of his colleagues that they do the same. One of them adopted the idea and started his own ritual, inviting employees and their family to Friday night dinner with his family.

Most managers we interviewed learned about the spouse indirectly from the employee. They talked to the employee about family matters, learning about family needs and abilities. If these conversations were open and sincere, the manager could learn what the spouse thinks about the manager. Most cases were not open, and the manager did not know the spouse's perception.

Whether the relationship is direct or indirect, the main point is the extent to which the manager perceives the employee's spouse as a stakeholder and therefore, considers the spouse when thinking about or making decisions regarding or affecting the employee. This means bearing in mind that the employee's spouse is influenced by and influences the work dyad. Moreover, it is important that the employee's spouse feels worthy and that the manager cares about him or her.

The findings show that the manager has two motivations to perceive the employee's spouse as an important stakeholder whose opinion is important. The first is affect-based motivation, a humanistic motivation, as demonstrated by the following quotes. A spouse noted: "*It was very important for me when the manager of William [her husband] called me on our anniversary, thanked me, acknowledging my role, and gave us a weekend in a hotel*". A manager stated: "*I know my employees' spouses, and if I know one of them has couple difficulties, I will not throw on him a complicated and demanding project that will make things worse*". Conversely, an employee mentioned that: "*My boss doesn't care about my family. I am very frustrated. It is as if I am only good as an employee*". In the same line of thought, another employee told us: "*When my daughter was born, my boss didn't send anything to my wife, didn't ask if we need something. He ignored the event. That was when I understood he really doesn't care*". These quotes demonstrate that the spouse is an important person for the employee and should be seen as such by the manager and not as irrelevant. This is the trust dimension of concern.

Source: Images taken from the STRESS MAP card tool. Used with permission of the developers-publishers and copyrights owners Simon L. Dolan and Avishai Landau ©(2021). Illustrations by Eitan Daniel.

The second motivation to manage the manager–spouse dyad was calculus based. The spouse has an important role in the employee's life, and so it is cost effective to know (directly or indirectly) and consider the spouse when managing the employee. Olivia, a manager, told us: "*If I ask Ava [the employee] to work on Friday, Frank [her spouse] won't like it and it will affect her work. If I want Ava to function at her best, I need Frank to be supportive*". In one case, the manager learned from the employee that her husband was angry about her work terms. She offered a meeting to talk about the terms. In another case, the manager, learning from the spouse the attitude of her husband, recommended that she consult with him regarding a role in the company she rejected.

Another example of the calculus-based motive is the case of Emily, an employee in a demanding job, who told us: *"My husband respects and appreciates my manager, so when I come late, he sees it favorably. In my previous job, it was the opposite. He despised my manager and influenced me to invest less in the work"*. Luna, a spouse in another triangle, clarified that point: *"My place in the triangle is assured. His [the manager's] is not. If he is clever, he will make sure I like him and want my husband to continue working for him"*.

It may seem that the more the manager knows and considers the spouse's needs and abilities, the better it will be. Nevertheless, a too-tight dyad was perceived as not appropriate and invasive. Findings show that the relationship between the manager and spouse can be described as a diagram of three intensity spaces, as shown in Figure 6.7.

The stars represent mismanagement of the dyad by the manager, whereas the dots represent effective dyad management. The three spaces describe three relationship frameworks. We named them invasiveness, involvement and disengagement. An invasive dyad is one in which the manager makes decisions for the couple, as in an example wherein a military commander told his officer: *"You are not going out on this mission; it's dangerous, and your wife is pregnant"*. The officer was very annoyed that the commander decided for him what he can or cannot do because of his wife. An involvement dyad is one in which the manager takes an interest in the spouse, bears the spouse in mind when managing the employee, and is considerate when possible. For example, *"I know that your wife has an important test; you can leave earlier this month to let her study"*. A disengaged dyad is one in which the manager ignores the spouse. As one manager told us: *"I manage the employee and he manage his relationship with his spouse. I don't care how he does it, and I don't think I have to take it into account when managing him"*. We found that work–family triangles that kept the manager–employee's spouse dyad in the involvement space enabled a better synchronized work–family triangle.

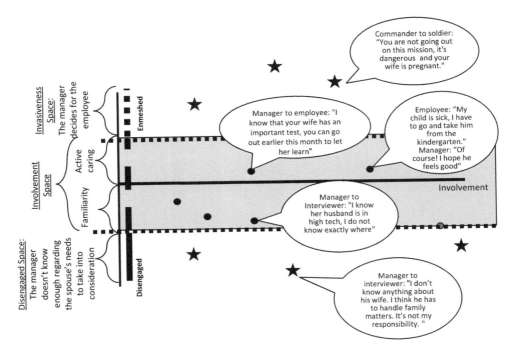

FIGURE 6.7 Manager–spouse intensity spaces.

The Triangle Trust Relationships

To synchronize things with cooperation, the stakeholders have to acknowledge their interdependencies – especially that the manager affects the couple dyad and the employee's spouse affects the work dyad. Several trust scholars propose that when dependence exists, trust is an efficient mechanism to help manage stakeholder interdependencies. Analysing how co-opetition triangle relationships manage WFC, we noticed that they all include the three dimensions of Tzafrir and Dolan's (2004)[5] trust model: harmony, concern and reliability. The authors concluded that the three dimensions build a dyadic trust relationship. Harmony is a shared combination of feelings, interests, opinions, purpose and values; concern occurs when one party believes that the other party considers her or his interests when making decisions; and reliability reflects a positive expectation based on reciprocated interactional history when promises and obligations are kept.

Expanding the dyadic trust model to a triangle trust relationship, the findings indicate that in a co-opetition triangle relationship, the three stakeholders are synchronized regarding the work–family hierarchy and work–family mixture. This thematic synchronization develops the harmony trust dimension. For example: *"I know he [the manager] sees it as I do. The family has to adjust to the work needs. My wife*

---

5 Tzafrir, S.S., and Dolan, S.L., (2004). Trust Me: A Scale for Measuring Manager-Employee Trust. *Management Research* 2(2): 115–132.

understands that as well. It makes things much easier"; *"If she [the manager] calls at 22:00, both I and my wife know it is important. She will never call late for something that can wait to the morning"*. This saying means that beyond harmony, there is reliability in the relationship. Another example of harmony and reliability is a manager who said: *"I know his [the employee's] work–family way of thinking. If he doesn't want to fly to the client because of home issues, I can trust his judgment. I know both he and his wife understand that the family has to adjust to work needs. They proved it many times"*. Beyond harmony and reliability, the stakeholders talked about the importance of feeling that the other parties care about and consider their interests. As one spouse punctuated: *"We are in it together"*.

That is, in WFTS, the three trust dimensions are met. The stakeholders feel that the work–family themes are synchronized (harmony) and the management of every case is evaluated in light of the synchronized themes with flexibility, leaning on positive past interactions of concern and reliability between the parties involved. One employee explained:

> *I know both my husband and my boss understand that when I'm at work, I have to handle family matters, and vice versa [harmony]. If I don't take care of a work or home issue, they [husband and manager] know it's because I'm busy and cannot take the time to address the issue. They know me. I always stand for my words [reliability] and I will never abuse their understanding [concern]. They trust I will do it the moment I can.*

The co-opetition process involves understanding the stakeholder's favourable work–family hierarchy and work–family mixture and finding together through a trust relationship a synchronized solution that respects all needs and abilities. Adopting such a process requires a fundamental change in the individual's perception, attitudes and behaviour, pushing trust to become the building block and basis of the work–family structure. Therefore, WFTS is a change from the second degree. Each stakeholder is required to adopt a broad vision instead of a narrow one. Instead of perceiving the manager as responsible for work, the employee's spouse for the family, and the employee between a rock and a hard place because the two spheres are important to him, the motivation is holistic: three stakeholders who want to meet the needs of both spheres. In this process, risk is built in and requires mutual reliance and interdependence for effective function. These aspects indicate the need for trust as a coping mechanism. Sabel (1993)[6] defined trust as "the mutual confidence that no party to an exchange will exploit another's vulnerabilities" (p. 1133). WFTS is a trust relationship wherein the abilities of the spheres are honestly and openly communicated to provide a maximum response to the various needs with a mutual confidence that no party to an exchange will exploit another's vulnerabilities. This is line with Werbel and Walter's (2002)[7] work–family mutualism analogy, illustrating the interdependence of the work and family systems as allies.

---

6 Sabel, C.F. (1993) Studied Trust: Building New Forms of Cooperation in a Volatile Economy. *Human Relations*, 46(9), 1133–1170.
7 Werbel, J., and Walter, M.H. (2002) Changing Views of Work and Family Roles: A Symbiotic Perspective. *Human Resource Management Review*, 12(3), 293–298.

Summary and Postscript

 INTERESTING TO KNOW

A survey conducted by the EU EUROFOUND on the nature and occurrence of parents and family-work conflicts, reveals the following:

- *Family–work conflict was strong for 16% of the parents interviewed. Women more often experienced greater pressure than men in juggling work and family responsibilities*
- *More than half of the respondents (56%) claimed that they often came home from work too tired to do necessary household chores*
- *Nearly half of the respondents (45%) indicated that they often face difficulties in performing family commitments because of spending too much time at work.*
- *The survey also revealed that a probability of strong work–family conflict is highest in people with an incomplete secondary education*

Source: www.eurofound.europa.eu/publications/article/2010/parents-and-family-work-conflict

Nowadays, as managers and families cope with the COVID-19 crisis, the WFTS process has become more essential than ever. Every work–family triangle system copes with different challenges and has to make different adaptions. For example, some dual-earner families became single-earner families, which dramatically changed the work–family triangles system. Other employees become remote workers, changing work–family patterns. Every work–family triangle system has to tune, via trust relationships, its work–family synchronization according to its unique system constraints. The COVID-19 pandemic has been more than a crisis; it has been a global wake-up call to change our paradigms and how we perceive the world. These days, more than ever, employees expect to be seen as a whole person and not only as an employee. Organizations are also undergoing perceptual changes and inspire the employee to bring his wholeness to work, for example, in teal organizations, resulting in significant variance in how different human resources management systems and people manage work and family systems. This conclusion was emphasized by Powell in an interview with Jaskiewicz,[8] saying that a one-size-fits-all work–family policy is no longer appropriate in the current reality. WFTS enables all stakeholders to manage WFC according to this new normal.

---

8 Powell, G.N., Greenhaus, J.H., Jaskiewicz, P., Combs, J.G., Balkin, D.B., and Shanine, K.K. (2017) Family Science and the Work-family Interface: An Interview with Gary Powell and Jeffrey Greenhaus. *Human Resource Management Review*, 28(1), 98–102.

TABLE 6.1 Theory development: WFTS main innovations, compared to the familiar WFC

WFC familiar paradigm	WFTS
The employee is the main responsible for managing the conflict	The three stakeholders (manager, employee, employee's spouse) are equally responsible for managing the conflict
Two dyadic relationships: couple relationship at home and manager–employee relationship at work	A triangle relationship: manager, employee, employee's spouse
Managing direct relationships: couple relationship at home and manager–employee relationship at work	Synchronizing direct and indirect relationships: manager–employee direct relationship, couple direct relationship, and manager–employee's spouse indirect relationship
The manager sees the employee through a narrow angle of his work effectiveness and sees the family constraints as a deterrent	Wholeness: manager sees the employee as a whole, and the relationship between them includes caring for all of the employee's systems, including his family
One size fits all: work–family programs, family-friendly workplace policies (employee assistance programs)	Tailormade: every work–family triangle system has to tune, via trust relationships, its work–family balance according to its unique system constraints

Moreover, the WFTS model encourages scholars to change their perceptions and how they address WFC. Expanding the perception of Beckman and Stanko (2020)[9] that "organizations should seek to understand the larger relational system in which their employees operate, and to understand the organization as but one actor in that system" (p. 435), we argue that recognition that WFC can be studied as a triangle system of three stakeholders can open the field to a new research area, revealing the sensitive, sometimes hidden dynamics in unconventional dyads of WFC, particularly the indirect influence of the manager–employee's spouse dyad. Table 6.1 summarizes the main innovations of the WFTS model, compared to the familiar WFC involving two dyads (couple relationship and manager–employee relationship).

"In order to act differently, one must first learn to see the world differently" (Watzlawick, 1987, p. 91).[10] When organizations and families understand the dynamics of the triangle and address WFC as a triangle system, they can possess the tools with which to manage the conflict effectively. To achieve an effective approach to WFC, it is important to understand the stakeholders of daily WFC, the role of each stakeholder, and how each stakeholder should address the other two stakeholders, especially how the manager should address the employee's spouse, and vice versa.

---

9 Beckman, C.M., and Stanco, T.L. (2020) t Takes Three: Relational Boundary Work, Resilience, and Commitment among Navy Couples, *The Academy of Management Journal*, 63(2), 411–439
10 Watzlawick P (1987) If You Desire to See, Learn How to Act. In J. Zeig (Ed.), *The Evolution of Psychotherapy*, New York: Brunner/Mazel, 91–106.

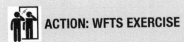

ACTION: WFTS EXERCISE

1. REFLECT ON CURRENT FAMILY–WORK CONFLICT MANAGEMENT

Reflect with your spouse and with your manager on your current work–family psychological contract. Have an open dialogue regarding how you manage nowadays the work–family interface and how you would like to manage it.

2. DESIGN YOUR WORK–FAMILY PSYCHOLOGICAL CONTRACT

Design your work–family psychological contract using the following guide. This should be a continual process of many synchronization discussions in different settings. It takes several iterations to make sure everyone is synchronized, thinks they can make the necessary adjustments, and feels that their needs have been addressed, even if not entirely fulfilled. Please adjust the templates for couple sync talks, work dyad sync talks, and triangle sync talks.

WORK–FAMILY HIERARCHY

Please mark how you would prefer to manage the work–family hierarchy of your triangle system. Place points on the ensuing Figure 6.8 template that shows the right balance for you regarding who adjusts to whom. Mark two points, one in relation to the work of Partner A and the other in relation to the work of Partner B.

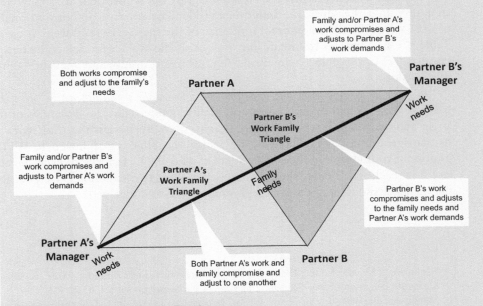

FIGURE 6.8 Work-Family Hierarchy Template.

Work and Family Triangle Synchronization 141

Explain your selection:
_____
_____
_____
_____

WORK–FAMILY MIXTURE

Please mark how you would prefer to manage the interaction between work and family. Indicate the right place for Partner A's work–family mixture (Figure 6.9) and for Partner B's work–family mixture (Figure 6.10).

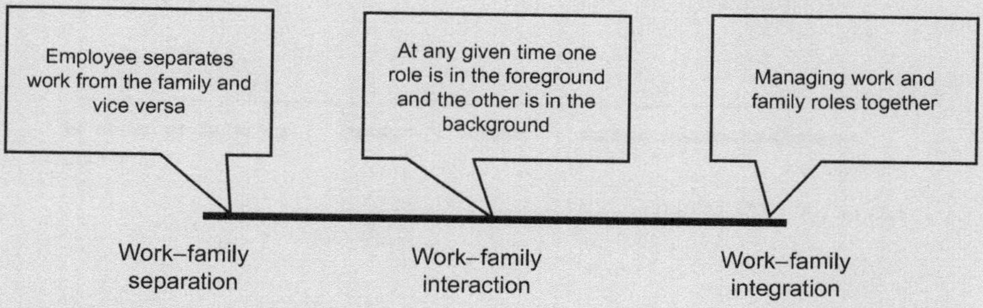

| Employee separates work from the family and vice versa | At any given time one role is in the foreground and the other is in the background | Managing work and family roles together |

Work–family separation   Work–family interaction   Work–family integration

FIGURE 6.9 Partner A's work–family mixture.

Explain your selection:
_____
_____
_____
_____

| Employee separates work from the family and vice versa | At any given time one role is in the foreground and the other is in the background | Managing work and family roles together |

Work–family separation   Work–family interaction   Work–family integration

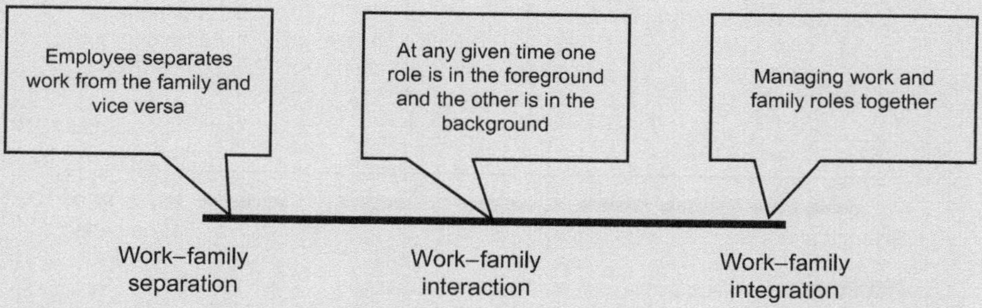

FIGURE 6.10 Partner B's work–family mixture.

Explain your selection:
_____
_____
_____

Relationship-intensity spaces of manager–employee's spouse dyad

Please mark how you would prefer that the manager–employee's spouse dyad be managed. Point the right place for Partner A's manager–employee's spouse dyad (Figure 6.11) and for Partner B's manager–employee's spouse dyad (Figure 6.12).

Explain your selection:

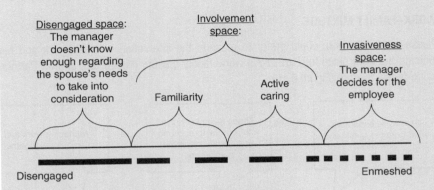

FIGURE 6.11 Partner A's manager–employee's spouse dyad.

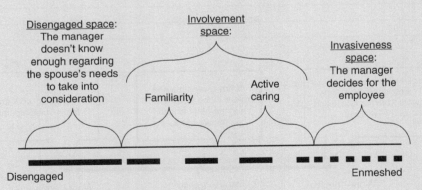

FIGURE 6.12 Partner B's manager–employee's spouse dyad.

Explain your selection:

Synchronize needs and KSA (**K**nowledge, **S**kills and **A**ttitudes)

Map the work and family needs and discuss them. Understand what each one means and its significance. Prepare a synchronized list of work and family needs that you all see as legitimate needs and try to see how you can address them.

Partner A's work need	Family/Partner B's work KSA that can address the need
Partner B's work need	Family/Partner A's work KSA that can address the need
Family's need	Partner A/B's work KSA that can address the need

CHAPTER 7

The Stress Map as an Emerging Gamification Tool and Methodology to Combat Chronic Stress

Introduction

Over the course of the past 10 years, the concept of "gamification" is gaining steam as a methodology used by health professionals to enhance physical and mental health. And, with the pandemic crisis of Covid-19, the world has been forced to embrace the various possibilities of twenty-first-century technology in its totality. If the numerous technological options weren't a part of every aspect of daily life before the crisis, then they are most certainly now. Games and gamification have structures, rules, objectives, win and fail states, that can be used to observe and analyse the interactions and reactions in a person and use the conclusions taken from them to develop a more effective therapy and/or intervention.

Gaming, and by extension gamification, are powerful hence they engage and immerse participants in a non-threatening manner; the players lose themselves in the game, and they no longer "consciously" think about what they are doing – some enter a state of flow.[1] When they are in this state, therapists can observe their behaviours in various contexts and how they react to these.

This also applies to the field of detecting and managing chronic stress. The chapter will describe the underlying model for which the stress map was developed. Ever since it has been introduced to the market it is becoming more and more popular and is gaining notoriety.

The complexity of the stress phenomenon was reduced down to four pillars. The tool was designed to help therapists, psychologists, coaches to help working people understand their stress, place the sources on a map, understand their proneness to stress due to their personality and some traits characteristics, and all this in view of planning (alone, with a professional or with a trustworthy work team) strategies to alleviate the stress and enhance their well-being.

---

1 Flow is a state of mind in which we operate at our absolute best. When the world around us seems to fade away, we lose our sense of time and self and enter a mode of hyper-focus.

Our experience in developing a similar game called *"The Value of Values"*, convinced us that developing a simple but powerful game can become an effective tool for transformation and better manage stress in our working lives and beyond. The chapter will describe a step-by-step process to engage in the game and progress to until the outcome (diagnosis). Once a diagnosis has been made, 50% of the problem is already solved hence people are becoming aware of their stress and the risks involved. The other 50% depends on a coherent strategy to engage in. A strategy can be selected from the menu of tools and techniques presented in Chapter 8 or a unique additional strategy can be sought of.

The Four Pillars Parsimonious Model of Chronic Stress

The first step in the stress map was to reduce the complex model offered by Dolan and Arsenault (presented in Chapter 2) to something that is simple or more parsimonious, so that it can be used in a therapeutic or assessment easily. Respecting, the logic and the scientific rigour, the model has been reduced into four pillars as presented in Figure 7.1. All the components of the model are offered in a deck of super illustrative and colourful cards.

The First Pillar (I) assesses the density of the stress signs and symptoms. The higher the density, the more stressed is the person. People are asked to think about the last four months in their lives and identify all signs and symptoms that they have experienced and for which it was frequent and severe. There are a total of 22 signs and symptoms, but an important innovation is to also offer two wild cards, where people can add signs or symptoms that do not appear on the list (i.e. cards).

The Second Pillar (II) of the stress map is the possible sources or origins of chronic stress. Here, based on the logic provided in former chapters, the focus is on typical

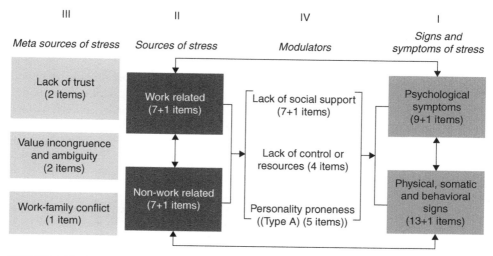

FIGURE 7.1 The four pillars of the stress map in action.
Note that the sequence of playing or using the game is by following the roman numbers I, II, III, ad IV. Also, in future production of the stress map, more information to diagnose about "Low Self-Esteem" will be added.

work-related stressors and family related stressors. As we all know, given that for the majority of people stress at home affects work, and vice versa, both were included in the stress map. Similar to the former, two wild cards were added and here the client may add additional stressors that do not appear on the list of 14 cards.

The Third Pillar (III) of the stress map was labelled meta sources of stress. This is an interesting innovation that comes from years of clinical experience but has not been validated empirically as of today. We labelled them meta sources, because we assume that they affect directly the consequences (the sign and symptoms of stress) without being modulated by modulators. These include sources such as living constantly in situations of values incongruence, not trusting the people that you work for or live with and having constant unresolved conflicts between work and family life. It is based on our (and others) independent research.[2]

The Fourth Pillar (IV) of the stress map places emphasis on the modulators of stress. As have been proposed throughout the chapters, to a great extent stress results from the "eye of the beholder" manner to interpret threats and difficulties. The three classical families of modulators are used in this model: 1) Social support (for which it is hypothesized that having it might buffer the negative consequences of stress, and not having it might make the situation worse; 2) control and resources for which a perception of having them may buffer stress, and the perception of having a deficit or not having them will aggravate the stress. And 3) personality proneness to stress and especially the type A personality trait.

In sum, The Stress Map is rooted in the principles of gamification and provides a visual way to *Explore, Evaluate* and *Execute* (A triaxial "3Es") the overall stress system of a person. In the *Exploration stage*, the client/cochee/patient/person will be invited to identify his/her most important:

- Signs and symptoms of stress (presented in a cyan colour in the game)
- Sources of stress (presented in a magenta colour in the game)
- Meta sources of stress (presented in grey colour in the game)
- Modulators of the stress response (presented in yellow colours in the game)

Then, the client along with the supervision of a therapist/coach be encouraged to *Evaluate* the *sources* and the *modulators* which by changing will help him/her see a significant change in the way they cope with their stress. Finally in the *Execution stage*, the client (with the help of a coach or therapist) will create a course of action that will bring about that change, which will result in reducing the signs and symptoms – ***they will manage their stress.***

---

2 See for example: Bao, Y., Vedina, R., Moodie, S., and Dolan, S.L. (2021) The Relationship between Value Incongruence Bad Individual and Organizational Well-Being Outcomes: An Exploratory Study among Catalan Nurses. *Journal of Advanced Nursing*, 69(3); Mach, M., Dolan, S.L., and Tzafrir, S (2010) The Differential Effect of Team Members' Trust on Team Performance: The Mediation Role of Team Cohesion, *Journal of Occupational and Organizational Psychology*, 83(3), 771–794; Tzafrir, S., and, Dolan S.L. (2004) Trust Me: A Scale for Measuring Manager-Employee Trust. *Management Research*, 2(2), 115–132.

Obviously, the best way to follow up this chapter is to also have at hand the original card game. However, as not all readers will have it, please imagine that you have a deck of cards and the stress map as basic tools to follow. The game itself is colourful and made of high-quality products hence it was designed as a tool to help mental help professionals in their work.[3] Nonetheless, in this chapter we will do the best to describe the content and process of using this unique tool to diagnose chronic stress.

Diagnosis via Gamification Process: A Stage by Stage Process

Exploration stage – 1st Pillar: *Signs and Symptoms of Your Stress*

Instructions: *Think about your life in general. Focus on your experience in the past four months. Review genuinely and honestly the cards that will be introduced to you in a 4-step sequence, each bearing a different colour scheme.*

Before you select the cards, here are some general observations and conclusions based on our (and other scholars) research. In the last decade, stress scientists define the phenomenon as a state or a condition where there is **"wear and tear"** to the body (physically) or the soul (psychologically). If you have no (or few) signs or symptoms of stress, it means that there is no *"wear or tear"* – which means no or very limited stress. However, if you are showing some signs/symptoms of stress, it is of utmost importance to identify and assess them and to engage in a strategy of "stress management". Otherwise, research shows that serious health consequences are likely to take place.

In exploring the *signs and* symptoms *of stress*, you will be presented with 22 cyan colour cards; they are divided into nine psychological symptoms and 13 physical, somatic, and behavioural signs. Please select **up to five cards** (of the 22) and place them on the **Stress Map**. In making your choice, it is important to assess them in terms of density. Density is a term used in physics to test the strength (or resistance of a material). We have adapted it here in a simple manner to help you understand the multiplied and interactive effect of the **frequency** and the **severity** of each sign/symptom. If something is happening relatively frequently and it has a severe impact, the stress density is very high, and it is indicated in the corresponding star systems on the stress map: High density *signs or symptoms* means 5 stars and relatively lower density means less stars. If you have placed no *cards of this colour* on the stress map (which is rare), it means that you have no stress whatsoever.

If you feel that there is an important stress-related sign/symptom that you have experienced in the past three months but is not included in the 22 signs and symptoms cards offered here, please add it (write it down) by placing it in the corresponding cyan wild card (this is an empty card with no description – we label this card a wild card).

If you use this tool with a group that knows each other well, you may engage in a short discussion about your selection, and perhaps after the group discussion you may improve the selection of the signs and symptoms cards. It is a way to validate and improve your diagnosis.

---

3 You can order the game at the following site: https://zinquo.com/tienda-zinquo/herramientas/el-mapa-del-estres/ . The stress map is bilingual and is offered in English and in Spanish.

Some typical signs and symptoms of stress included in the Stress map (presented here in alphabetical order) are:

Buzz in the ears, Clenching Jaws, Colds and Viral infections, Depression, Dandruff, Dryness in the moth, Emotional exhaustion, Excessive drinking, Excessive eating, Excessive sweating, Headaches, Heartbeat-Chest pain) , Impatience, Indifference (Apathy), Irritation (Aggressiveness), Lack of motivation, Lack of strength (Vigor), Nervous (Shaking), Physical exhaustion, Ticks in the eyes, Trouble in Intimate relations, Trouble sleeping, etc.

Exploration stage – 2nd Pillar: *Sources of Stress*

For exploring the *Sources of Stress*, you will be presented with 14 magenta colour cards divided into seven work-related sources of stress and seven non-work-related sources of stress (home, family and friends). You may select **up to five cards** (of the 14) and place them on the corresponding portion of the Stress Map. Similar to the selection of the signs and symptoms, exploring the sources of stress is important to apply the concept of density (**frequency** and **severity**). If something is happening (or has happened in the past four months) relatively frequent and if it has been serious, the source density is very high, and it is indicated in the star systems on the stress map. High density source means five stars, and lower density source means less stars. It is your decision to place the cards on the corresponding level of density.

If you feel that there is an important source of stress that you have experienced in the past four months but is not included in the 14 *Sources of Stress*, please add it (write it down) by placing it in the magenta-coloured wild card (this is an empty card with no description).

Once again, if you use this tool with a group that you know, you may engage in a short discussion that may result in some changes and improvement of your selection of *Sources of Stress* cards. It is a way to validate and improve your diagnosis.

Some typical sources of stress included in the stress map (presented here in alphabetical order) are:

Conflicts at work/home, Overload with tasks/chores, Overwhelmed by responsibilities at work/home, etc.

Exploration Stage – 3rd Pillar: *Meta Sources of Stress*

There is also a special class of factors that are assessed and are labelled the *meta sources of stress*. The five cards *have* been divided into two cards representing living in conditions of lack of trust, two cards representing situations of value incongruence, and an important card that represents difficulties in managing work-family conflicts and tensions. You should select **up to two** cards from the five in case it applies to you and place them on the corresponding stress map (five stars for the relatively highest density and four stars for the relatively lower density). Exploring the density of the meta sources of stress is of utmost importance; hence they directly affect the signs and symptoms of stress. Once again, if you use this tool with others you know, engage in a short discussion with the aim of improving your selection of the relevant meta sources of stress.

Exploration Stage – 4th Pillar: *The Stress Modulators*

The factors that can either filter or amplify the stress reaction are presented in the yellow card deck. Now, you will assess them and end up better understanding your personal capacity to manage the stress in your life/work. The modulators are divided into three groups: six cards connected to the issue of "lack of support", four cards connected to "lack of control or resources", and five cards connected to see if you possess a "personality proneness to stress". Please select **up to seven** cards and place them on the corresponding stress map category. The more stars you have selected means that you have a personality trait that is prone to stress, you do not have sufficient support systems to moderate the negative consequences of stress, or you are engaged in activities with no or little control over the situation. Research shows that effective *stress modulators* (high perception of control, strong support systems and resilient personality) can play an important positive role leading to fewer signs and symptoms of stress. The modulators should be considered later in this tool when stress management will be discussed. If you use this tool with others, a short discussion is recommended to improve the selection of *stress modulator cards*.

An important note for the selection process during the exploration stage: Remember that you cannot select more than the maximum cards allowed for each pilar (**five** cyan cards – 1st pillar, **five** magenta cards – 2nd pillar, **two** grey cards – 3rd pillar, and **seven** yellow cards – 4th pillar). At the same time, remember that you do not have to select all possible cards. You place whatever number of cards that you assess relevant, and the total can be from 0 cards (no cards none whatsoever) to the maximum cards allowed for each category. The more you think and reflect in your choice of cards, the more accurate the stress map will become and will naturally enable you to enter the evaluation stage forcefully and authentically.

Evaluation Stage

In this stage you need to select **up to three** cards from the grey, magenta and yellow cards placed on your stress map. Choose the cards which you think by working on them you will make a significant change that eventually will reduce the stress you have been experiencing.

Now follow the two-step sequence described herein, which will help you evaluate those three cards you will work on.

- **1st step**: Each participant explains to the rest of the group (if you use this tool in a group) or a therapist/coach (in the context of therapy/coaching) the meaning and reasons for your selection. Start by inspecting the density of the signs and symptoms of stress (cyan cards). Remember that the star system can help you in this evaluation. The more stars the more stress. Then you can examine the magenta cards and grey cards in your stress map and identify the principal reasons for your stress (these are the sources). Finally, you may inspect the modulator factors that can either filter or amplify the stress reaction (these are the yellow cards). The more stars you select the more vulnerable you are. Hence you either have a personality trait that makes you more prone to stress, that you do not have sufficient support systems to moderate the stress, or that you are engaged in activities with no or little control over them. Start evaluating the stress map through the high-density cards (identified by the relative star system for each category) and explain what you have learned from this short diagnosis. If time permits, discuss the low-density cards as well.

As you explain your stress map to the participants, check whether you want to update it by changing the cards in the different categories or changing the density of the cards on the map. Make sure that before you continue to step 2, the Stress Map is final, and you agree with it.

- **2nd step**: Together with the group (or a coach in the context of coaching), evaluate which three cards (or less) from the grey, magenta, and yellow cards you discussed in step 1 are the ones that you wish to work on to reduce the stress experience and improve the quality of your life.

Execution Stage

The last stage is designated to shape a **plan of action**. These can be discussed in a separate professional session (with a therapist, a coach, a mentor, a consultant, or an educator) or in a support group, in the case of family, or the team that works together so that the level of mutual trust is high. Design a strategy of **Stress Management**; it should be relatively easy; hence now you clearly understand the various components of your Stress Map. Otherwise, serious health consequences are likely to show in the future.

Write down a "**psychological contract with yourself**" (you may use the form provided herewith (Figure 7.2)) to engage in action and sign it as an obligation. Ensure that the contract contains a **timetable**. Choose who you wish to **accompany** you through the process. As part of the contract, this person needs to accept and join you in signing the psychological contract document. Then, take a photo of the initial map. This will be your baseline to start the journey towards stress management. A replay with the **designated accompanier** (a coach/therapist) or the same group should be scheduled three to six months afterwards. We hope that you can note the difference.

Sharing Stories of Success in Using the Stress Map

In this section, I have invited four therapists who have completed training and certification in the use of the stress map to share their experience. Obviously, the client/patient/cochee name remains anonymous. By contrast, all three therapists have accepted to provide their names and emails so that readers who wish to obtain more information are encouraged to contact them.

Case 1: The Story of the Middle-aged Manager in a Pharmaceutical Company

Case experienced and presented by **Glòria Forns Rodríguez**[4]

---

4 Gloria is a pharmacist, Coach, Organizational consultant, Chief happiness officer and a certified expert in the use and application of the **Stress Map**. https://Felizing by Gloria Forns Email: coach@gloriaforns.com

The Stress Map® · El Mapa del Estrés®

Execution Stage · *Etapa de Ejecución*

A contract with myself · Un contrato conmigo

After completing the Examination and Evaluation of "The Stress Map", and accepting it as an accurate map of my situation, I hereby commit to
Después de completar las etapas de examen y evaluación de "El Mapa del Estrés", y aceptarlo como un mapa preciso de mi situación, por la presente me comprometo a:

Please be precise and specify where, when, with whom, how much · Sé preciso y especifica dónde, cuándo, cómo y con quién.

The anticipated consequences that I expect to have when this contract is kept: · Las consecuencias que espero obtener al cumplir este contrato son:

1)
2)
3)

Expectations from my accompanying person · De la persona que me acompaña en este proceso espero:

Date of signing the contract (or Replay date)
Fecha de firma del contrato (o fecha de repetición)

Date · Fecha

Name of witness & accompanying person
Nombre del testigo y/o acompañante

Signature · Firma   Signature of accompanying person · Firma del acompañante

FIGURE 7.2 A template to sign a contract with yourself.

The client has been working in the pharmaceutical sector and occupies a management position. She is divorced with a 10-year-old child (full custody). She lives in a large metropolitan area. The person is super dynamic, and initially claimed that she has handled stress effectively all her life.

About six months ago she had a panic attack that ended up in the hospital as a cardiac event and, as a result her daughter is now suffering from anxiety, and has started psychological therapy (she declares "my daughter suffers from anxiety because of me"). She has become aware that she wants to change the situation. Her company was willing to help in subsidizing the purchase of a relaxation music APP and/or cover the cost of an online psychological support. Although she has used the means offered by the company, her situation has not improved and finally she had to take sick leave from work due to anxiety. At this time, she was determined to take actions to improve her quality of life in the face of the stress she is suffering. She thought, perhaps understanding her stress from a different angle might be more instrumental.

The client did the pre-session stress self-assessment (paper and pencil), in which she obtained a high score indicating high level of stress. She came to the session commenting that she feels anger at the situation and guilt, and at this point we began to use the stress map, ending with her selecting many signs and symptoms, but it being difficult for her to select the top 5 with the highest density.

She became astonished as she played the game. She couldn't believe that such a simple "game-tool" could give so much information and clarity about her situation. She learned that her stress is the result of her DECISIONS (it is the word that came looking at the map) and that she has a 50% "guilt" because "all that I see is what I am accepting and experiencing every day and, that's why I feel angry". Definitely, the tool helped her to realize that she had responsibility in her current situation, starting a new phase where she is willing to take lead of her own stress, creating new habits that can support her stress management strategy.

Here is a snapshot of the initial stress map of the client developed in the first session. Even if the quality of the image is poor, one can notice that the map was full (all three pillars). Lots of signs and symptoms, lots of sources and multiple modulators.

She has acknowledged each source of stress, having discovered the "Unfair Pay" in the form of lack of RECOGNITION (she has understood that recognition is part of her emotional salary). The acceptance of this factor has allowed her to compare her present with previous experiences in other companies she has worked for, where she was working from a more satisfying position due to this. The session ended here because the client was short of time.

The client arrived at the second session having evaluated her sources and modulators and with an action plan drawn up for each of them, demonstrating a firm commitment to the change she wants for her current situation. During this evaluation, she found that her sources are external in nature and the modulators depend on her.

So, the second session started with the Evaluation stage, although the client had already begun incorporating some slight changes in her life.

At the beginning of the evaluation, the client chose the WORK-LIFE BALANCE card for her action plan, but she realized, through the dialogue, that it is a goal, not a tool for her, so she should work better with other factors to achieve it.

During the session she became aware that she was burdened with TOO MUCH RESPONSIBILITY. With the new vision from the stress map and having been conscious of her own decisions, she declared that "I have let others charge me in the past, but being aware of the consequences, I want to learn how to say no to them", since she would like not to fulfil others' expectations.

Moreover, she noticed that it is her (herself) who "has accustomed people to have eternal availability". That is why we have worked on the distinction of being INDIVIDUALISTIC vs HELPING, which are values that appear in her conversation. Our dialogue gave her a new perspective where she can HELP & BE INDIVIDUALISTIC by "HELPING MYSELF FIRST", honouring both values but changing her "readiness to be available" not for others as a priority but for herself.

During that moment of the session, in the view of experiencing the power of values, a NEW card appeared on the stress map with even greater relevance to her stress: It was the meta-source of LIVING IN INCONGRUENCE WITH HER CORE VALUES. The client became aware of her fundamental values, which she clearly sorted out (values like, HONESTY, EFFORT, EQUITY) and these were not reflected in her day to day life because she is spending too much time dedicated to her professional life, where the organizational culture is not aligned with her values and, therefore, she does not feel that she can act in congruence with them.

Moving to modulators, the client understood the extreme type A personality traits she has and had fully acknowledged them.

During the session multiple plans of actions were proposed by the client (maybe a typical sign of type A personality), but I proposed her to focus only on three cards in order to better manage her stress, which were:

1. Too much responsibility
2. Pay inequity (in the form of lack of recognition)
3. Hyperactivity always in rush

154   The Stress Map

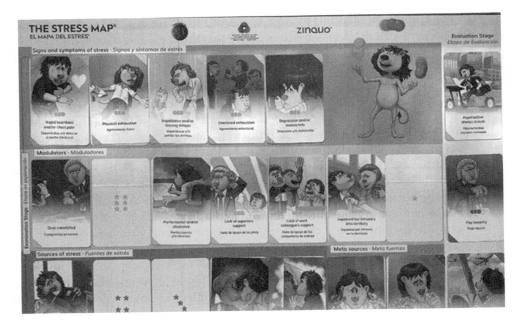

In sum, here are my principal conclusions and observations:

- The client did not believe that such a simple "game-tool" could yield such an effective diagnosis, in such a short time with a relatively high precision.
- The client commented on how easy it has been for her to enter and see her own stress map, and although she has felt it for many days (even months) she could not put the finger on it; The stress map did the job eloquently, professionally and rapidly.
- Given the COVID situation, the session was done online. But, with the camera focusing on the tool and the client only seeing my hands, has not been an impediment for her to feel comfortable and to explore her stress with comfort and confidence.
- The first session pointed out that any of the meta-sources related to VALUES could have something to do with their stress, which appeared during the second session. This fact is key to understand that a coaching process is needed to look into our own stress and find valuable insights that can really help us to move from stress to balance through the action plan.
- Additionally, I recommend using the Value of Values game-Tool in combination with the assessment of the stress map. It may bring more relevant information that can later be incorporated in the picture.
- By having done this stress map particularly, I was more convinced of the proposal from Simon about the theory that meta-sources can play a relevant role in highly stressing situations without being filtered or affected by modulators. In particular, when the meta-sources related to values appear in a stress map, this can explain why someone who has a type A personality can lead to a burnout syndrome in some working environments but not in others where his/her values were aligned. This link of values meta-sources with burnout syndrome, as extreme consequences of stress, could be a powerful investigation line to be considered in the future.

- My own experience as a coach is that the stress map and its evaluation stage need a minimum of two sessions to be built in order to have maximum effectiveness of the tool and that later coaching sessions are needed to move the client from a difficult situation to accomplish his/her vision of balanced life.
- All in all, this is an amazing and effective tool.
- I recommend in the future to also use the value of values game-tool to the assessment. It may bring more relevant information that can later be incorporated in the stress map.
- I also think that not following the therapy/coaching for a couple of more sessions after using the stress map, will deter from the effectiveness of the tool. Some complementary paper and pencil measures can be a perfect companion to the stress map.
- But all in all, this is an amazing, effective tool. This is my opinion, and these are the words spoken by the client.

Case 2: "I'm tired, I can't relax and when I relax something bad happens to me"

Case experienced and presented by **Carlos Sanchez Muñoz**.[5]

Frank is a 45-year-old male, and current professional trader (buying and selling financial assets). Two years ago, I had a coaching process with NLP with him to manage an important change in his life. Frank was formerly an entrepreneur selling computer products. His wife is employed part time with the UN staff in NY, and he was offered an important position in New York.

Both consensually decide to accept the positions and make a change to their lives and move away from Spain. Frank then ceased this opportunity to realize one of his dreams *"to dedicate myself to trading"* (his current profession). At the same time, he realized that trading generates stress and frustration: coming to see me again he said: *"Carlos, I'm tired of suffering stress, I can't relax, and when I relax something bad happens"*.

Taking advantage of one of his trips to Spain, we had a coaching session but this time I used "The Stress Map" to help us assess and measure the chronic stress that he may have experienced. The first thing I did was administer congruence and self-esteem paper and pencil tests, to be able to focus on his mental scheme a bit more deeply.

By exploring the 4four pillars of the stress map, Frank felt instantly comfortable in identifying and sorting the various cards from the game/tool. When he explored the signs and symptoms, he saw two very significant cards that applied to his case: **Emotional Exhaustion and Chest Pain.** When exploring the other pillars of the stress model, he had identified the card indicating dissatisfaction in life. And when he was invited to use the wild card, he added a "lack of professional success" as prime source for his stress.

As he progressed through the game and explored the meta-sources cards, he selected the cards indicating that he lives in incongruity with his core values, and

---

5 Carlos is a certified expert in the use of the stress map. He is also a PNL certified coach and an osteopath. He runs a successful clinic in Mataro (Spain). His email is: www.facilitotucambio.es and his web site: www.facilitotucambio.es

also that he is experiencing high levels of distrust at work. You should have seen his face when he suddenly understood what is happening to him; the game was very insightful. For him, professional success was and is very important at that point in his life – so what do you do when you do not feel confident at work? He realized that he depends on computer platforms, which he does not trust.

The stress map simulation also opened his eyes and made him reflect on how he lives and how he sees the world; he realized that there is nothing objective in this worldly perspective, it is his own subjective perception of reality that counts. Furthermore, when personality traits were assessed in the modulator pillar, he has identified in two cards that indicate his high intensity, obsessive and perfectionist traits. Once he understood that these traits are part of his type A personality, he realized that perhaps a large portion of the stress he suffers is generated by himself, by being self-demanding and self-imposing.

I asked Frank to summarize his experience after using the stress map, and he came back to me with two words: clarity and awareness. The map opens your eyes and at the same time provides for a new window of opportunities to sink in your mind. The latter can be instrumental to facilitate a change of perception of how you see and live your own reality of the world. Eventually, this reflection leads to new possibilities and options to reduce your own stress levels, not to mention that it leads to design some concrete action plans.

In some, my experience in applying the stress map is super positive. The tool enables you (as a coach) to be able to go further and connect the dots and go deeper to reveal the underlying conditions that generate stress among a cochee. It allows the coach to ask questions to know more about the cochee map, and from there to help modify unhealthy customs and behaviours including help to reduce the hormones connected with stress (like cortisol) and even increase the levels of dopamine and oxytocin, in order to be able to live with less stress and greater well-being.

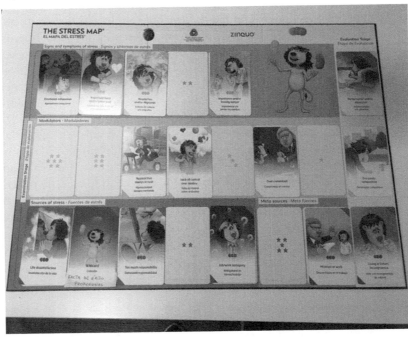

Case 3: The Restaurant Owner[6]

Case experienced and presented by **Alícia Calzada**

The case is taken from the hospitality industry. In many parts of the world, especially in places near the coasts, restaurants and hotels are one of the largest sources of income in the country.

The client is an owner of a small family restaurant. We met at the end of the season where apparently the level of stress touched the roof. He has made a retrospective analysis of the season and became aware that something is happening to him: at the end of every season he ends up emotionally destroyed, without energy and this year he even suffered from a mild stroke.

Until now he always thought that this situation was the normal way of managing a business in this sector, where there are incensed seasons in a restaurant and that it was very normal to suffer stress. He associated stress with energy load and that if he did not feel that stress and pressure during working hours, the staff he was in charge of did not perform the way they had to.

It was then that he decided to discover if there was any other way to work without so much pressure, because every time his body showed more signs and symptoms of a problem. The man is 67 years old. He reached the conclusion that he could not withstand that pressure anymore and perhaps needed help.

In coming to see me and completing the stress map a huge revelation took place.

Here are the three big discoveries made by our restaurant owner after completing the stress map:

- He found out that he had many of the traits of a type A personality. He confessed that it was very difficult for him to delegate tasks to his workers because many times they did it wrong and it had an impact on the image towards customers.

- He realized that he had become super-expendable and that he could not leave the establishment for a minute with what led him to great arguments with his wife and could not see his son almost during the entire summer season.

- In addition, selecting cards from the meta-sources deck of cards, he discovered that he was constantly in ambiguity with his core values – he lives a constant state of values-incongruence.

---

[6] Alícia Calzada. is the founder of Aijoobmind. She is an international expert in values development in adolescents. And a Specialist in the use of the Stress Map. https://aijoobmind.com/descubre-tu-nivel-de-estres-2/ Her email is: hola@aijoobmind.com

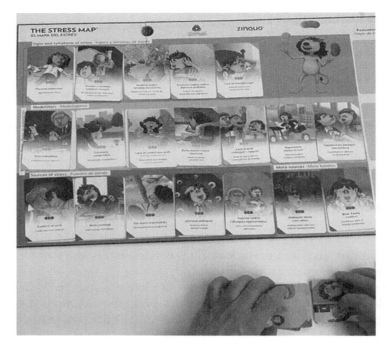

Following the completion of the stress map we moved to the next stage of the process, where he had to select up to three cards (goals) to work in the future in order to alleviate and manage the stress better. Here are the three objectives selected:

Manage better the issue of *"Excess in Commitment"*.
Improve manners for which he will not suffer from the feeling of *"Lack of control at work"*.
Work on identifying and aligning his core values in order to reduce the consequences of *"values incongruence"*.

Thanks to the information gathered during the coaching session where the stress map was used as the principal tool, he was able to discover his origin of all of his symptoms and signs of stress he had throughout the work season (from March to November each year). An action plan was proposed so as not to repeat it in the next season and of course enhance his emotional and physical health.

He chose to learn how to delegate. I n order to do so, he wrote each task in detail so that the staff, whatever the season, could follow that without problem and always do it the same way as if he had done it himself.

In parallel, he also set out a plan for how to better organize each person's roles and really dedicate himself to tasks that were productive and absolutely necessary to make the business viable.

And finally, he set aside on a daily basis time to devote to himself, his wife and his son, so he can harness the social support from the family, enjoy their company and reduce any potential work-family conflicts.

Conclusion: The stress map was very revealing. Results were accurate, fast and the use of gamification principles helped the process. It really makes the difference when you sense, experience and visualize what is happening to you. As a coach I am committed to using this tool, and it will be interesting to reconstruct the stress map with this man after the experiences in the next season.

Case 4: Solving the Couple Stress[7]

Case experienced and presented by **Dr Anat Garti**

A husband and wife asked to come to couple therapy because of constant quarrels. He is self-employed in the restaurant business, and she is a medical doctor working in a public hospital. They have three children ages 9–16. They felt that the therapy is the last resort and if they weren't able to sort thing out, they will most likely end up with a divorce. From the Intec meeting it was clear that they both suffered from a lot of stress, some from work and some from home. Since my impression was that they were overwhelmed and did not know how to manage the personal and marital tension they experienced, I used the pressure map in the first meeting.

I asked each of them to play the role of the other. Each one was to choose the signs and symptoms of their spouse's stress, as they see it, the sources of their spouse's stress as they understand it and the stress modulators. It was important to me that they engaged with the experience of the other and helped their spouse to understand and organize experience, with obtain, regulate and support. That each one of them feels that the other sees their pain and wants to be there to help.

While designing the map, each asked the other questions to find out and be precise about the intensity of the symptoms, to pinpoint the sources and symptoms, including sources of stress related to himself/herself as a partner. The interesting part was when they chose the cards of the modulators, the yellow cards. There they realized how much they aggravate the pressure of the spouse.

After they both designed the spouse's map and checked with the other to see if they correctly identified things, I asked each of them to choose three cards from the sources of pressure and mediators that would allow their partner to significantly improve the stress they are currently experiencing in life and reduce the intensity of the symptoms. Physiological symptoms and no less important, psychological symptoms that harm the relationship and create many tensions between them.

As a mediator, they both chose for the other "lack of partner support" and from there we started making the change, working on the sources of stress and providing support to the other.

After three months they asked to use the game again. It was important for them to see how the things they worked on were able to make a broader systemic change in factors, mediators and of course in symptoms. In their words: "The map invited us to understand the experience of the spouse and especially our opportunity to be significant for him in formatting and promoting change. We did not realize the situation until we saw it on the board. The map gave us a language and the process gave us the way".

---

7 Dr. Anat Garti is a therapist and a coach. She is the co-developer of the Stress Map and the chief psychologist of the Israel Value Center (www.values-center.co.il . Her email is: anatgarti@gmail.com

Chapter Summary and Postscript

The stress map is a novelty. It is the first available tool for professionals to be used in diagnosing chronic stress and planning the first actions in managing it. As recently, we have offered training and certificates in using the stress map, the following description provides a neat summary of this chapter.[8]

Game card **The Stress Map**	A tool to help people and professionals assess the density of stress that is present in their lives and to have alternatives to be able to manage it successfully.

The Stress Map is the result of more than 35 years of scientific research by Dr. Simon L. Dolan and his team in the field of occupational stress. It is aimed at professionals who want to help their clients identify the factors that cause stress in their lives and want to know how to reduce them. By creating your stress map, you will see clearly what plan to follow and to learn how to reduce stress and take action.

Identify through the 4 Pillars Model, the symptoms that cause stress. Through the game and its instruction manual we will guide you to build your Stress Map, identifying, through the 4 Pillars Model, the signs and symptoms that measure your density of stress, the sources and meta-sources that are causing it, and the modulators that play a role so that you can understand how they are influencing how they are influencing the stress consequences..

---

8 Note that in this chapter we do not provide a section on action. We recommend that you obtain the card game and move to action. If you wish to become an expert in using the tools, some online certifications and training are available throughout the year, currently namely bin Spanish but shortly will be offered in English as well. For more information see: https://zinquo.com/profesionales/coaching/especializaciones-coaching/especializacion-en-el-mapa-del-estres/

CHAPTER 8

A Kaleidoscope of Individual and Corporate Remedies to De-stress and Enhance Resilience and Well-being at Work

Introduction

It has been repeatedly demonstrated so far that work-related stress results in as many painful consequences for individuals as for organizations. For this reason, it is necessary for us to learn to prevent stress or, at least, to know how to control and combat it. There are no universal formulas to fighting stress. It is true that since *Hans Seyle introduced the term stress*[1] in 1950s we now know much more about this phenomenon, its causes and consequences. Nevertheless, statistics also indicate that more and more people are affected by stress-related problems. Equally, stress is causing low productivity and a host of negative consequences to organizations. Stress basically, is a loss-loss condition for which one needs to address and combat it to the best of our ability.

We labeled this chapter a kaleidoscope of individual and organizational remedy hence this is no single remedy that works perfectly to either the person or to its organization. Thus, in this chapter we provide a menu of remedies and experiences by experts, therapists and organization consultants to broaden the landscape of possibilities. Like a menu, after reading the former chapters, you have good understanding of the phenomenon at hand, and you can pick and choose whatever you think might be the most suitable to you personally or to your organization.

In the following pages we are going to discuss some of the most effective individual and organizational strategies for tackling stress. Nevertheless, and in contrast to what has been held as fact for many years, we consider that these are not enough. Increasingly, more data is being revealed confirming the enormous relationship that stress has with organizational and work factors, for instance: organizational culture, the type of structure adopted by the company, the leadership style exerted, and how jobs are designed, amongst others. *Is it enough for workers to practice relaxation techniques and/or improve time management?* We are inclined to consider that they are necessary but insufficient, since these types of actions imply involvement only at an individual level though stress also has an organizational component.

DOI: 10.4324/9781003217626-9

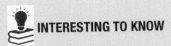

> **INTERESTING TO KNOW**
>
> **ANNA DIAMANTOPOULOU, FORMER EUROPEAN COMMISSIONER FOR EMPLOYMENT AND SOCIAL AFFAIRS:**
>
> *"It is necessary for all the interested parties to recognize that occupational stress is a real risk and one that is deeply rooted in the workplace. Industrialists, workers, and governments will have to step up preventive measures in this field. Good stress management practices in the workplace are required for tackling this ever-increasing problem".*

Because we are aware of the fact that an entire book can be written on almost each remedy offered, we realize that the presentation and discussion will be brief and perhaps incomplete. Recently, we have published an interesting (albeit philosophical) paper of the "design of life".[1] It is worthwhile reading hence we claim that a person can control to a great extent his/her level of stress by planning respective life philosophy, where needs, desires, talent, work setting and family setting are considered altogether. We will elaborate a bit more on this concept in our last chapter where we discussed the future. Nonetheless, we trust your level of judgement and curiosity and we are sure that once a concept has been introduced you will be able to further explore with recent resources.

Organizational Strategies to "De-stress"

In the collective management of stress-causing factors, the predominant objective is to minimize the situations that create tension within the company or organization. Specific actions to do this are aimed at the organizational structure, communication styles, the decision-making process, corporate culture, work functions, and hiring and training methods.

Within the work environment, it is important to consider physical improvements, including ergonomic factors, safety and hygiene. These are particularly relevant concerns for workers. For the company, they represent a latent effort with the aim of improving employees' well-being.

As a general rule, organizational changes are aimed at the restructuring of processes and tasks, which allow workers to develop their skills and increase their responsibilities while improving communication. This is achieved by means of assistance programs for workers, quality circles, assessment groups, support groups, active participation, teamwork, solidarity, professional development, pro motion of creativity and continued improvement methods.

Different strategies can be used, such as the development of a "healthier" culture, adapting leadership styles, the redistribution of power and authority, and responsible and active participation in decision making, developing both formal and informal

---

1 Raich M., and Dolan S.L. (2022) The Art of Life Design. *Kindai Management Review,* June 2022

internal communications, improving the general work atmosphere, and creating a favourable environment for the sustained, healthy and complete development of workers' productive life in the company.

However, the first stage in managing stress at the company level is to understand its causes and to know which specific measures must be introduced from a wide-ranging list of options. The classic European Commission Communication "How to adapt to changes in society and the workplace: A new European strategy (2002-2006)", defines different ways to combat occupational stress, including the following:

- It begins with, the communiqué stressing that "real well-being – physical, moral and social – has to be promoted in the workplace; it should not be measured solely by the absence of work-related accidents or illnesses". Within this new, global focus, one of the objectives is defined as follows: "To prevent social risks: stress, harassment, depression, anxiety, and the risks associated with dependence on alcohol, drugs or other medicines".
- It highlights that the preventative services within the company should in fact be multidisciplinary and that they should consider social and psychological risks.
- Lastly, it states how important it is for this social dialogue to include new risks, "stress in particular, whose diverse and multiform character – especially due to the wide variety of pathologies manifested – completely justifies a proposal of this type, with the implication of the social representatives".

Main Obstacles to Stress Intervention in the Company

 INTERESTING TO KNOW

WHY THE CEO WOULD REJECT A STUDY ON WORK-RELATED STRESS IN HIS ORGANIZATION?

The director of a large hospital in Catalonia declared (literally) to researchers offering to carry out research on stress among hospital staff:

> "We know our personnel are
> very stressed. We have more and more work to do, with patients
> and more aggressive families, and with fewer and fewer
> resources (human, technological and financial). My staff is
> stressed now, but if we have a formal diagnosis of this, they'll be
> even more stressed. I'm afraid to open a Pandora's Box, so we're
> not going to carry out a formal study; I accept the status quo ".

When a problem such as stress occurs within a company, those in charge of occupational health are faced with various obstacles that must be overcome. Although it is subject to debate whether the organization of a human group should be based on technical limitations or in terms of jobs, generally, the company's technology and job organization go hand in hand. In many cases, human resources and the possible ways to organize employees have already been determined. However, new management trends favour the re-evaluation of the "company's human capital", incorporating a new vision of the business reality in which greater relevance is increasingly being given to employees, applying a range of knowledge, methods andtechniques from the field of behavioural sciences. Studies, carried out by various scholars in social and behavioural sciences, are being successfully put into practice in many companies. It is recommended that those in charge of occupational health be allowed to carry out these types of tasks while, at the same time, the company charter or bylaws enable them to do so.

Intervention in these types of problems is difficult, generally due to:

- A greater knowledge among managers of the "technical" or "economic" functioning of the company, rather than the "human" functioning.
- A non-specific presentation of the problem to managers.
- A lack of conviction regarding the scale of the associated costs of problems or the lack of trust that these costs can be controlled by planning, organization and management.
- The non-existing relationship between preventative goals and management's goals.
- The fear of many managers that running a formal diagnosis would open a "Pandora's Box".

To overcome these obstacles, adequate tools need to be used, which enable quantification of the problem. The use of these tools by those responsible for occupational health cannot be limited solely to developing a good diagnosis. They must be able to provide clear, unequivocal and comprehensible data, which will allow for the different groups within the organization to become aware of the problem.

Very frequently, economic profit is the main reference used in terms of whether a given measure is convenient or inconvenient. For this reason, those responsible for occupational health must provide data, which demonstrates that the measures to be taken in terms of employee organization are in fact profitable.

By the same token, proposals for change must be carefully planned, adapting them to frameworks in terms of utility, profitability and practicality and considering costs, partial objectives, goals, processes, etc., and controlling the entire process of change while searching for a convergence between management's goals and those related to prevention within the company.

Stages and Methodologies for Occupational Stress Management

The program for this epidemiological control can be structured in six stages as shown in Figure 8.1.

Stage I: Diagnosis

As described above, the identification of the psycho-social risk factors requires the use of different strategies, including: personal interviews, direct observation and a

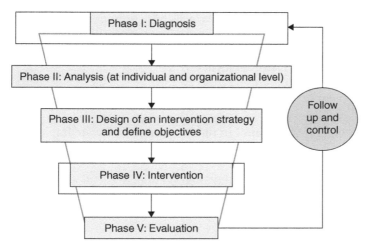

FIGURE 8.1 The main stages in occupational stress management.

tool designed to measure the answers provided by the workers and their perceptions regarding the presence and frequency of the different psycho-social risk factors and where they stem from.

1. The individual
   – Personal, psychological appraisal.
   – Use of psycho-technical tests.
   – Clinical psychological history.
2. The internal working conditions
   – Measurement tool.
   – Direct observation.
3. The conditions outside of work
   – Report in personal interview.

Stage II: Analysis of Results

1. Special cases of individual therapy are identified.
2. Group weaknesses by job title are identified.
3. Along with the results from the tool, more complete and accurate information should be provided in terms of every category measured. This analysis will determine not only the most frequent psycho-social risks, but also to what degree these have affected the organization's employees and executives leading to occupational stress.

Stage III: Design of the Intervention Strategy

Once the most representative risks affecting workers have been identified, the most appropriate methodology to minimize the risk factors, both at their source and in terms of their effects on the workers, should be studied and determined. By the same token, an intervention schedule is needed in which those responsible for each activity are specified, along with the corresponding time limits and objectives. In order to evaluate the program's impact, management indexes must be determined to verify the increase or decrease in the risk factor incidence.

Stage IV: Intervention

At this stage, all the established measures in the intervention plan are implemented to control the risk factor. The objective is to:

1. Minimize the risk agent (source): the methodologies to eliminate these risk factors are implemented and the administrators are incorporated so that they commit themselves to the change and help achieve the success of the program's goals in managing the psycho-social risks.
2. Control the risk factors present in the work environment: upon identifying the risk factors present in the workplace, the ideal methodology to improve the organizational atmosphere is determined, generating greater commitment as a result, the sense of belonging, and a better atmosphere and work environment in the workplace.
3. Develop skills (individual) so that employees can more easily adapt to their environment and cope with the various daily problems. They should have the applicative and practical tools necessary and develop their skills to modify their behaviour and environment, encouraging a better quality of work life.

Stage V: Evaluation of the Results

Once the intervention stage has been completed, the tool for measuring results should be implemented to measure and quantify the psycho-social risks, their incidence or absence, determining the change in the risk factor and the efficacy of the program for this epidemiological control.

Stage VI: Follow-up and Control

The development of this stage is divided into two-time segments: one consists of periodic controls to determine the prevalence and/or reduction of the risk factor; the other comes at the end of the control program to determine whether it has met its objectives by means of control measures.

When referring to the aspects, which commonly lead to occupational stress, we should not only refer to certain conditions that the individual has to cope with. In their specific area of work, employees undergo an adaptative effort. This effort will be greater when the characteristics or conditions of the job put their abilities to the test and/or less significant when the conditions are less than their expectations or needs. Given that stress factors are accumulative, the greater the number of aspects requiring an intense, frequent or long-lasting adaptative effort, the greater the possibility that workers' adaptation abilities will be overwhelmed. As such, the greater the number of stressors, the greater the sense of threat and the higher the level of stress produced.

To alleviate the effects of the different stressors, different measures can be applied at different levels; some are focused on the reorganization of the work tasks, others on the organization of the branch or headquarters; some are focused on the reorganization of resources and means, and others on personal intervention.

In general, and depending on their flexibility, the alternative systems proposed allow for a better adaptation to workers' abilities, needs and expectations. All these types of measures could be described as an increase in the attention and trust shown to workers. The fact that these types of measures imply a different orientation for the company focused on process, technology and production does not, however, imply a rejection of aspects such as productivity or profitability. Simply put, however, workers' health is not subordinated to these objectives.

At the same time, the implementation of these measures in the organization implies intervention at the personal level, and trains workers in order to obtain the best possible results from these measures. However, when intervening at the organizational level, and in order to avoid causing stress, four important elements responsible for generating stress have to be remembered: the presence of stressful demands or work conditions; the perception of these conditions as threats; the difficulty in coping with these demands; and the corresponding, inadequate physiological and emotional responses they provoke.

First, these objectively stressful work demands, and conditions have to be reduced or minimized.

Generally, certain work demands have to be determined depending on the workers' abilities (not only considering the service or production needs) while an increase in demands should only occur when there is a correlative increase in the workers' abilities.

Working conditions should not only be determined by the criteria set by the market, the productive process, technology, etc., but also by certain needs (safety, affiliation, a sense of belonging, status, etc.), expectations and the legitimate aspirations of employees. However, this, in and of itself, would not be completely effective if the workers continued to perceive that some conditions and demands were stressful. The fact that an individual perceives a certain demand as threatening is also a result of the individual's ability to cope with this situation. For this reason, it is important to provide the individual with the behavioural abilities and skills to cope with these situations. The company should provide clear and unequivocal information about the worker's responsibilities and functions, the objectives (product quantity and quality), the methods and means of work, deadlines, etc.

Implementation Plans – Some conditions that need to be taken into account when implementing any measure within the company include:

- The workers' and their representatives' active participation should be counted on regarding the changes to be made, not only so that these are accepted by the workers, but also because it is helpful to contrast opinions in order to adopt the most appropriate decisions.
- Conflictive company-worker situations or general crises are contraindications for carrying out changes as they may interfere both in the adequate implementation of the measures or in their functioning. It is extremely important to choose the right moment to implement any change in order to avoid the risk of failure.

- It is advisable that changes be made progressively, by means of pilot programs. This will allow the comparison between two systems at the same time, to try out different models without high costs (in case of failure) and, in reduced groups, experimentally control the different variables that arise in the new work systems, changes in information channels, etc. At the same time, the advantages of the new system will be perceived by workers who have not been included in the study group and will have a motivating effect on them.
- The advantages and disadvantages regarding who is promoting the change (whether it is someone within the organization or an external consultant) have to be considered. It is possible that people within the organization will have greater knowledge of the organization's idiosyncrasies, but, on the other hand, may express greater resistance to change.
- The experiences prior to the implementation of the measure have to be controlled in all their extremes, attempting to periodically track all the circumstances and comparing the results with the original hypotheses.
- For best results, it should be remembered that a certain period for the workers to adapt to the new situation is necessary and that the implemented measures may require a certain amount of fine-tuning.

Intervention within the Company: Focus on Classic Origins

For good stress management within the organization, the specific characteristics that may be sources of stress, as described in the previous section, have to be identified. It must be remembered that these problems arise progressively. In other words, we will find them in different stages of development from their initial appearance onwards, both at the individual and collective levels. As such, it is worth detecting the symptoms that indicate stressful situations within the organization, and what provokes them, quickly.

Various studies have identified some classic causes of this problem:

- Excessive work demands;
- An imposed work pace;
- Role ambiguity and conflict;
- Bad personal relationships;
- Inadequate management and supervision styles;
- Lack of adaptation to the job;
- Important responsibilities;
- Instability at work;
- Carrying out dangerous tasks (by the nature of the tasks themselves or the conditions in which they are carried out).

Improving Employees' Sense of Control

With reference to the possibility that a situation is perceived as threatening (or otherwise), the final determination will be based on the individual's ability to successfully control and cope with the situation. At the same time, controlling the situation depends on the effective possibility the worker has of working directly on the situation and whether he or she has the necessary strategies available to cope with it.

To this end, one of the measures that must be taken is increasing workers' degree of control over their jobs, this is a necessary condition and ensures workers' health and boosts their job satisfaction level.

Studies have shown that this type of measure is particularly effective in situations involving heavy workloads with few possibilities for the person to control the variables affecting task performance.

When referring to worker's control over their own jobs, we refer to the control over the following aspects:

- What the worker is expected to do (functions, competencies, responsibilities, quantity and quality of the results of their job);
- The way or method of carrying out their job;
- Time schedule and breaks (temporal autonomy), work pace, choice of shifts, flextime, etc.;
- Participation in decision-making concerning those aspects related to their jobs.

With an increase in the worker's discretionary control, there must also be adequate and precise training provided for the worker's specific job and general training to successfully carry out these types of measures (time management, decision making, etc.). It is important not to forget that giving employees freedom with respect to their job, without being adequately prepared for this freedom, may be a great source of stress in itself.

Improving Information and Communication Systems

Given the significant problems which can arise from poor information and communication, in order to correct this situation, effective information and communication systems (including top-down, bottom-up or horizontal) need to be developed, not only directed at achieving productive efficacy, but also to respond to workers' needs and to help them adjust to the new work organization.

A given work demand involves the person concerned carrying out a specific task. Situations where what is expected of the worker is not clearly defined, when their role is ambiguous or there is a lack of free-flowing communication, are among the most important stressors in the workplace. Not knowing exactly what to do, how to do it and what the specific job responsibilities are, create a sense of doubt and threat. It is no longer a question of responding to a demand, but, rather, the worker not knowing what the demand actually is.

That and how it is presented to him can lead to questions of the following type: Can he ask for clarification? Will it be provided? Are these tasks contradictory? Are different things assigned to him at the same time?; Is advice provided?; Can he disagree with what has to be done?; Is it easy?, etc. The problems that can arise from this poor communication and lack of information and the ambiguity or conflict in roles that may develop as a result are two of the most potent stressors. In addition, they are factors, which most affect the company's efficiency.

For these reasons, it is extremely important to revise the company's information system, paying special attention to the following variables:

- Precision of information;
- Coherence between information provided;
- Congruency of the decisions made based on the information provided (both with the same objective);
- Use of appropriate language for the specific recipient;
- Frequency of communication adequate to the needs;
- Adequate procedures to collect, process and transmit information.

A good information system will allow everyone to understand exactly what is expected of them (tasks or objectives to be met) and access the results of the work already carried out. We can differentiate between horizontal communication (among people at the same hierarchical level) and vertical communication (among people at different hierarchical levels).

Within vertical communication there is top-down communication from a higher level to a lower level and bottom-up communication from lower to higher levels.

Top-down Communication – The objective of this type of communication is to:

- Coordinate the members of an organization in order to achieve their objectives;
- Inform people so that they contribute to meeting the objectives and have a better understanding of their tasks and the organization, thereby boosting their motivation. Knowledge and understanding the job and organization can have motivational effects.

It is worthwhile to bear in mind a couple of points, as described by various researchers. In terms of message content, precision must be sought to provide good information. Content simplicity and clarity facilitate message assimilation.

In terms of messages transmitted through a hierarchy, it must be remembered that the following problems may arise:

- If the same message is delivered to all the recipients (irrespective of their hierarchical level), its meaning ma y require it be interpreted differently at each level.
- If the message is adapted for different levels, distortions may arise with respect to the meaning of the original message.

Also worth noting is that the recipients' interest in the message content may be a more determinant factor than the degree of information contained. Good information is characterized not by its scope or frequency but by its ability to respond to employee's expectations.

Bottom-up Communication – Although management generally tends to view bottom-up communication less positively than other types of communication, bottom-up communication is particularly useful because it fosters the working of the organization, as well as having a positive role in personal relationships:

- It allows for points of view to be expressed and channels workers' initiatives regarding different working aspects of the company.
- It encourages feedback regarding top-down communication and the degree to which workers have taken on the organization's objectives.
- It constitutes a basic condition for facilitating worker participation.

In reality, this type of communication is generally problematic in two respects. On the one hand, some companies restrict this type of communication when dealing with certain issues; on the other hand, in some context's workers are reluctant to use this type of communication. When the upper hierarchical levels are the recipients of this information and the source of retribution or reward, employees may have reservations about the content of their messages and will tend to modify the possibly negative aspects, filtering that information which may provoke negative reactions or undesired consequences for the sender.

Another problem in terms of communication originating from the lower ranks occurs when the hierarchical pyramid is extremely narrow at the top, in other words, when the information has to travel up through various levels before reaching the final recipient.

Horizontal Communication – Horizontal communication refers to the exchange of messages between members of the same hierarchical level within the organization. This type of communication enables activity coordination and conflict resolution (although in highly bureaucratic organizations these coordination and conflict resolution functions may be reserved for upper levels).

Generally, it is a means of facilitating emotional support among employees and, at the same time, a source of satisfaction.

Tackling Methods for Conflict Management

In any company there are generally people or groups of people whose objectives and interests are different and, at times, conflicting. The emergence of conflict can be considered normal and foreseeable, and this is why it is necessary to create the means to resolve these conflicts. These measures must be designed to foster:

- Reduction in the appearance of conflicts;
- Creation of arbitration and mediation procedures;
- Training for workers in non-traumatic conflict resolution.

One of the greatest sources of conflict in any company is related to problems arising from the non-definition of employees' roles. To avoid this role ambiguity and conflicts between individuals and instructions that may be the source of these conflicts, a clear and unequivocal definition of each person's tasks and their role within the organization must be sought, as well as the means and contents of their interactions with others. In addition, adequate coordination of all their activities and a sustained coherence in terms of the instructions they are given are necessary. In this respect, the establishment of adequate information channels is especially important.

Nevertheless, given that companies are prone to change, it is necessary to design systems to regulate conflict and to develop structural procedures for the mediation and arbitration of possible conflicts. In addition, employees should be given training in how to interact with others.

Improving or Initiating Socialization Processes

Interpersonal relationships are one of the most important aspects when we refer to the problem of stress within organizations. This is due to the fact that they are in themselves a source of stress and dissatisfaction as relationships are one of the aspects most appreciated by workers in terms of their job satisfaction. As such, it is now considered common practice to pay special attention to the socialization process and training in interpersonal relationships as a way to avoid inadequate relationships becoming possible sources of stress and dissatisfaction.

By the same token, social support must be considered a resource in dealing with a stressful situation: it has been demonstrated that a positive social atmosphere in the workplace eases the emotional impact of stressful situations and the development of physical and psychological consequences.

In terms of a worker adapting to a specific job, it is worth noting that it is necessary to clearly explain the job to the candidate as well as provide necessary training prior to beginning the job or when the job changes.

Many of the measures proposed so far need to be complemented by employee training programs (both managers and workers) regarding how they must act within the redesigned organization. When faced by change, individual intervention is necessary and complementary. It entails providing the individual with the strategies to adapt to some aspects, which are difficult to cope with by means of organizational measures.

Intervention within the Company: Focus on Human Resource Practices and Policies

From a human resource management perspective, prevention has to be initiated from the outset, intervening during the design phase, and bearing in mind all the elements regarding the new job, the physical and social environment and the possible repercussions on health.

To this end, intervention is required on aspects related to controlling tasks and work organization:

- Excessive work demands;
- Imposed work pace;
- Work schedule;
- Organization of one's own task;
- Complexity of the administrative processes;
- Role ambiguity and conflict;
- Employment instability;
- High degree of responsibility;
- Systems for promotion;

- Performance evaluation;
- Interpersonal conflicts;
- Deployment of work engagement programs.

Some of these are a part of good human resource management practices and policies, which are briefly described hereafter.

Improve the Employee Selection and Promotion Processes – The employee selection and promotion processes should broaden the criteria normally used with the aim of encompassing the descriptive elements of the psycho-social dimension of the demands of the job. The physical health risks that individuals will be exposed to should be assessed at the beginning, and the expectations and personal needs of each candidate should be mapped out. In addition, and with the aim of avoiding candidates fostering unreal expectations regarding their future job, they should be informed about the general requirements expected of them within the organization and the philosophy behind human resource management.

Improve Task Descriptions – In the area of human resource management, the aim is to offer the optimal degree of challenge and complexity. No matter how compassionate human resource managers' intentions are when redefining tasks as part of an enrichment or development program, the observed results are disappointing when those new descriptions are implanted without any sort of discrimination in the organization as a whole. This type of enrichment program offers an excellent means for reducing stress among workers who want to take on more responsibilities and want more autonomy regarding their own management. However, for other workers, the consequences may be harmful in terms of their health and job performance. Ever more frequently, it is admitted that, even among those wanting more responsibility and autonomy, a lack training or self-control can lead to the risk of producing dire consequences. Other factors causing stress have to be taken into account when redefining tasks, for example, role clarification, the inherent workload and the skills level required. Without a doubt, in these three cases, the existence of role ambiguity and conflicts, work overload, or under-use, are actual sources of stress.

Develop More Innovative Professional Career Plans – When developing career plans, it is essential to outline the criteria used for promotion as clearly as possible. Organizations have been rightly criticized for neglecting to define career plans. None, however, would dare forget to develop the company's financial or production plan. In an organization, stress is drastically reduced when workers perceive less ambiguity in terms of their professional career. If the promotion criteria are clearly established and if each individual knows what they have to do to advance within the organization, there will be less risk of suffering from stress. In human resource management, efforts must be made to offer different options in terms of professional careers, which take into account both horizontal readjustments as well as vertical promotion.

Personnel Training: Keeping Skills Up-dated – In this aspect, employees' skills should be maintained. This practice is justified by the fact that the individual tends to mistrust his ability to carry out his job correctly. This is even more important when the worker is highly specialized and works in an area where knowledge tends to become obsolete very quickly. Also included in this area are the different programs and techniques aimed at reducing the symptoms of stress described above.

Improve Performance Evaluation Systems and the Techniques to Recognize Effort – The current trend is to involve subordinates in evaluating their own performance. All bilateral appraisal techniques, such as management by objectives, are especially aimed at stimulating individual motivation by allowing the individual to take part in the evaluation process, diminishing the perception of unilateral judgments and at the same time reducing feelings of doubt or injustice.

Develop More Equitable Retribution Systems – The current trend to increasingly individualized salary programs based on the needs of each worker must be further accentuated. Many advantages could be obtained through the use of recently acquired knowledge regarding theories of compensation, theories of equity and the theory of expectations. In terms of expectations, human resource managers argue that a solid salary plan would clearly establish the relationship between effort, performance and relationships. They should ensure that these relationships are as clear and explicit as possible so as to avoid generating tension. In terms of equity, the company's pay policy should be public. This supposes that the changes made to the policy as well as the criteria used are communicated to the workers and are not kept under lock and key. Without a doubt, the aim is to reduce the tensions that may arise from retribution in a context where salaries tend to be personalized.

Offer Flexible Work Schedules – There is increasingly more talk about flextime, flexible work schedules. This approach is also becoming popular among human resource managers. For an organization, this type of schedule resolves a good part of the problems related to late coming since it allows workers to choose the start and finish times that most suit them. This concept could also be extended to include weeks with a variable number of hours.

Establish Well-being Programs – Corporations are focusing more often on maintaining their workers' health instead of helping them recuperate from illness. They are investing in well-being programs, which seem to help employee morale and performance, while at the same time reduce absenteeism and health costs.

Deploy work engagement programs – Work engagement is not only linked to organizational outcomes, but also to individual health outcomes. It is thought that engaged workers are full of energy and are less likely to develop **work related stress complaints**, which can have severe negative impact on workers' health. All in all, employee engagement includes three components: 1) building career and supporting employee career, 2) Enhancing competence-boosting opportunities to ensure that employees always have higher level skills, and 3) sustain caring. Small day to day caring by management making employees feel that they belong to the organization. Work engagement has become a buzz word (very popular) among organizational consultants in the last couple of years, but actually it includes many principles that were treated and used by visionary HR professionals for many years.

Here are some of the 15 most popular strategies for employee engagement:

1. Encourage Knowledge Sharing
2. Building Open and Transparent Communication
3. Involve Employees in Business Planning Processes
4. Build Internal Information Bulletin
5. Help in Creating Individual Growth Path

6. Create a Culture of Social Responsibility
7. Initiate Wellness Programs
8. Regular Employee Surveys and Feedback (Show them you listen)
9. Encourage Employee Learning Initiatives
10. Select the Right Managers and Coach them for Employee Engagement
11. Competitive and well-defined Compensation Structure
12. Rewards and Recognition System
13. Be Fair and Realistic
14. Provide Regular Breaks to Rest
15. Work-Life Balance

Individual Techniques and Strategies to "De-stress"

Strategies to Manage Stress Connected with Physiological and Motor Characteristics

What can we do when stress has already begun to show? In the first place, *try to control it* or, at least, to have the *"perception of control"* over it. To be stressed means to perceive that we have no control over what surrounds us and even over ourselves. When we feel relaxed and happy, we have the sensation of exerting greater control on the things around us. On the other hand, to try to have everything always under control can be a self-defence mechanism behind which is a lack of self-confidence and security in oneself.

Some people have the type of personality profile in which they like to control all the inputs that take place around them (for example, clients, boss, co-workers, children, partner, business trips, stock market decisions, holidays, etc.). At the same time, it is usually very difficult for them to do *de-stressing* daily activities, such as communicating with their partner, practicing a sport, turning off their mobile phone, and so on. However, there is another personality profile of people who can live *happily* without this excessive need for control. Who will be more stressed? In all probability, the person who most resembles the first of the two previously described profiles.

Not everybody has the same need to control their surroundings and themselves. The person with an internal locus of control tends to always want to dominate the situation that confronts him/her and considers that this situation will depend on the decisions, attitudes and behaviour that he /she adopts. In contrast, the person with an external locus will believe in luck, causality, destiny, or the power of others. Let's imagine how a person with an internal locus of control would react to a stressful situation. What would he do? Most likely he would tend to over-activate and launch into several activities to deal with the situation. However, a person with a more external locus of control, may instead become inhibited and avoid the situation, given that "it is the outcome of bad luck, chance, and that nothing can be done about it". Probably, higher levels of stress would be found in the first profile as opposed to the second profile. This suggests that those who stress most are people with a certain degree of commitment to the work they do, and who are dedicated and motivated to improving themselves every day.

How many days like this one would a person be able to put up with? Tolerance to stress is related to the amount of stress that a person is able to put up with without it significantly affecting normal functioning. A person with a high level of stress tolerance will normally show symptoms of the negative consequences of stress much later than someone with a low level of tolerance. What does the tolerance level depend on? There is an individual component, related overall to personality characteristics (levels of anxiety, impulsiveness, reflection, etc.). However, it is also related to socio-cultural and organizational factors, as we shall see further on, factors on which we can also try to act.

Relaxation Techniques

Relaxation techniques are a very highly sought-after tool in present-day society where the stress and fast pace of modern life is a source of psychological disorders for a large part of the population. Relaxation, a classic technique in psychology, is still being widely used as an end in itself as well as a means of complementing other types of therapies. Research has demonstrated the effectiveness of relaxation techniques (including progressive muscle relaxation, meditation, hypnosis, and autogenous training) in the treatment of many problems related to tension, such as insomnia, essential hypertension, headaches brought on by tension, bronchial asthma and tension in general.

Relaxation techniques are used as a means to alleviate the symptoms of stress; nevertheless, they can hardly be considered to be a radical treatment in and of themselves for the causes of stress. If stress is generated by the alteration of an individual's subjective perception of his work, it is therefore necessary to work on the perception or the idea that this individual has of his work. If, on the contrary, a work related problem does in fact exist, the individual is of little importance, and there will always be adaptation problems; in this situation it will be necessary to analyze the job, its content and its context.

There are many different types of relaxation techniques. Nevertheless, not all of them are suitable for everybody. Each person will have to choose the relaxation technique that is best suited to his or her personality traits. And so, for example, techniques involving muscle relaxation will be appropriate for those people who have considerable muscle tension derived from stress.

The following are two of the most widely-known relaxation techniques:

- Jacobson's *progressive muscle relaxation* technique, and
- Schultz' *Autogenous training*.

Progressive Muscle Relaxation (Jacobson)[2] – At the beginning of the twentieth century, Edmund Jacobson conceived a relaxation method that was intended to induce a state of mental calmness as a result of progressively suppressing muscular tension. This method introduces learning how to progressively relax all parts

---

2 If you are interested in this technique, I recommend that you read the BBC story: The man who invented relaxation, by W. Kremer (2015) www.bbc.com/news/magazine-34714591

of the body. The number of hours proposed by Jacobson for learning how to use the progressive relaxation technique is a serious limitation in terms of applying the technique. Jacobson demanded that trainees practice for an hour a day. If they said they didn't have time he told them to wake up an hour earlier, as his exercises were more important than sleep.

In his writings, Jacobson asks patients to tighten their muscles and then release them slowly, paying close attention to the sensations of tiny amounts of residual tension. The idea is that after much practice, they become able to detect any tension and then work on eliminating it.

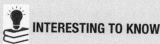 **INTERESTING TO KNOW**

Throughout the twentieth century, the practice of yoga in the West moved from being a niche activity for those interested in Eastern spirituality to a more secularised exercise program with wide appeal to the mainstream. While pictures of the Maharishi Mahesh Yogi practising yoga with the Beatles were beamed around the world, government-funded evening classes were starting in London.

One of Jacobson great supporter was Herbert Benson, who published a blockbuster book called: The Relaxation Response,[3] Benson catalogued, in his book, a long list of modern ills, ranging from job insecurity to the rapid change in the role of women in society, to the ever-present fear of sudden nuclear annihilation. The result, Benson wrote, was that our innate "fight-or-flight" mechanism was working in overdrive, leading to an "epidemic" of hypertension. Thus, taking a pause, relaxing, can slow down the process.

Autogenous Training (Schultz) – From 1912 onwards, a German psychiatrist, Johannes Schultz worked on the principles of autogenous training, based on his observations on the use of hypnosis, which he mastered perfectly. The denomination of autogenous training was etymologically based on the Greek words "autos" (oneself) and "gen" (to happen) and could be translated as: an exercise or training, developed from the individual's own "self" and which shapes this "self".

According to Schultz:[4] "*The principle on which the method is based consists of producing a general transformation in the subject under study by means of using certain physiological and rational exercises (heaviness exercise, heat exercise, pulsation exercise, respiratory exercise, abdominal regulation) and which, in analogy with the oldest exogenous hypnotic practices, enables the subject to obtain identical results to those obtained by the real suggestive states*".

Yoga, Meditation, and Other Relaxation Techniques – Yoga is a broad term for a series of practices that were developed over several millennia to bring

---

3   The first ed was published by Benson in 1975. Here is a reference for the latest edition: Benson H. and Klipper M.A. (2009) The Relaxation Response. Harper Collins.
4   Autogenic Training developed by Dr. Schultz, J. H.: A gentle way to relax is available for free download in several formats – including epub, pdf, azw, mobi and more. [PDF] Download Autogenic Training developed by Dr. Schultz, J. H.: A gentle way to relax *Full Books* ~ Justice pdfbookfinest

practitioners into a state of wholeness and completeness. The sanskrit word *yoga*, which literally means "to unite", has many branches, including **Hatha Yoga**. Hatha Yoga consists of concentration techniques, breathing exercises, dietary guidelines, and a series of stationary or moving poses – also called **asanas**. These body movements are what we commonly refer to today when we use the word "yoga".

Yoga postures balance the different systems of the body, including the *central nervous system*, the *endocrine* (or glandular) *system*, and the *digestive system*. By slowing down the mental activity, and by gently stretching the body and massaging the internal organs, yoga creates a climate of dynamic peacefulness within. This relaxing and rejuvenating experience momentarily removes us from involvement with the stressors in our lives – our "to-do" lists, unresolved issues from the past, or worries of the future. By practicing yoga on a regular basis, we build up a natural response to stress, and bring the relaxed state more and more into our daily lives.

The health benefits of yoga are tremendous. Feeling better physically counters the effects of stress. Yoga, according to advocates of this method, claim that it produces the following physical health benefits:

- improves flexibility and muscle joint mobility
- strengthens and tones muscles
- increases stamina
- relief from back pain
- increases vitality and improves brain function
- improves digestion and elimination
- decreases cholesterol and blood sugar levels
- increases circulation
- boosts immune response

Meditation – The history of meditation goes back even further than that of Hatha Yoga, with its origins beginning around 3,000 B.C.E. Meditation evolved as a way for the ancient spiritual seers – known in India as *Rishis* – to gain direct knowledge of the nature of the Ultimate Reality. Today, meditation is recognized for its myriad health benefits, and is widely practiced as a way to counteract stress. Meditation brings together all the energies of the mind and focuses them on a chosen point: a word, a sound, a symbol, an image that evokes comfort, or one's own breathing. It is typically practiced in a quiet, clean environment in a seated posture with the eyes closed.

As with yoga, a regular practice of meditation conditions you to bring the meditative state into your daily life. Holistic-online.com reports that "hormones and other biochemical compounds in the blood indicative of stress tend to decrease during (meditation) practice. These changes also stabilize over time, so that a person is actually less stressed biochemically during daily activity".

In meditation there is both *effort* and *passive participation*. You continually bring the attention back to a chosen focus (effort), and simply become **a witness** of all that transpires (passive participation) – incorporating thoughts, sensory input, bodily sensations, and external stimulus into the meditation experience. The result of centering the mind in this way is a corresponding calming and relaxing of the body, down to the cellular level, providing stress reduction.

And, back to Benson who managed to combine Jacobson's **Relaxation Response**, with meditation in a manner that is easy to understand and apply. Perhaps this was the secret for his book to become a best seller. Some claim that Benson made "relaxation" a buzzword in much the same way that "mindfulness" is now (see next section). Indeed, the approaches have some common ground. Benson was a cardiologist who had become convinced of the benefits of transcendental meditation techniques on physical health, and he instructed patients to adopt a passive attitude and hold a thought or word in their minds for an extended period. Here are the procedures (steps) to elicit the relaxation response:

1. Sit quietly in a comfortable position.
2. Close your eyes.
3. Deeply relax all your muscles, beginning at your feet and progressing up to your face. Keep them relaxed.
4. Breathe through your nose. Become aware of your breathing. As you breathe out, say the word, "one", silently to yourself. For example, breathe in ... out, "one", in .. out, "one", etc. Breathe easily and naturally.
5. Continue for 10 to 20 minutes. You may open your eyes to check the time, but do not use an alarm. When you finish, sit quietly for several minutes, at first with your eyes closed and later with your eyes opened. Do not stand up for a few minutes.
6. Do not worry about whether you are successful in achieving a deep level of relaxation. Maintain a passive attitude and permit relaxation to occur at its own pace. When distracting thoughts occur, try to ignore them by not dwelling upon them and return to repeating "one".

With practice, the response should come with little effort. Practice the technique once or twice daily, but not within two hours after any meal since the digestive processes seem to interfere with the elicitation of the relaxation response.

Throughout history, people have chosen spiritual teachers to help them reach a more profound spiritual connection via meditation. Table 8.1 is a synopsis of the biggest (or most famous) contemporary gurus of meditation. Notice that they all have the Indian connection.

Mindfulness – is the practice of purposely bringing one's attention in the present moment without evaluation. It is a skill one develops through meditation or other type of similar training. Mindfulness derives from *sati*, a significant element of Buddhist traditions, and is based on Zen, *Vipassanā*, and Tibetan meditation techniques. Though definitions and techniques of mindfulness are wide-ranging, Buddhist traditions explain what constitutes mindfulness such as how past, present,

180 A Kaleidoscope of Individual and Corporate Remedies

TABLE 8.1 The six biggest meditation Gurus

Guru's name	Description and short Bio	Comments and further references
Paramahansa Yogananda 1893-1952	Is best known for his literary masterpiece *Autobiography of a Yogi* – was born as Mukunda Lal Ghosh in Gorakhpur, India to a wealthy Bengali family. His parents were disciples of Lahiri Mahasaya, who was known for reintroducing *Kriya Yoga* (the scientific technique of God-realization through the practice of a specific form of meditation) in modern India.	The seeds of Yogananda's teachings have lived on through his self-realization centers, which are located around the world. Many locations have beautiful meditation gardens such as Lake Shrine Gardens in Pacific Palisades, California and the Encinitas Hermitage, Retreat & Gardens in Encinitas, California **Famous quote:** *Read a little. Meditate more. Think of God all the time".*
Maharishi Mahesh Yogi, 1918-2008	Was a guru to many singers and Hollywood stars in the 1960s, became interested in a spiritual path after obtaining his Master's degree in physics at Allahabad University in 1940. After studying under guru, Swami Brahmananda Saraswati, he began the Spiritual Regeneration Movement and his world tour to teach meditation. He named his technique **Transcendental Meditation** and expanded his teachings to the United Kingdom and the U.S.	Maharishi Mahesh Yogi founded his first international university, now situated in Fairfield, Iowa. There are more than 5 million meditators who have learned and practiced the Transcendental Meditation technique **Famous quote** *"The important thing is this: to be able, at any moment, to sacrifice what we are for what we could become".*
Sri Sri Ravi Shankar, 1956-present	known as a spiritual leader and an ambassador of peace, founded The Art of Living Foundation and developed the **Sudarshan Kriya** breathing technique. In 1997, Sri Sri founded the International Association for Human Values (IAHV), a humanitarian organization with a vision to uplift human values. IAHV delivers disaster-relief funds throughout the world and includes programs such as prisoner rehabilitation and trauma relief for veterans	As ambassador of peace, Sri Sri has brought a message of non-violence and conflict resolution to countries such as Iraq, and the Indian states of Kashmir and Bihar **Famous quote** *"You should be ready for any challenge. This readiness will make you happy".*
Amma (Mata Amritanandamayi), 1953-present	Mata Amritanandamayi or *Amma*, which means "Mother" as her devotees call her, is known worldwide as the "hugging saint". When on tour, Amma sometimes spends up to 22 hours a day embracing people who come to her for healing and blessings. In her work, she and her trained volunteers have taught more than 1.3 million people to meditate through her simple meditation technique called **Integrated Amrita Meditation** (IAM).	Through her organization, Embracing the World, Amma not only offers love and comfort, she gives back through selfless service (*seva*). Embracing the World feeds 10 million poor people in India every year, has built 45,000 homes for the homeless, and has built a 1,300-bed hospital in Kerala, India **Famous quote** *Our highest, most important duty in this world is to help our fellow beings".*

TABLE 8.1 Cont.

Guru's name	Description and short Bio	Comments and further references
Deepak Chopra, **1947-present**	Deepak Chopra, who began his career as a medical doctor in Boston, is the author of more than 80 books, co-founder of the Chopra Center for Wellbeing, and founder of The Chopra Foundation. He became increasingly frustrated with Western medicine. He experienced patients who only wanted relief through prescription medications. He began studying alternative medicine, met meditation guru, Maharishi Mahesh Yogi with whom he learned Transcendental Meditation, and began a successful career in alternative medicine and holistic practices. He formed the **Primordial Sound Meditation** technique rooted in the ancient Vedic tradition of India. Although the roots of this mantra-based meditation technique have been around for thousands of years, Dr. Chopra has mentored and taught thousands of modern meditators, including many Hollywood celebrities,	His book *Ageless Body, Timeless Mind* moved him to celebrity status after it sold one million copies in hardcover. **Famous quote** "I, of course, meditate for two hours every morning. I wake up at 4 a.m. every day and I love it".
Rajinder Singh* **1946–present**	Sant Rajinder Singh Ji Maharaj is head of Science of Spirituality (SOS), an international non-profit organization with over 3,200 centers worldwide, headquartered at the International Science of Spirituality Meditation Center in Lisle, Illinois, and Sawan Kirpal Ruhani Mission, headquartered at Kirpal Ashram, Delhi, India. He is internationally recognized for his work toward promoting inner and outer peace through spirituality and meditation on the inner Light and Sound and his worldwide charitable work. With a background in spirituality and science, earning his B.Tech degree in Electrical Engineering from IIT (Indian Institute of Technology) Madras, India, and an M.S. degree in Electrical Engineering from IIT (Illinois Institute of Technology) in Chicago, Illinois, he presents meditation in an easily understandable way to help people achieve physical, mental, emotional, and spiritual growth.	He received his spiritual education from two of India's leading spiritual Masters: Sant Kirpal Singh Ji Maharaj (1894–1974) and Sant Darshan Singh Ji Maharaj (1921–1989). His training in both disciplines has helped him express age-old spiritual teachings in clear and logical language. Sant Rajinder Singh Ji Maharaj is internationally recognized for teaching meditation globally to millions through meditation seminars, his many books and audiobooks translated into over 50 languages, including *Meditation as Medication for the Soul* and *Inner and Outer Peace through Meditation,* videos, audios, articles, appearances on TV, radio, and Internet broadcasts, and through social media. More info is available at www.sos.org **Famous quote** "If each person attains inner peace through meditation and develops love for all, it will not be long before peace prevails on our planet"

* Note: The information about Sant Rajinder Singh Ji Maharaj has been provided and validated by his son, Dr. Kenny Duggal. I wish to thank Dr Duggal for his kind collaboration.

and future moments arise and cease as momentary sense impressions and mental phenomena. Individuals who have contributed to the popularity of mindfulness in the modern Western context include **Thích Nhất Hạnh**[5] and **Jon Kabat-Zinn**,[6] among others.

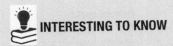 **INTERESTING TO KNOW**

SOME RECENT CONCLUSION AND SCIENTIFIC EVIDENCE FOR PRACTICING MINDFULNESS?

There is no doubt that it is trendy; this is the "in" concept in the field of management.

There is no doubt that any form of stress reducing technique blended with some spiritual elements, produces positive results for those who practice (but not necessarily more than those who practice praying, Yoga, and other techniques of relaxation).

Remember that Mindfulness is not a panacea to resolve all human or organizational problems. In fact, for some people practicing mindfulness might even be counterproductive, especially when the practice has become an obsession.

It is extremely difficult to show the direct impact of this practice on organizational outcomes (such as creativity or productivity). However, several studies show effects on indirect measures of productivity such as lower absenteeism rates, lover levels of work accidents, and other indirect outcomes.

Source: Dolan S.L. (2017) Mindfulness for Dummies (GFWF Blog)

At the time that this book was published, mindfulness meditation had become a multi-billion-dollar industry. The question is: Is it just another health fad? And how do Buddhists feel about it being secularized and commercialized? The US meditation industry is now worth $1B. By 2027, the global alternative healthcare industry – including meditation, acupuncture, breathing exercises, yoga and tai chi, and chiropractic mindfulness services – will be worth $296.3B.[7] This trend is being driven by a few key factors, including smartphone apps, new research, wellness culture and the

---

5 As a Vietnamese Thiền Buddhist monk, peace activist, prolific author, poet, teacher, and founder of the Plum Village Tradition, historically recognized as the main inspiration for engaged Buddhism. He is known as the "father of mindfulness". (Thích Nhất Hạnh – Wikipedia)

6 **Jon Kabat-Zinn** (born **Jon Kabat**) is an American professor emeritus of medicine and the creator of the Stress Reduction Clinic and the Center for Mindfulness in Medicine, Health Care, and Society at the University of Massachusetts Medical School. Kabat-Zinn was a student of Zen Buddhist teachers such as Philip Kapleau, Thich Nhat Hanh and Seung Sahn, and a founding member of Cambridge Zen Center. His practice of yoga and studies with Buddhist teachers led him to integrate their teachings with scientific findings. He teaches mindfulness, which he says can help people cope with stress, anxiety, pain, and illness. The stress reduction program created by Kabat-Zinn, mindfulness-based stress reduction (MBSR), is offered by medical centres, hospitals, and health maintenance organizations, and is described in his book Full Catastrophe Living. (Jon Kabat-Zinn – Wikipedia)

7 Source: What's Next For The Meditation Startups and The Mindfulness Industry? (fitt.co)

rise of burnout. Here are a few interesting observations about mindfulness. You will be able to decide if it is a fad or a fact to DE-STRESS:

- **Technology** – The integration of technology into traditional mindfulness practices makes meditation accessible and affordable for people all over the world. How accessible? On iTunes, for instance, there are nearly 1,000 mindfulness and meditation apps to choose from.
- **Science** – Recent research on mindfulness and meditation has proven the practice's benefits, even for people who practice for as little as 10 minutes. From controlling and managing pain to lowering blood pressure and lessening the symptoms of depression; the results seem to be real.
- **Wellness** – The rising popularity of wellness culture and self-care have thrust mindfulness into the spotlight. Perpetuated by the Wellness Industrial Complex, meditation and mindfulness are perfectly aligned with our never-ending pursuit of optimization and productivity.
- **Burnout** – An American Psychological Association (APA) poll conducted in 2018 shows that 40% of Americans are more anxious than they were at this time a year before. And it is estimated that during and after the COVID-19 pandemic, the percentages have risen significantly. Today's teenagers report higher rates of anxiety and depression, too. Mindfulness, then, seems like a natural remedy to combat these difficult trends.
- **An ethical conundrum** – Some experts have gone so far as to call this industry boom "McMindfulness", referencing the fact that a 10-minute, app-assisted meditation, or a technology-enabled meditation headband stray incredibly far from the original intent of a Buddhist meditation practice, which has no end goal. In traditional Buddhist meditation practices, there is no opportunity to "do it right" because the process isn't something you judge. Additionally, meditation and mindfulness programs are also traditionally offered for free, which presents an interesting market tension.

Biofeedback-assisted relaxation – is a technique that, with the aid of detectors placed on various organs or different parts of the body, enables the individual to perceive signals by sight or sound. Perceiving these signals allows the individual to control a function that would normally evade his voluntary control. Biofeedback uses electronic devices to teach you to produce changes in your body that are associated with relaxation, such as reduced muscle tension. The objective of the training in biofeedback is to get the subject to process the biological data he receives and use it to gain control over specific processes and biological parameters.

There are three main approaches to biofeedback:

- Skin temperature methods: Adrenaline diverts blood from the body surface to the core of the body, in preparation for response to danger. As less warm blood is going to the surface, skin temperature drops.
- Skin electrical activity methods: When you are under stress you sweat more. Skin that is damp (sweating) conducts electricity more effectively than skin that is dry. These methods of biofeedback measure the amount of electricity conducted between two electrodes on the skin.

- Muscle electrical activity: These methods measure the electrical activity of muscles under the surface of the skin. This is useful in measuring the tension of these muscles.

These techniques have been the object of considerable criticism and occupy a certain position in the psychosomatic treatment of the consequences derived from stress. As such, in certain cases, migraines respond well to biofeedback treatment, and results in individuals under treatment reducing their arterial tension by using the same type of technique.

Final observation about the relaxation techniques: All these techniques have some similar effects – Benson's techniques and meditation methods, and mindfulness and muscle relaxation and breathing techniques – they all have some common effects in relaxation. Although they also have some very specific effects because they work by different pathways. Nonetheless, these techniques seem to be instrumental and promote wellness, which is a wonderful way to DE-STRESS. What is a bit worrisome is that meditation and mindfulness are paving the way for mental health startups hoping to address depression, anxiety and burnout and convert it into prosperous profits. Only a minority of firms or associations offered these in a benevolent manner in order to help the person develop spiritually.

Humour and Laughter Therapy[8]

A smile is the shortest distance between two people.

Victor Borge

Is there a correlation between stress, particularly negative perceptions and emotions, and disease? Can the body-mind connection help to reduce stress and anxiety? The premise of humour therapy is that if negative thoughts can result in illness and disease, positive thoughts should do the opposite and enhance health.

In the movie **Patch Adams**, based on a true story, the late Robin Williams acts as a medical student who is scrutinized by the medical administration for his non-conventional medical clown playfulness to bring empathic joy, laughter and humour to the patients.

Researchers at the University of California have been studying the effects of laughter on the immune system. To date their published studies have shown that laughing lowers blood pressure, reduces stress hormones, increases muscle flexion, and boosts immune function by raising levels of infection-fighting T-cells, disease-fighting proteins called Gamma-interferon and B-cells, which produce disease-destroying antibodies. Laughter also triggers the release of endorphins, the body's natural painkillers, and produces a general sense of well-being.[9]

---

8 Note: this section was reviewed and enhanced by Mr Avi Liran, a person that dedicate his professional life to delight people in organizations. For more information visit his web site: www.deliveringdelight.com

9 Wooten, P., (1997) Psychoneuroimmunology of Laughter: An Interview with Lee Berk, Dr. PH. *Journal of Nursing Jocularity*, Fall 7(3), 46-47.

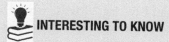 **INTERESTING TO KNOW**

The value of humour has been confirmed to the point that many hospitals and ambulatory care centers now have incorporated special rooms where materials – and sometimes people – are there to help make people laugh. Materials include movies, audio and videotapes, books, games, and puzzles for patients of every age. Movies and TV shows by popular comedians from Laurel and Hardy to Bob Hope and Bob Newhart, humorous songs, the joke of the day on the Internet, the one paragraph jokes and funny stories from the Readers' Digest, all have value in helping patients who would otherwise have little to laugh about.

A hospital in North Carolina created a "laughmobile" that visits bedridden patients. Many hospitals throughout the U.S. now use volunteer groups who visit patients with carts full of humour devices, including slapstick items such as water pistols and rubber chickens. They visit patients who are fighting cancer and other serious illnesses, providing an oasis of laughter during an otherwise difficult time.

Source: www.phoenix5.org/humor/HumorTherapyACS.htmLaughing

is aerobic, providing a workout for the diaphragm and increasing the body's ability to use oxygen. Experts believe that, when used as an adjunct to conventional care, laughter can reduce pain and aid the healing process. For one thing, laughter offers a powerful distraction from pain. Norman Cousins, an influential writer and editor in chief of **Saturday Review** who wrote the book "**Anatomy of an Illness**" is considered as the man who triggered the interest of the medical community in the healing properties of laughter. In the 1970s, Cousins was hospitalized with a mysterious, crippling degenerative bone disease with no known treatment. Facing the doctors diagnosed that his progressive paralysis or a disease that would eventually kill him, Cousins checked himself out of the hospital, and into a hotel. He prescribed to himself a mega dosage of vitamin C, watched funny movies such as Candid Camera and the Marx Brothers and read funny books. He later wrote: "I made the joyous discovery that 10 minutes of genuine belly laughter had an anesthetic effect and would give me at least two hours of pain-free sleep".[10]

In 1995 Dr Madan Kataria had started a movement called Laughter Yoga. Laughing for no reason without humor or comedy. The yoga part of Laughter is the combination of Laughter Exercises with yoga breathing techniques (Pranayama). There are more than 20,000 free social Laughter clubs in 110 countries.[11]

My friend and colleague Avi Liran who went to Laughter Yoga teacher accreditation in 2006 share that he laughed 9 hours a day and lost 2kg in five days. He reported a significant improvement in his stress levels that lasted about four months.

---

10 Note: Cousins was portrayed by actor Ed Asner in a 1984 television movie, Anatomy of an Illness, which was based on Cousins's 1979 book, Anatomy of an Illness as Perceived by the Patient: Reflections on Healing. Cousins was not pleased with the commercial nature of the movie, and with Hollywood's sensationalistic exaggerations of his experience.

11 Videos of Madan Kataria Laughter Yoga can be watched at: www.bing.com/videos/search?q=madan+kataria+laughter+yoga&qpvt=madan+kataria+laughter+yoga&FORM=VDRE

Avi shared with me why he stopped teaching Laughter Yoga after a few months: "As I researched more about happiness and wellbeing, I resonated with what Dr. Patch Adams said: "Laughter is not the best medicine, friendship is". In good relationship finding something to smile and laugh about comes naturally as a result, not as a goal. I found that playfulness on the other hand usually induces frequent and genuine laughter".

For example, in a study published in the *Journal of Holistic Nursing*, patients were told one-liners after surgery and before painful medication was administered. Those exposed to humour perceived less pain when compared to patients who didn't get a dose of humour as part of their therapy.

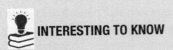

INTERESTING TO KNOW

Two tips by Avi Liran

The best way to increase and extend your joy is to share it. If a joke tickled your funny bone, chances are that other people will appreciate it and laugh with you. If you want to remember a joke, first use the power of repetition: First tell it to as many friends as possible. Second make a mental note or write in a notebook the keywords of the joke so you will not forget it.
Steps to initiate humour therapy may include the following elements:

- Look for the funny. Watch comedies, stand-up comedians and read funny books.
- Learn not to take yourself too seriously.
- Laugh at yourself; find one humorous thing a day.
- Laugh with people not on people.
- Learn to hyper exaggerate when telling a story.
- Build a humour library.
- Find a host of varied humour venues.
- Access your humour **network**.

Intake of Products that Boost the Immune System

The Importance of Vitamin C

Study after study report that in addition to benefits related to the common cold and cancer, vitamin C helps reduce both the physical and psychological effects of stress on people. It's already everybody's favourite nutritional supplement, linked, however controversially, to preventing the common cold and fighting cancer. But Vitamin C recently added a new notch on its belt. The vitamin helps reduce both the physical and psychological effects of stress on people.

According to the Nobel price winner Linus Pauling, whom I had the chance to meet in person in 1979 (Monte Carlo-Monaco), Vitamin C is one of the best remedies to fight stress as it works directly on boosting the immune system. There has been more research about the immune-boosting effects of Vitamin C than perhaps any other nutrient. Pauling asserts that Vitamin C – also known as ascorbic acid or sodium ascorbate or calcium ascorbate – is involved in a great number of biochemical reactions in the human body. Two of its major interactions are in potentiating the immune system and aiding the synthesis of the protein collagen, which is a very important substance that holds together the human body. Collagen strengthens the blood vessels, the skin, the muscles, and the bones. You cannot make collagen without Vitamin C.

Vitamin C increases the production of infection-fighting white blood cells and antibodies and increases levels of interferon, the antibody that coats cell surfaces, preventing the entry of viruses. Vitamin C reduces the risk of cardiovascular disease by raising levels of HDL (good) cholesterol while lowering blood pressure and interfering with the process by which fat is converted to plaque in the arteries. As an added perk, persons whose diets are higher in Vitamin C have lower rates of colon, prostate and breast cancer. Pauling developed his Vitamin C theory extrapolating from animal food consumption. Most animals, except humans, monkeys and apes, manufacture Vitamin C. They don't rely on vitamin pills or on foods—they make Vitamin C in their liver in amounts proportional to body weight. For an adult man the proportion turns out to be on the average about 10 or 12 grams (12,000 mg) a day. That's 200 times the Recommended Dietary Allowance (RDA)–200 times the amount people get in an ordinary diet! This is why Pauling suggests that we should be getting 200 times the amount of Vitamin C that the Food and Nutrition Board recommends. The RDA, 60 mg, is far too small and indicates the importance of taking Vitamin C supplements.

Apparently, people who have high levels of Vitamin C do not show the expected mental and physical signs of stress when subjected to acute psychological challenges. What's more, they bounce back from stressful situations faster than people with low levels of Vitamin C in their blood. In one study German researchers subjected 120 people to a sure-fire stressor – a public speaking task combined with math problems. Half of those studied were given 1,000 mg of Vitamin C. Such signs of stress as elevated levels of the stress hormone cortisol and high blood pressure were significantly greater in those who did not get the vitamin supplement. Those who got Vitamin C reported that they felt less stressed when they got the vitamin.[12]

There is quite controversy over Pauling theory in general, and the quantity of vitamin intake. In the 1960s, Dr. Pauling published his theory on Vitamin C and the common cold. The "Establishment" quickly branded him a "Quack" while suggesting he remain a chemist, for which he received a Nobel Prize. When he suggested that Vitamin C had efficacy with cancer, the "Establishment" as well as the mainstream media considered it nonsense. They demeaned and vilified the altruistic Dr Pauling for years afterward.

---

12 Source: Psychology today . www.psychologytoday.com/us/articles/200304/vitamin-c-stress-buster

The Importance of Vitamin D

Vitamin D has become a star supplement during the COVID-19 epidemic. The question is if it is really boosting the immune system and secondly if it also helps to combat stress and mental illnesses. Research done before and during the pandemic suggest clearly that Vitamin D has important roles in addition to its classic effects on calcium and bone homeostasis. As the Vitamin D receptor is expressed on immune cells (B cells, T cells and antigen presenting cells) and these immunologic cells are all are capable of synthesizing the active Vitamin D metabolite, Vitamin D has the capability of acting in an autocrine manner in a local immunologic milieu. Vitamin D can modulate the innate and adaptive immune responses. Deficiency in Vitamin D is associated with increased autoimmunity as well as an increased susceptibility to infection. As immune cells in autoimmune diseases are responsive to the ameliorative effects of Vitamin D, the beneficial effects of supplementing Vitamin D deficient individuals with autoimmune disease may extend beyond the effects on bone and calcium homeostasis.[13]

Vitamin D functions as a steroid hormone in the body. Other steroid hormones that you may be familiar with are testosterone and estrogen. Once Vitamin D is synthesized (or consumed), it still needs to find a receptor in order to become active in the body. Vitamin D has its own receptor, called Vitamin D receptor or VDR. A special class of hormones called glucocorticoids is known to decrease expression of Vitamin D receptor. The most well-known glucocorticoid is cortisol. And cortisol is one of the keys "stress hormones". It is produced by the adrenal glands and helps the body adapt to stressful situations. Cortisol also helps the body adjust to the rhythms of the day: in a person with well-regulated cortisol, levels will peak in the morning, around 8 am. Cortisol will reach its lowest levels in the middle of the night, from midnight to 4 am. In sum, without a receptor, Vitamin D is left with nothing to do and nowhere to go; it remains inactive in the body.

The Effects of ZINC and Curcumin on the Immune System

The World Health Organization reports that between 17% and 30% of the world population has a zinc deficiency, potentially affecting health outcomes. Zinc is a trace mineral with crucial effects on the effectiveness of the cells and cytokines of our innate and adaptive immune systems. Zinc aids in fighting viruses, protects us from free radical damage to our cells, and has been shown to shorten the duration of a cold when given as a supplement.

Curcumin is the main active ingredient in turmeric root and has been shown to bestow multiple health benefits. In fact, there are more than 120 human clinical trials showing the effectiveness of curcumin in treating diseases ranging from autoimmunity to Alzheimer's disease. The magic of curcumin is how it decreases inflammation at multiple levels in the body, not only helping with symptom relief from pain and arthritis but also blocking inflammatory cytokines driving autoimmune disease, heart disease and diabetes.

---

13 Source: Aranow C. (2011) Vitamin D and the Immune System. *J Investig Med.* 2011 Aug, 59(6), 881–886.

Strategies to Manage Stress Connected with Cognitive, Behavioral and Emotional Characteristics

Using and Practicing Cognitive Reconstruction

Cognitive restructuring is a useful tool for understanding and turning around negative thinking (see the proposed template in Table 8.2). It helps us put unhappy, negative thoughts "under the microscope", challenging them and in many cases receipting the negative thinking that lies behind them. In doing this, it can help us approach situations in a positive frame of mind.

This is obviously important because not only are negative moods unpleasant for us, but they also reduce the quality of our performance and undermine our working and social relationships with other people. In addition, research has now substantiated the hypothesis that negative thoughts can suppress the immune system.

The key idea behind this tool, as with the other tools in this section, is that our moods are driven by what we tell ourselves, and this is usually based on our interpretations of our environment. Cognitive restructuring helps us evaluate how rational and valid these interpretations are. Where we find that these assumptions and interpretations are incorrect, this changes the way we think about situations and in the process changes our moods.

We must distinguish between positive and negative thoughts. Positive thoughts are those that help us to reach our objectives. Negative thoughts are those that prevent us from reaching our objectives and which, at the same time, make us feel bad.

Both positive as well as negatives thoughts can be either rational or irrational. Irrational thoughts are those that are not based on sufficient real or objective data or may even contradict reality.

Techniques of positive thought – *Why do some people tend to see the glass half full while others see it half empty?* As we already commented in the previous section, thoughts can be of two types: positive and negative. The first type includes those that push us on and give us the energy to achieve personal objectives. However, the second type drains our energy levels and, in addition, makes us feel bad on an emotional level.

What we feel depends on what we think and vice versa. For this reason, thinking positive can help us to overcome situations that may be stressful and difficult for us. The following are some of the distorted negative thoughts that we can develop in a stressful situation:

- *Polarised thought*: thinking that things can only be black or white, without considering that there is a whole span of greys in between. This consists of always considering the two most extreme options, making it very difficult to come to a halfway agreement with other people.
- *Filtered thought*: this is a type of negative thought in which we tend to interpret the things that happen based on a series of "filters" or fixed and preconceived ideas, quite often biased, and which make us deform reality.
- *Catastrophist thought*: this consists of thinking that misfortune and negative events always have to happen to us.

TABLE 8.2 A template for use in the Cognitive Restructuring Process

Situation	mood	Automatic Thought and Images	Evidence that Supports Hot Thought	Evidence that does not support hot thoughts	Alternative Balanced thought	Mood now, Actions & Positive Thoughts

The template in Table 8.1 could be used as a work sheet in recording events and training in cognitive restructuring.

In order to do that, the following steps need to be undertaken:

1. **Write down the situation that triggered the negative thoughts:** (Make a brief note of the situation in the first column of the worksheet.)

2. **Identify the moods that you felt in the situation:** (In the second column, enter the moods that you feel in the situation. Moods here are the deep feelings that we have about the situation. They are not thoughts about it. "Mind over Mood" offers an easy trick to help tell moods from thoughts: It is usually possible to express moods in one word, while thoughts are more complex. Keep in mind, you may well feel several different moods at the same time. These reflect different aspects of the situation. For example, "he is trashing my suggestion in front of my coworkers", would be a thought, while the associated moods might be "humiliated", "frustrated", "angry" and "insecure".

3. **Write down the Automatic Thoughts that you experienced when you felt the mood:**

   In the third column, write down the thoughts that came into your mind when you felt the mood. Identify the most distressing of these. In the example above, thoughts might be:

   - Maybe my analysis skills aren't good enough…
   - Have I failed to consider these things?
   - He hasn't liked me since…
   - How rude and arrogant of him!
   - Everyone will think badly of me
   - But my argument is good and sound…
   - This is undermining my future with this company

   In this case, the person in this example might consider that the most distressing thoughts (the "Hot Thoughts") are "maybe my analysis skills aren't good enough", and "everyone will think badly of me".

4. **Identify the evidence that supports these Hot Thoughts:** In the fourth column of the worksheet, write down the objective evidence that you can find that supports the Hot Thoughts. Developing this example, the evidence written down might have been:

   - The meeting moved on and decisions were taken with no account being taken of my suggestion.
   - He did identify a flaw in one of the arguments in my paper on the subject.

TABLE 8.2 Cont.

5. **Identify the evidence that does not support the Hot Thoughts:**

   In the next column, write down the objective evidence that contradicts the Hot Thoughts. Evidence contradicting the Hot Thought in the example might be:

   - The flaw was minor and did not alter the conclusions.
   - The analysis was objectively sound, and the suggestion was realistic and well founded.
   - When I trained in the analysis method, I usually came close to the top of my class.
   - My clients respect my analysis and my opinion.

6. **Now, identify fair, balanced thoughts about the situation:**

   By this stage, you will have looked at both sides of the situation as far as you can. This should have clarified the situation. You may now have all the information you need to take a fair, balanced view of the situation. Alternatively, you may find that there are still substantial points of uncertainty. If this is the case, then you may need to clarify this uncertainty, perhaps by discussing the situation with other people who have a view or by testing the question in some other way. Obviously, the amount of effort you put in does depend on the importance of the situation. Do what is needed to come to a balanced view and write the balanced thoughts down in the sixth column of the worksheet. The balanced thoughts in this example might now be:

   - I am good at this sort of analysis. Other people respect my abilities.
   - My analysis was reasonable, but not perfect.
   - There was an error, however it did not affect the validity of the conclusions.
   - The way he handled the situation was not correct.
   - People were surprised and a little shocked by the way he handled my suggestion (this comment would have followed a conversation with other people at the meeting).

7. **Finally, observe your mood now and think about what you are going to do:**

   You should now have a clearer view of the situation. Look at your mood now. You will probably find that it has changed and (hopefully!) improved. Write this in the final column.

8. The next step is to think about what you could do about the situation. You may conclude that no action is appropriate. By looking at the situation in a balanced way, it may cease to be important. Alternatively, you may choose to do something about the situation. If you do, you may find that some of the techniques explained elsewhere on this site are useful. The Assertiveness tool is most likely to be particularly useful in dealing with problems with other people! Make a note of these actions in the final column, but also put them on your To Do List so that you act on them. Finally, think through positive affirmations that you can use to counter any future negative thoughts of this type, and see if you can spot any opportunities coming out of the situation.

Mood: Compared with the moods felt at the start of the example, the mood experienced by the person completing the worksheet will have changed. Instead of feeling humiliation, frustration, anger and insecurity, this person is most

likely to feel only anger.

Actions: A first action will be to use relaxation techniques to calm the anger. Having done this, this person

may take away two actions: First, to check his or her work more thoroughly and second, to arrange a meeting to discuss the situation in an assertive manner.

Positive Thoughts: This person could also create, and use, the following positive thought in a similar situation: *"My opinions are sound and are respected by fair-minded colleagues and clients. I will rise above rudeness"*.

Thinking positive can help us confront stressful situations with a greater guarantee of being able to control the situation:

- *Minimization:* this allows us to relativize the importance of the consequences resulting from the problem or situation that is generating stress: "I've decided I don't need it as much as I thought".
- *Spacing or emotional cooling down*: protecting ourselves against the impact of the problem.
- *Selective attention*: this consists in focusing attention on the positive aspects of the problem.
- *Positive comparisons*: this is a mechanism to induce satisfaction based on contrasting differences.
- *Drawing positive values from negative events*: putting this into practice makes it easier for negative situations to be perceived more positively

Seeking Social Support

Many people when stressed tend to set aside those things that normally satisfy them, including their closest circle of family and friends. There is an escalating and "unreal" feeling that they don't need anybody, that they will be able to solve their problems on their own. Nevertheless, we see how this is not how it works: quite the opposite in fact. The more stressed we are, the more we will need to get support from others, although in many cases it may be that we do not ask for it and may even refuse the help offered by others.

People are social creatures by nature. This implies that we need to feel a part of a social structure that we are satisfied with, at work as well as in our personal and home life. Social support refers to the perception that we have concerning quality interpersonal relations for dealing with difficult situations. It acts as a shock absorber for stress.

Research in various disciplines from medicine to psychology and management show that social support has an impact on reducing stress. Studies show that social support decreases the stress response hormones in our bodies. People who have close relationships and a strong sense of connection and community enjoy better health and live longer than those who live in isolation or alienation.[14] People, who suffer alone, suffer more.

Benefits of social support include:

- **Emotional support and encouragement**: a shoulder to lean on and an ear to listen. Talking about feelings (ventilation) reduces stress and helps us to work through problems and feel better about ourselves.
- **Logistical support**: at times of overload, illness or injury, people can take care of our children, help with tasks or errands or drive us to medical appointments.
- **Mentoring and coaching**: after a job loss or relationship break-up, it helps to talk to people who have been through a similar experience and can share the lessons they've learned. They can also show us how to use a computer, build a deck, write a resume or prepare for an interview.

14 Source: Ornish, D., (1998) *Love and Survival*, Harper Perennial.

- **Networking**: people in our support system can tell us about a job opportunity, a good car mechanic or a new book club.

How to develop and use a support system? Here is a wishlist of actions that can be undertaken:

- Find people whom you trust and who care about you. You don't need a gallery of folks – a few close friends or relatives will suffice.
- The best time to develop a support system is before you need it. Don't wait till you're halfway up the twist and then run out to some passer-by on the street and say: "I have to tell you about my day!"
- The best way to develop a support system is to give support to others. This establishes a relationship and builds trust and goodwill. When you know someone is upset, ask if they'd like to talk about it. Then listen patiently and empathically. Call or visit someone who's sick or going through a rough time. Then, when you need a listening and caring ear, you'll have built a connection that can be reciprocated comfortably. As my father put it: "Just keeping giving and the taking will look after itself".
- Confide only what's comfortable for you. You don't have to divulge your entire life story. Venting feelings is more important than sharing details. A couple went through a very tough time when their child was hospitalized after a serious injury. "We called on our support system and told them what we needed. We knew we couldn't get through it alone".
- Turn to people with whom you feel comfortable (relatives, friends, neighbors, colleagues at work, family doctors, clergymen, or even specific professionals such as therapists–what a colleague of mine calls "renting a friend".).
- Don't judge yourself as weak or "less than" when you seek support. We all feel stressed, angry, frustrated or scared at times. It's a mistake to keep those feelings in. Having problems doesn't mean you're weak. It only means you're human. And there's a saying that "A problem shared is a problem halved".

Enhancing Assertiveness

"One half of words belongs to the one who utters them and the other half to the one who hears them"
   Montaigne

Human beings are social by nature. As a result, we use communication as a vehicle for interaction with others. Some of us speak more than others. But we don't always succeed in establishing effective interpersonal contact. This is something that is very complex, and it is not only a matter of making and listening to comments. Many factors influence the messages that are sent. For this reason, what we say is often not as "logical" and "quite so clear" as we might think. In addition, our communication is conditioned by our prejudices, attitudes, ideals, interests, feelings, defenses, anxieties and fears. On the other hand, we select what we hear according to our motivations. When it comes down to it, we hear what we want to hear. In addition, the same words can have a different connotation for different people, depending on previous experiences and cultural differences.

We can distinguish three different styles of communication: *aggressive*, *passive* and *assertive*.

- **The aggressive style** is characterized by a lack of respect towards the speaker where people try to impose their point of view and/or opinion, without listening to others. Behavioural signs of this type of communication are shouting and insulting the other person, a lack of argument or point and excessive gesticulating and/or movement of the upper extremities. It is normally accompanied by rage, emotional outbursts and scorn directed at others; it usually appears as a result of rage or anger and the inability to use self-control.

- The **passive style** is the opposite extreme of the aggressive. This is used to describe the passive person who does not know how to express his feelings and does not know how to defend his or her rights. This leads, in general, to the individual not feeling satisfied, since he/she is unable to say what he thinks or feels and does not get his point across to others. It usually produces insecurity, a feeling of being poorly accepted and of not being considered by others. All of this leads to a deterioration of personal self-esteem.

- **The assertiveness style** is between the aggressive and the passive style. Assertiveness is defined as a personal ability that allows us to express feelings, opinions and thoughts, at the appropriate time, in a suitable manner and without denying or failing to consider others people's rights. In order to give an assertive answer, the first step is to actively listen to others and give them signs that we understand what they are thinking or feeling (Step 1). Next, we express what we think or give an opinion (Step 2). And, finally, we communicate to the person what we want to happen (Step 3). Traditionally, assertiveness has had little recognition in our society in terms of its importance in human communication. Thus, for example, success has been associated more with verbal and nonverbal behaviours more commonly associated to an aggressive style. Nevertheless, this stereotype is changing.

Although in the middle of the last century, the image of a leader was associated with an image of a person who was sure of himself/herself, with clear ideas, who knew how to impose his criteria and opinions on others, without caring if he was being more or less threatening and/or contemptuous of his collaborators. Luckily this situation is changing.

At the moment and, more so in the years ahead, the person who wants to be successful in business will have to be skilled not only in finances, marketing and strategic planning, but also in communication and interpersonal skills. In this sense, they will need to develop their emotional intelligence more than their technical intelligence.

Why should we use assertiveness when we feel stressed at work? We have seen that many of the factors leading to stressful situations have a lot to do with the interpersonal relationships established in the workplace (relationships with people on the same hierarchical level, relationships with people from outside the organization, relationships with superiors and with those under our command. Also, as we have commented previously, people can use different styles of communication (aggressive, passive and/or assertive), although due to tradition, we have grown especially accustomed to using the first two of these styles. In terms of our work, this can lead to us being exposed to situations that represent sources of stress. The use of assertiveness at work has numerous advantages for the person who puts it into practice:

- It allows them to express positive and negative feelings and desires effectively, without denying or disregarding the rights of others and without creating or feeling shame.
- It allows them to defend themselves, without aggression or passivity, from the uncooperative, inappropriate, or unreasonable behaviour of others.

TABLE 8.3 Typical behaviours and corresponding characteristics the imply aggressive, assertive, or passive expressions

Behaviours	Aggressive	Assertive	Passive
Posture	Leaning forward	Firm posture	Cowering
Head	Head held high	Head held firm	Head lowered
Eyes	Fixed stare, penetrating	Looking directly at people, normal eye contact	Poor eye contact, avoids looking directly at people
Face	No facial expression	Expression matching words	Smiling even when displeased
Voice	Raised voice	Voice modulated, in accordance with what is being said	Hesitant, low voice. Faltering words and sentences
Arms/hands	Arms controlled, gestures pronounced and marked, pointing fingers	Arms and hands relaxed, moving with ease	Arms held still
Movements/manner of walking	Slow and laboured movements	Movements in accordance with the situation	Brusque movements, rapid or slow
Speech patterns	Rigid	Structured	Disordered
Listening	Unidirectional, does not listen	Active, asks for confirmation, clarifications, asks questions when something has not been understood	Passive, does not ask questions
Attention	Gets the attention of others when speaking. Uses repetitive resources	Gets the attention of others when speaking. Uses creative resources	Does not get the attention of others when speaking
Problem solving	Does not give in, tends to get own way	Looks for consensus	Accepts others' ideas
Empathy	Does not put him in the place of others	Is capable of putting him in the place of others	Shows understanding
How disagreement is expressed	Says no emphatically	Knows how to say no without upsetting others	Has difficulty expressing disagreement

This way, it will help to reduce stress levels since it increases the perception of control over the situation, self-confidence and with it the feeling of personal self-esteem. The advantage of learning and practicing assertive behaviours is that these get through to other people, the messages themselves expressing opinions, showing that they have been taken into consideration. They obtain feelings of security and social recognition. Without a doubt, assertive behaviour helps to maintain high self-esteem. A comparison of typical behaviors and expressions is provided in Table 8.3.

 SELF ASSESSMENT OF ASERTIVENESS

The purpose of this quiz is to help you understand better if you are more "ASSERTIVE" or "NON-ASSERTIVE" in your communication style.

Rate on a scale from 1-5 the following 12 statements. Be honest (this assessment is for you to know)

1	2	3	4	5
not really	more or less	a bit	a lot	a great deal

1. Are you openly critical of others' ideas, opinions, and behaviour? ____
2. Do you speak out in protest when someone takes your place in line? ____
3. Do you often avoid people or situations for fear of embarrassment? ____
4. Do you usually have confidence in your own judgement? ____
5. Do you insist that your spouse or roommate take on a fair share of household chores? ____
6. Do you find it hard to say "NO" to salespeople? ____
7. Are you reluctant to speak up in a discussion or debate? ____
8. Are you disturbed when someone watches you? ____
9. Do you find it difficult to maintain eye contact when talking with another person? ____
10. Do you return faulty merchandise? ____
11. Are you able to openly express love and affection? ____
12. Are you able to accept unreasonable requests from friends? ____

TOTAL SCORE AND INTERPRETATION:

A. *Total up your scores for questions: **1,3,4,5,10,11** (the range is between 6-36). The higher the score, the **more assertive you are**. And vice versa, the lower the score the more nonassertive you are in your communication style.*

B. ***Total up your scores for questions: 3, 6,,7, 8, 9, 12*** *(the range should be between 6-36). The higher the score, **the more non-assertive** you are in your communication skills and vice versa: the lower the score the more assertive you are.*

> **Note**: Remember, this quiz is valid if you get high score on dimension A and low score on dimension B, or if you obtain lower score on Dimension A, you also obtained high score on dimension B.
>
> If both your scores are closer to each other, it means that you are in between assertiveness and non-assertiveness.

Delegating Effectively

We often wish that there were more than 24 hours in a day because, if there were, we would have enough time to do all the activities and tasks that we have to do. Is this good time management? The answer is more likely than not going to be no. Effective time management for individuals requires good delegation. To delegate means to yield the authority and the means for carrying out a task without renouncing responsibility over the final result. The difficulties that we face in delegating are due to several factors, both individual as well as organizational. The following is a detailed list of some of the most frequent factors:

- Excessive desire for perfection, lack of time, fear of being outshone by the person who is being delegated to do the task. Behind this attitude, the person is usually someone who is excessively controlling, who has a lack of self confidence and who is insecure, in other words, who has a lack of personal self-esteem.
- Difficulties in finding a person in whom to delegate through a lack of professional competencies.
- Lack of a delegation "culture" (there is no tradition of this in the company). The person who delegates is described as one "who tends to slope off from doing the work themselves", and "who does not get involved and take responsibility for their work".

The advantages of delegating include all the following:

- It frees up more time for managing and supervising tasks.
- It alleviates tension. A frequent error lies in *wanting to do things* instead of *supervising*.
- It improves know-how amongst personnel.
- It provides a climate that facilitates motivation.
- It provides standards for evaluating performance.
- It improves results.
- It increases team participation.

Employing Effective Time Management Techniques

Expressions such as *"I don't have time"* or *"I need time"*, form part of every-day language. In the work environment, these expressions are associated in many cases to a situation of professional and personal success in life in general. Nevertheless, behind this superficial image is a heartrending reality, and one, which in many cases masks a situation of stress and tension at the personal and family level.

There is a certain paradox in our present society. On the one hand, employees are expected to learn to manage the time they dedicate to their work in order to optimize the resources that are destined to it. This in turn is supposed to entail a qualitative improvement in working conditions (for example, better ways of combining professional and personal life, offloading certain tasks and more routine activities). In many cases, companies provide their employees with training on how to optimize their working time. Nevertheless, those who claim, "to have free time" and are proud of it are described as being "work-shy" or "irresponsible".

When a person suffers stress, their "internal clock" becomes altered. Being able to manage their professional and personal time well will help them to recover this internal rhythm. Knowing how to manage work time does not mean working more, it means working better. When a person feels stressed, they have more likelihood of being robbed of their time. Time thieves are situations, behavioural patterns, others' attitudes (external thieves) and our own personal attitudes (internal thieves) that make effective management of working time difficult. In Table 8.4 we summarize the more common time thieves.

Once the main time thieves have been identified, it is important to differentiate between what is urgent and what is important. Stressed people tend to confuse both. According to the economist, Pareto, 20% of our activities at work should provide approximately 80% of our output results. If this is not the case, we will have to analyses whether or not we are leaving aside important activities in order to do those that are urgent, but which do not contribute toward obtaining the results we have set ourselves.

In short, *does managing time effectively reduce stress?* This will depend on the sources causing the stress. If the cause resides in a lack of planning and/or an unexpected increase in the volume of work, then it can be an ally. Nevertheless, if the stress factors are related more to the nature of the work in itself, independently of the volume of activity that there might be, learning to manage personal time will be of little help in reducing stress levels.

TABLE 8.4 Principal internal and external time thieves

External Time Thieves	Internal Time Thieves
- Television	- Lack of prioritization
- Unexpected telephone calls	- Absence of a daily work plan
- Telephone calls from work during free time	- An "open doors" policy and a feeling of having to be permanently available
- Unexpected visits	- Excessive perfectionism
- Bureaucratic proceedings	- Inability to say no (lack of assertiveness)
- A disorganized mind	- Being disorganized

SELF-TEST OF YOUR TIME MANAGEMENT EFFICACY

The following list contains questions on how you organize your time. Please, circle "YES" or "NO" to indicate your response.

1. Do you tackle the most difficult tasks first thing in the morning? YES/NO
2. Do you write a list of "things I have to do today"? YES/NO
3. Do you sometimes say "NO" when asked to do something? YES/NO
4. Do you ever ask "WHY?" when you are invited to attend a meeting? YES/NO
5. Do you think that your bosses waste less time than you do? YES/NO
6. Do you give more priority to the urgent matters than to the important ones? YES/NO
7. Do you arrange tasks by priorities and carry them out following that order? YES/NO
8. Do you undertake a single task, finish it and then move on to the next one? YES/NO
9. Do you try to have a minimum of paperwork and notes at meetings? YES/NO
10. Do you accept all unexpected interruptions? YES/NO
11. Do you regularly take work home at night or at the weekends? YES/NO
12. Do you prefer doing things yourself rather than getting other members of your staff to do them? YES/NO
13. Do you meet deadlines on time? YES/NO
14. Do you talk to your boss about daily work events? YES/NO
15. Do you mention your work to colleagues? YES/NO
16. Do you ask other people how you should organize your time? YES/NO
17. Do you leave the factory to work somewhere else if you have something important to do? YES/NO
18. Do you hire your staff personally? YES/NO
19. Do you try to avoid problems before they arise, instead of having to solve them after they have cropped up? YES/NO
20. Do you set aside a little time every day during which you can work in peace, without interruptions? YES/NO
21. Do your employees cooperate enthusiastically in the tasks that are assigned to them? YES/NO
22. Do you delegate well? YES/NO
23. Do you do something every day that takes you nearer to your long-term goals? YES/NO
24. Can others take on most of your responsibilities if you are absent from work? YES/NO

Interpretation:
Check the total number of YES and NO to each of the 24 statements. Then conclude by yourself what is the meaning of it. It should be easy and straightforward.

Developing and Strengthening Change Management Skills

We live immersed in constant situations of change: at work and in our personal life. Nevertheless, this does not imply that we know how to adapt to these constant changes. Generally, any situation of change is associated with a certain amount of stress. Depending on our capabilities to manage this stress, we will be able to adapt better or worse to the new situation. To do so, we can act on our own and/or seek the help of others. In the next chapter, we will see some of the resources that can be used by organizations to help their employees successfully confront situations of organizational change.

What Happens to People during Change?

Changing and making changes is no easy task. If I want to introduce a change in the way my team works and in how we communicate, I have to be aware that any change will produce in people – those who are affected by this change – a series of reactions, including *stress* (see the typical manifestations in Figure 8.2).

The most common error is to think that people will change just because they have been told to do so. Change begins when people perceive that the change is necessary and that it is possible. It is important to understand that the people in whom change causes a feeling of loss are not weak or old-fashioned. It is healthier to recognize and to express loss when it takes place, so that the participants can cope with the transition process more quickly.

When the loss is not recognized, it is common for this to be translated into resistance and disorganization in the future. During change, people look back on the past and deny the change. Then, they go through a period of worrying, during which they ask themselves where they fit into the new scheme of things and how the change will affect them. This is normally when resistance arises, and stress occurs.

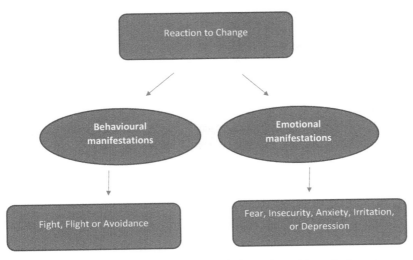

FIGURE 8.2 Typical manifestations connected with change (or resistance to change).

The following factors explain why individuals may pose resistance towards change:

- **Habits:** We individuals are influenced by our habits in our ways of working and accept or reject a change depending upon the effect which a change may have on the existing habits of the individuals. For example, change in the office location might be subjected to resistance from the individuals as this might compel them to change their existing life routine and create a lot of difficulties in adjustment or coping with the schedule. The individuals might have to drive a longer way for reaching their office, or start early from home for reaching their office in time, etc.
- **Lack of Acceptability or Tolerance for the Change:** Some individuals endorse change and welcome a change initiative happily while few individuals fear the impact of change. Over a period of time change fatigue also builds up.
- **Fear of a Negative Impact Economically or on the Income:** During the process of organizational restructuring or introduction of organization-wide change as a strategic move on the part of the management, several inhibitions, and fear rule the thought process of the individuals. Fear of possible loss of a job as a result of change or a change in their income structure or may be a change in their work hours could be one amongst the possible reasons.
- **Fear of the Unseen and Unknown Future:** Individuals develop inertia towards the change due to the fear of unknown or uncertainties in the future. This can be tackled through effective communication with the participants of change and making people aware of the positives of change and the course of action which individuals are expected to follow to cope with the changing requirements successfully.
- **Fear of Losing Something Really Valuable:** Any form of threat to personal security or financial security or threat to the health of the individuals may lead to fear of losing something precious as a result of the implementation of change.
- **Selective Processing of Information:** It can be considered as a filtering process in which the individuals perceive or make judgements by gathering selective information which is greatly influenced by their personal background, attitude, personal biases or prejudices, etc. If an individual maintains a negative attitude towards any kind of change, then they are having a usual tendency of looking at the negativities associated with the change and involve all the positive aspects of it.
- A rigid belief that changes cannot bring about any facilitating change in the organization and it only involves the pain and threats to the individuals.

So, getting out of the comfort zone takes some courage, and look for the positive factors of change. If you are definitely stressed, you should realize that no change and staying in the comfort zone will eventually make you sick or even kill you. If you cannot or do not have the skills to change, a consultant or a coach can come handy. We will further explain it in the next section.

Can We Reduce Stress on Our Own or Do We Need Help?

Self-diagnosis and Self-guidance

If you are experiencing the symptoms and signs of stress for a prolonged period (using the diagnostic tools offered in this book), and if you feel they are affecting your everyday life or are making you feel unwell, you should try and find a solution. Before seeking external help (psychologist, medical doctor, therapist, or a coach) you should, perhaps attempt your own action.

Here are three steps to take when feeling or diagnosing chronic (or acute) stress:

- Realize when it is causing you a problem. Try to make the connection between feeling tired or ill and the pressures you are faced with. Look out for physical warnings such as tense muscles, over-tiredness, headaches, or migraines.
- Identify the causes. Try to identify the underlying causes. Sort the possible reasons for your stress into three categories 1) those with a practical solution 2) those that will get better given time and 3) those you can't do anything about. Try to release the worry of those in the second and third groups and let them go.
- Review your lifestyle. Could you be taking on too much? Are there things you are doing which could be handed over to someone else? Can you do things in a more leisurely way?

To act on the answer to these questions, you may need to prioritize things you are trying to achieve and re-organize your life. Getting life priorities is another strategy that over the years we have provided a concept, a methodology and tool. It is based on a triaxial model of values. Read my other book with this publisher, in order to follow an effective stress combatting strategy that will be well aligned with your core values.[15] This will help to release pressure that can come from trying to do everything at once.

Contracting External Help: A Family Doctor, A Family Member, A Coach, or A Consultant

Remember, that it is okay to ask for professional help. If you feel that you are struggling to manage on your own, then you can reach out. It is important to know that you can get help as soon as possible, and that you deserve to get better.

The first person to approach is your family doctor. He or she should be able to give advice about treatment and may refer you to another local professional. If the doctor only treats your symptoms, don't accept it hence this is not a solution. This can be a solution for an acute situation, where pain or suffering can be alleviated. But for chronic stress, medicines are not the solution. You can also share your signs and symptoms with a close family member (i.e. level of trust is high and healthy) that perhaps jointly can help refine the assessment and look for a solution.

But remember, that today there are a variety of coaches, consultants, psychologists, and therapists that are equipped with all kinds of Cognitive Behavioral Therapies

---

15 Read: Dolan, S.L., (2021) *The Secrets of Coaching and Leading by Values: How to Ensure Alignment and Proper Realignment*, Routledge.

(this is a type of therapy that works by helping you to understand that your thoughts and actions can affect the way you feel) as well as experts in relaxation techniques (the popular mindfulness included), all geared to help reduce stress. There are also a number of voluntary organizations which can help you to tackle the causes of stress and advise you about ways to get better. Perhaps, one of these external resources can also help you boost your self-esteem, which we summarize in our next section

Boosting Our Self-esteem?

In former chapter we dealt with details with the concept of self-esteem. We have already proposed that low self-esteem can negatively affect virtually every facet of your life, including your relationships, your job and your health. But you can boost your self-esteem by taking cues from types of mental health counseling. In order to be very practical, in this section I will enumerate steps and ideas that can be used to boost self-esteem. Already mentioned that we are not born with this trait, and if we practice and practice we can improve the situation. Obviously, as mentioned in the previous section, a good professional can help accelerate the process.
Consider these steps, based on cognitive behavioral therapy.[16]

Identify Troubling Conditions or Situations
Think about the conditions or situations that seem to deflate your self-esteem. Common triggers might include:

- A work or school presentation
- A crisis at work or home
- A challenge with a spouse, loved one, co-worker or other close contact
- A change in roles or life circumstances, such as a job loss or a child leaving home

Become Aware of Thoughts and Beliefs
Once you've identified troubling situations, pay attention to your thoughts about them. This includes what you tell yourself (self-talk) and your interpretation of what the situation means. Your thoughts and beliefs might be positive, negative, or neutral. They might be rational, based on reason or facts, or irrational, based on false ideas. Ask yourself if these beliefs are true. Would you say them to a friend? If you wouldn't say them to someone else, don't say them to yourself.

Challenge Negative or Inaccurate Thinking
Your initial thoughts might not be the only way to view a situation – so test the accuracy of your thoughts. Ask yourself whether your view is consistent with facts and logic or whether other explanations for the situation might be plausible. Be aware that it can be hard to recognize inaccuracies in thinking. Long-held thoughts and beliefs can feel normal and factual, even though many are just opinions or perceptions.

---

16 Section is based on information provided by the Mayo Clinic Staff (Self-esteem: Take steps to feel better about yourself – Mayo Clinic) and also on the NHS on Raising low Self-Esteem (www.nhs.uk/mental-health/self-help/tips-and-support/raise-low-self-esteem/)

Also pay attention to thought patterns that erode self-esteem:

- **All-or-nothing thinking.** You see things as either all good or all bad. For example, "If I don't succeed in this task, I'm a total failure".
- **Mental filtering.** You see only negatives and dwell on them, distorting your view of a person or situation. For example, "I made a mistake on that report and now everyone will realize I'm not up to this job".
- **Converting positives into negatives.** You reject your achievements and other positive experiences by insisting that they don't count. For example, "I only did well on that test because it was so easy".
- **Jumping to negative conclusions.** You reach a negative conclusion when little or no evidence supports it. For example, "My friend hasn't replied to my email, so I must have done something to make her angry".
- **Mistaking feelings for facts.** You confuse feelings or beliefs with facts. For example, "I feel like a failure, so I must be a failure".
- **Negative self-talk.** You undervalue yourself, put yourself down or use self-deprecating humor. For example, "I don't deserve anything better".

Adjust Your Thoughts and Beliefs

Now replace negative or inaccurate thoughts with accurate, constructive thoughts. Try these strategies:

- **Use hopeful statements.** Treat yourself with kindness and encouragement. Instead of thinking your presentation won't go well, try telling yourself things such as, "Even though it's tough, I can handle this situation".
- **Forgive yourself.** Everyone makes mistakes – and mistakes aren't permanent reflections on you as a person. They're isolated moments in time. Tell yourself, "I made a mistake, but that doesn't make me a bad person".
- **Avoid "should" and "must" statements.** If you find that your thoughts are full of these words, you might be putting unreasonable demands on yourself – or on others. Removing these words from your thoughts can lead to more realistic expectations.
- **Focus on the positive.** Think about the parts of your life that work well. Consider the skills you've used to cope with challenging situations.
- **Consider what you've learned.** If it was a negative experience, what might you do differently the next time to create a more positive outcome?
- **Relabel upsetting thoughts.** You don't need to react negatively to negative thoughts. Instead, think of negative thoughts as signals to try new, healthy patterns. Ask yourself, "What can I think and do to make this less stressful?"
- **Encourage yourself.** Give yourself credit for making positive changes. For example, "My presentation might not have been perfect, but my colleagues' asked questions and remained engaged – which means that I accomplished my goal".

You might also try these steps:

Identify Troubling Conditions or Situations

Again, think about the conditions or situations that seem to deflate your self-esteem. Once you've identified troubling situations, pay attention to your thoughts about them.

Step Back from Your Thoughts

Repeat your negative thoughts many times or write them down in an unusual way, such as with your nondominant hand. Imagine seeing your negative thoughts written on different objects. You might even sing a song about them in your mind. These exercises can help you take a step back from thoughts and beliefs that are often automatic and observe them. Instead of trying to change your thoughts, distance yourself from your thoughts. Realize that they are nothing more or less than words.

Accept your Thoughts

Instead of fighting, resisting or being overwhelmed by negative thoughts or feelings, accept them. You don't have to like them, just allow yourself to feel them. Negative thoughts don't need to be controlled, changed, or acted upon. Aim to lessen the power of your negative thoughts and their influence on your behaviour. These steps might seem awkward at first, but they'll get easier with practice. As you begin to recognize the thoughts and beliefs that are contributing to your low self-esteem, you can counter them or change the way you think about them. This will help you accept your value as a person. As your self-esteem increases, your confidence and sense of well-being are likely to soar.

In addition to these suggestions, try to remember on a daily basis that you're worth special care. To that end, be sure to:

- **Take care of yourself.** Follow good health guidelines. Try to exercise at least 30 minutes a day most days of the week. Eat lots of fruits and vegetables. Limit sweets, junk food and animal fats.
- **Do things you enjoy.** Start by making a list of things you like to do. Try to do something from that list every day.
- **Spend time with people who make you happy.** Don't waste time on people who don't treat you well.

Summary and a Postscript

Combatting stress is not an easy task. Because the origins of stress can be work related, non-work related, personal and personality issues and of course the circumstances. Thus, we could not offer a panacea for solving all stress problems. There is no "aspirin" to become "DE-STRESSED". Stress cannot be eliminated. Therefore, the emphasis in this chapter was on managing stress more than anything else. We have divided the chapter into two sections. The first part of the chapter dealt with organizational stressors and what management can do to alleviate some of these. The second part of the chapter was focused on individuals and what they can do or experiment in order to manage the stress in their lives. In each section an attempt was made to provide a menu of options and a short description of each strategy or technique was offered.

We labeled this chapter a kaleidoscope because we offered a range of tools, ideas, techniques, and strategies. Obviously, for management to offer or employ a strategy in involves additional costs, and it is advisable to develop and algorithm where costs and benefits will be calculated from the firm perspective. This is not an easy task hence 1) some parameters cannot be quantifying and 2) not all parameters and consequences are easily detectable (especially in the case of chronic situation. So, some sort of stress audit, or sometimes it is called social-psychological risk factors can be developed.[17]

As to the person, there are tools like the STRESS MAP that was presented in the former chapter. The most important for a person is to become aware of the stress in his/her life (at work or outside) and engage in actions to manage it, The STRESS MAP is a professional tool, but there are hundreds of other tools available on the net and allow some limited assessment. I personally like the 10 points assessment that has been offered by my colleague Prof. Manfred Kets de Vries from INSEAD to assess life stress:[18]

Consider your life today and answer the following questions:

1. Do you feel that your life is out of control and that you have too many things on your plate?
2. Do you often feel confused, anxious, irritable, fatigued or physically debilitated?
3. Are you having increased interpersonal conflicts (e.g. with your spouse, children, other family members, friends or colleagues)?
4. Do you feel that negative thoughts and feelings are affecting how you function at home or at work?
5. Is your work or home life no longer giving you any pleasure?
6. Do you feel overwhelmed by the demands of emails, messaging tools and **social media**?
7. Do you feel that your life has become a never-ending treadmill?
8. Are you prone to serious pangs of guilt every time you try to relax?
9. Have you recently experienced a life-altering event such as a change of marital status, new work responsibilities, job loss, retirement, financial difficulties, injury, illness or death in the family?
10. When you are stressed out, do you feel that you have nobody to talk to?

Prof. Kets de vries offers the following interpretation to this short individual stress audit: *If you have answered "yes" to most of these questions, stress might have started to build up. If you feel close to your breaking point, it's high time to act.*

---

17 I recommend reading this short paper for those who wish to be inspired: Newton, L., Hayday, S., and Silverman, M. (2005) *Stress Audits: What You Need to Know.* Institute for Employment studies (www.employment-studies.co.uk/system/files/resources/files/mp48.pdf)

18 Manfred, F.R., and de Vries, K. (2018) *The 10 Point Stress Audit.* Source: https://knowledge.insead.edu/blog/insead-blog/the-10-point-stress-audit-9836

Because this book is focusing on DE-STRESS, rather on doing a stress audit (which has always negative tone), I rather focus on resilience. I therefore recommend that you assess yourself on the resilience quiz that I have developed and is offered hereafter in the action section.

 ACTION I: DOLAN QUICK RESILIENCE QUIZ (DQRQ)*

Rate yourself from 1 to 5 (**1** = strongly disagree; **5** = strongly agree):

- I'm usually optimistic. I see difficulties as temporary and expect to overcome them.___
- Feelings of anger, loss and discouragement don't last long.___
- I can tolerate high levels of ambiguity and uncertainty about situations.___
- I adapt quickly to new developments. I'm curious. I ask questions.___
- I'm playful. I find the humor in rough situations and can laugh at myself.___
- I learn valuable lessons from my experiences and from the experiences of others.___
- I'm good at solving problems. I'm good at making things work well.___
- I'm strong and durable. I hold up well during tough times.___
- I've converted misfortune into good luck and found benefits in bad experiences.___

Total Score: _____

QUICK INTERPRETATION

Less than 20: Low Resilience – *You may have trouble handling pressure or setbacks and may feel deeply hurt by any criticism. When things don't go well, you may feel helpless and without hope. Consider seeking some professional help, a good coach or support in developing your resiliency skills. Connect with others who share your developmental goals.*

10-30: Some Resilience – *You have some valuable pro-resiliency skills, but also plenty of room for improvement. Strive to strengthen the characteristics you already have and to cultivate the characteristics you lack. You may also wish to seek some outside coaching or support.*

30-35: Adequate Resilience – *You are a self-motivated learner who recovers well from most challenges. Learning more about resilience, and consciously building your resiliency skills, will empower you to find more joy in life, even in the face of adversity.*

35-45: High Resilient – *You bounce back well from life's setbacks and can thrive even under pressure. You could be of service to others who are trying to cope better with adversity.*

* **Note**: *Adapted by the author of this book based on the early work of the late Al Siebert, founder of "The Resiliency Center" in Portland, Oregon. Remember that this test has been developed for training purposes only and has not (yet) been validated scientifically.*

ACTION II: DOLAN STRESS MANAGEMENT AND WELLNESS QUIZ (DSMWQ)[*]

This checklist can give you an idea if your organization is really proactive in managing stress in your organization. Simply tick the yes or no answer for each item.

Item	Description	Yes	No
1	Does your company have any clear wellness promotion program		
2	Does your company provide on a regular basis a stress management training program?		
3	Does your company collect actively data (conduct a survey) on emotional health of the employees on a regular basis		
4	Does your company engage professionals (psychologists for example) to help employees who have emotional problems?		
5	Does your company have a clear policy, communicated to all levels of management, on what to do when an employee seems to be stressed?		
6	Does your company bother about improving the physical and ergonomic conditions of the work environment?		
7	Does the company provide places and policies allowing employees to meditate or practice Yoga during work hours?		
8	Does your company provide or encourage employees to work in teams and meet regularly to discuss common stress related issues/problems?		
9	Does your company provide regular physical activity programs or support through gym membership, healthy eating, team sports etc.?		
10	Does your company promote a healthy work-life balance and encourage all levels of manages to act accordingly? (i.e. going home on time, work from home, flexible hours, regular break times, etc.)		

INTERPRETATION

- If you marked 8 or more "yes", you are lucky to be working in a company that really cares about your emotional wellbeing and actively promotes wellness
- If you marked 5-7 "yes" your company cares about your emotional health but still needs to offer more practices and policies to help you de stress and enhance your emotional wellbeing
- If you marked less than 4 "yes", your firm needs to invest more resources to offer you and the rest of the employees a reasonable stress management and wellness program
- If you did not mark any "yes", this might be indicative of an indifferent or even a toxic company; it does not look like they care about your stress and emotional wellbeing.

[*] This quiz was developed for training purposes only. It has not, yet, been validated empirically.

CHAPTER 9

Workplace Stress and the Future

Looking Beyond

Introduction

Nobody knows what the future holds. Yet we need to prepare for it, hence the ambiguity about our future will become a permanent source of chronic stress. Moreover, the world of work is intimately linked to the global world in which we live. So, challenges of terrorism, global conflicts, immigration, ecological challenges and the fast developments in artificial intelligence will all have an impact on ourselves and on other generations. Obviously, the experience of the two pandemic years shows the instant impact on the stress of people, corporations and political leaders altogether. Many were stressed to the point of committing suicide. The WHO reports that during the pandemic every 40 seconds someone committed suicide in one part of the world. On the other hand, people and organizations learned how to be resourceful, and in the name of survival engaged in a new set of behaviours, adopted a new type of attitudes, and learned to harness technology to its fullest. Virtuality became the "name of the game".

In this chapter I will attempt to maintain my academic rigour based on my traditional scholarly manners of presenting ideas, but I will allow myself to fly and describe future work scenarios. The idea in this chapter is to perhaps prepare you, the reader, to the future and once you are conscious of the situation, fear is reduced, ambiguity and uncertainty is reduced, and perhaps all in all stressed will be reduced. Here are the typical questions that the average employee asks himself/herself given the transformation that is occurring and the future changes:

Will I be able to get a job? Will technology replace me?
Will I be able to get a stable employment, or I should prepare for multiple job hopping?
Will my firm/employer survive (still be around)?
Will I be able to compete or to collaborate with machines equipped with AI (Artificial Intelligence)?

How long it will take before I become obsolete? Will I be able to reskill and retook every few years to not become obsolete?

Will jobs in the future be meaningful to me? Or should I need to compromise and accept meaningless jobs that guarantee flow of income?

To answer these questions (and more) we will address a potpourri of related themes. Some of these issues were addressed already by our team and published in *The European Business Review*. It is part of the branding of the Global Future of Work Foundation, and as I am writing these lines, you can download (free of charge) many of our papers free.[1]

For those who do not have the time to invest in further reading, I hope that this chapter will provide a nice summary or synopsis. I will always connect the dots and refer to DE-STRESS to render the relevance to the title of this book

Are You Prepared for the New Future of Work?

Getting Your Value Compass

The world of work is changing. We are in the middle of critical evolutionary and paradigmatic transformations which according to Raich and colleagues are driven by three powerful forces: globalization, digitalization-virtualization and creation-innovation.[2]

- **Globalization** is causing people to work midst paradoxical tensions that simultaneously are flattening and rounding, uniting, and detaching, the connections between and across organizational ecosystems, stakeholders and resources.
- **Digitalisation** is increasing the pace of work; people the world over have instant access to more information, relationships and inputs than they can easily handle with their time and brain capacities; the related virtualization is weaving a tapestry of handshakes as people work across cultures, boundaries and borders, demanding trust and near-simulated relationships and environments. We live in a "technologically-intoxicated zone" that is characterized by a continual search for quick fixes and lives that are distracted and distanced – while causing us to give up the "high touch" aspects of life that give our lives meaning: hope, fear, and longing, love and forgiveness, nature, and spirituality. Roll forward to today, and we see that the greatest demands for jobs are characterized by high tech, high touch, high growth – in industries such as information technology, health care and education – as well as in opportunities offered by the aging population market segment and demanding entrepreneurship, mathematics, and the sciences.
- And finally, **Creation** which represent the force for transformation and innovation. The definition of the word "innovation" has subtly changed over the last 30 years. In the 1960s and 1970s innovation was thought of as a process, as the introduction of change. Some, apparently, regarded innovation as simply the generation of a new idea. Today we imply that any new concept needs to be brought

---

1 Check the blog section of www.globalfutureofwork.com
2 Raich, M., Eisler R., and Dolan, S.L. (2014) *Cyberness: The Future Reinvented*. www.amazon.com.

into use before innovation could be said to have taken place. Moreover, in order for innovation to become sustainable and thus embed the concept of transformation, the concept needs to include some measure of success. The latter can be reflected in the words "effectively", "profitably", and "satisfied stakeholders". This hardening of the understanding of the word "innovation" to include the concept of successful commercialization is probably a result of the increases in business competitiveness, and the developing focus on sustainability, which have occurred in the last 30 years.

Technology that includes information and communication tools has been transforming workplaces the world over for years now and will continue to do so in the future. The development and refinement of new technologies like virtual reality and artificial intelligence have yet to make an impact on the workplace, but there is no doubt that such impact will be profound. The new generation of employees entering the labor force in the next decades will differ not only in the level and specialization of knowledge and skills they possess, but also in their work attitudes and preferences for work-life balance. Globalization, digitalization and virtualization will continue "shrinking" the world at a heightened pace, making work even more portable and detached from geography than we currently experience and understand.

These developments will surely result in changes in how work is done, how companies operate, and how organizations as well as its leaders and managers relate to their employees. As these shifts unfold, they present not only an opportunity for companies to increase their sources of both competitive and cooperative advantage but also the potential risk of strategic implosion – when the breadth, depth, and level of change, of informational and relational inputs simply overwhelms the human capacity to efficiently, effectively, and creatively function. New work principles, practices, and values will be needed, in order for firms to develop the human, managerial, and organizational capabilities to flourish, if not survive, into the twenty-second century.

The future of work will be shaped by transformation in cyber-technology and the social and physical contexts of work, as well as in attitudes towards work and lifestyle and the skills and education needed for work (See Figure 9.1).

Extrapolating from massive data that we have gathered over the years at the Future of Work Chair in ESADE, and later at the Global Future of Work Foundation (www.globalfutureofwork.com), I argue that managers, executives and employees in general need to assess their readiness to the new future of work in the following 10 key domains that will affect the new ways of working:[3]

- *The impact of technology and the cyber-age on the future of work and jobs*
- *The type of work that people will be performing*
- *Where will people work and what locations they consider desirable*
- *Work and Non-Work (leisure) combinations: the new mix (balance and integration) of activities in a typical day*
- *Portfolio employment*

---

3 Dolan, S.L., Makarevich, A., and Kawamura, K.M. (2015) *The European Business Review.* July Are You – And Your Company – Prepared For The Future Of Work In Tomorrowland? – The European Business Review

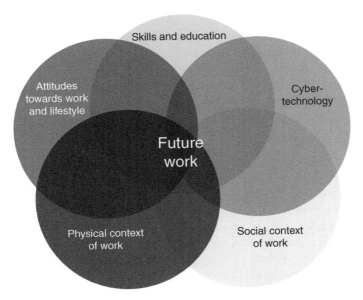

FIGURE 9.1 Facets and components of the future of work.

- *The social context in which work will take place*
- *The physical context in which work will take place*
- *The mix of skills and education that knowledge workers will need*
- *Perspectives on productivity and the factors that contribute to them*
- *Measures or attributes of work and life satisfaction*

The forces of globalization, digitalization, virtualization and creation are reshaping the world of work and will reshape it further in the future. Organizations that will not be able to guard against the risks and to capitalize on the advantages that these forces will be subjected to tremendous tensions as the risk of them being extinct is very likely. In the face of this transformative and paradoxical forces that are changing the future of work, employees will have to retool and reskill both their ha skills as well as the soft skills enabling better coping and preparedness. The same apply to corporations; web-based, cyber-based, and bricks-and-mortar-based, local and global – need first to assess their level of preparedness to operate, compete, and cooperate within the changing world of work.

In the ensuing sections we will highlight some of the principal challenges of the future of work with a focus on their impact on the well-being of people and organizations.

The Principal Stressors of the Future

Beyond contexts related to business, we are also facing global challenges threatening our sheer existence: demographics and global migration; environmental deterioration through global pollution; climate change; asymmetric conflicts and wars. Other contributing factors that are shaping, or will shape, the cyber-enterprise includes the emerging new "Intelligent Internet" (including the Internet of Things), combined with machine learning, mobile technology and new technologies encompassing people, artefacts, and cyber-entities (CE)1, which is on the way to becoming the first autonomous cyber-entity existing and acting in hybrid reality.

Beyond digital reality, a new, much-more potent and disruptive revolution is surfacing cyber-reality (CR). Cyber-reality is a powerful configuration of elements from digital reality, augmented reality, and virtual reality. Together with artificial intelligence (AI), it will lead to a far more radical transformation than anything we have seen before. In fact, digitalization is just one step, albeit a necessary one, in the transition towards virtual reality (VR). The progress of VR is tightly linked to the development of computer technology and artificial intelligence.

A new generation is joining the workforce and enter the markets is highly "cyber-savvy". Social and professional life will be shifting increasingly into virtual reality. People need to be willing and able to coexist, live and work side by side with smart machines and cyber-entities, **creating collaborative intelligence** (see section 9.4 hereafter).

The Competition to Become Smarter

To prepare for the big transformation ahead, we need to understand what is happening right now, what is on the horizon, and how and where all this will shape the cyber-organization and its corresponding effects on the workforce. Since transformation is already in effect, I wish to alert the readers that there are issues that need to be dealt with immediately (here and now), while other important issues can be left for the future.

Today, we may wonder how it is to live and work in a world characterized by permanent transitions, where highly smart cyber-entities are present as companions of humans. Make no mistake; this type of world is not far away; smart cyber-entities are already supporting people throughout the day, at home and at work, in politics, in the arts, in science and technology, in education, in entertainment, in "our reality" and in cyber-reality. Cyber-reality consists of digital, augmented and virtual reality.

Coexistence and collaboration will become an integral part of human civilization. Robots and smart machines will be taking care of a significant proportion of manual and administrative work.

A large part of the human population will live and work extensively in hybrid reality (reality and virtual). Imagine, in a not-too-distant future, situations where some people have physical and mental abilities way beyond the rest, simply because they have augmented their competences, thanks to advanced technologies and techniques. The mentally enhanced humans are considered to be the intellectual elite; they will create the talent pool of scientists, technicians, engineers, future researchers and future designers or even spiritual leaders. Imagine how social and professional life will shift into virtual reality. Obviously, it you belong to this group, you will have less stress, but if you depend on this group, you will have more stress due to dependability.

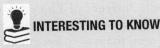
INTERESTING TO KNOW

*According to the annual plastic surgery procedural statistics, there were **17.5 million** surgical and minimally invasive cosmetic procedures performed in the United States in 2017, a 2 percent increase over 2016.*

The American Society of Plastic Surgeons (ASPS) on April 27, 2021, released the 2020 results of the organization's annual procedure survey. While the first wave of pandemic demand saw a rush on facial procedures in response to a significant surge in Zoom calls and downtime for discreet recovery at home, the national survey results show that Tummy Tucks (22%) and Liposuction (17%) are among the top procedures that women who are extremely or very likely to consider procedures within 6 months are seeking.

And how do you join the group? Will you be forced to take some chemicals to boost your brain? What will be your choice? If we judge by another phenomenon, the beauty industry, and especially for women, the question become: do you have to undertake a plastic surgery in order to improve the look? It's no longer a choice, ladies born with ugly look, have less chances to compete in the market for handsome men. Many develop complex of inferiority and use it as an excuse to undergo plastic surgery (see box). If this is an indicator, the dilemma of taking the pill or not will be much stronger than the dilemma during COVID-19 weather or not to be vaccinated.

Today, with the fear of becoming obsolete, there are some worrisome data that suggest that in some advanced professions (connected with the new technology) already the consumption of pills has skyrocketed.

Here are some pills to boost intelligence (cognitive, social and other competences):

- **Piracetam**. The so-called "original smart pill", Piracetam has been shown in studies to significantly improve cognitive and working memory at all levels.
- **Aniracetam**. A synthetic derivative of Piracetam, aniracetam is believed to be the second most widely used nootropic in the Racetam family, popular for its stimulatory effects.
- **Oxiracetam**. Popular among computer programmers, oxiracetam, another racetam, has been shown to be effective in recovery from neurological trauma and improvement to long-term memory.
- **Modafinil**. Modafinil, sold under the name Provigil, is a stimulant that some have dubbed the "genius pill". Originally developed as a treatment for narcolepsy and other sleep disorders,
- **Ginsenoside Rg1**. Is a molecule found in the plant genus panax (ginseng), is being increasingly researched as an effect nootropic.

If the current workplace is very competitive place the future seems to be even more competitive. Today stress, is produce because it makes people always on their tips and look for economic advantages and react fast, for otherwise, you'll get passed by those who do. Whether you're studying for a final exam or trying to secure a big business deal, you need a definitive mental edge. The question become: Are smart drugs and brain-boosting pills the answer for cognitive enhancement? If you're not cheating, you're not trying, right? Bad advice for some scenarios, but there is a grain of truth to every saying – even this one.

When 2011 Hollywood blockbuster movie **Limitless** hit theatres, the smart drugs industry erupted. Smart pills and nootropics aren't new. But, Limitless fueled the industry's growth by taking biohacking mainstream. If you haven't seen the movie, imagine unfathomable brain power in capsule form. Picture a drug from another universe. It can transform an unsuccessful lazy person into a millionaire financial mogul. Ingesting the powerful smart pill boosts intelligence and turns you into a prodigy. Its results are instant. Sounds great, right? If only it were real.

The truth is, taking a smart pill today will not allow you to access information that you have not already learned. If you speak English, a smart drug cannot embed the Spanish dictionary into your brain. In other words, they won't make you smarter or more intelligent. We need to throttle back our expectations and explore reality. Nonetheless, the possibility exists for either smart drugs or an implant of nano chip that will give you the edge to competition. If all this will happen, stress will rocket, and we will face a new scale of pandemic.

The Mix of Reality and Imaginary World

Digital reality has already made big inroads into all domains of our life. Augmented reality is expanding fast in gaming, education, and business. The market for augmented reality is expected to be worth $61.39 billion by 2023, growing at a 55.71% compound annual growth rate3. Virtual reality is establishing its presence in many industries in a number of ways, such as experiences and business processes.

The **"cyber-organization"** or **"cyber-enterprise"**. are growing rapidly. Once fully developed, these will be very different kinds of organizations. I am not proposing that all organizations will become cyber-organizations, as we will most likely see a mix of traditional forms side by side. Some organizations will be relatively stable, such as those in charge of infrastructure, but there will also be those who will constantly be adjusting in a highly automated environment, and these will struggle to satisfy the growing and changing needs, requirements and wishes of its multiple stakeholders. They will have a structure that is highly nimble and agile, creating and driving new markets in the hybrid reality as a substitute for, or an addition to, the more traditional markets.

Many working activities will be executed collectively by highly sophisticated, AI-based entities (machines and robots) in a joint effort with humans. Technology will accomplish routine, standardized tasks that are often seen as repetitive. Humans will spend their working years performing a mix of productive, creative and educational activities. An increasing part of work and education will be shifting into cyber-reality, in particular virtual reality.

The Future of Higher Education – Challenges in Combatting Obsolescence

If we look 25 years into the future from now, we can see a different world. The cyber-entities will be supporting people everywhere and in all aspects of daily life and work, in politics and arts, in science and technology, in education and in entertainment. A large part of the human population will live and works extensively in the hybrid reality and the metaverse. Are most people prepared for this type of world? Do they have the skills to de learn and relearn? One thing is certain. The current educational system where people are being trained to enter the labour market, will not be sufficient to ensure employment for the rest of their lives. The answer lies in the concept of lifetime education.

In the future, virtual-reality will become seamless to our-reality, and the boundaries between the different realities will be increasingly blurry; the world has dramatically changed, and many of us need to have the capacities to navigate in this new world. We have already mentioned the possibilities that our physical, and mental abilities would have to be augmented thanks to advanced technologies and techniques. No doubt that people must become "cyber savvy" in order to interact with the highly sophisticated and smart technology. Additionally, the social and professional life will shift increasingly into the virtual reality.

Peter Diamandis, best known for being founder and chairman of the X Prize Foundation, cofounder and executive chairman of Singularity University, presents a fascinating future model for future education based on five guiding principles: Passion; Curiosity; Imagination; Critical thinking and Perseverance in pursuit of long-term goals.[4] He also presents a fascinating layout of modules and deployment of exponential technologies in classrooms. Although his model is addressing elementary school level, it is also applicable for later stages of education.

Top universities' administrators and presidents suggest that the contemporary university will fundamentally be transformed by distance education and technology, mass enrolments, increasing vocational-focused programs and privatization. The early twenty-first century is a period of both crisis and transformation for higher education globally. And it is entirely possible that some sectors of higher education will change fundamentally or risk at vanishing altogether.[5]

Thus, we need to redefine education in relationships to this new reality. I argue that higher education will and should not be left to academic institutions alone, but should encompass other players such as corporations (i.e. corporate education and executive education), as well as new institutions. Some corporations and enterprises will become new important players in the new higher education. Lifetime learning, and unlearning, development and transformation are here to stay. The time of more of the same seems to be over.

In the future, we will need a two-tier higher education, with a dynamic balance of academic and corporate involvement. It will be a kind of "dual higher education" with two stages: formal higher education and post-formal education. Both levels will be using collateral education, peer consulting and tutoring; creation of personal education networks (PEN).

---

4 A Model for the Future of Education, and the Tech Shaping It, Peter H. Diamandis, MD, Sep 12, 2018, https://singularityhub.com/2018/09/12/a-model − for − the − future − of − education − and − the − tech − shaping − it/?utm _ source = Singularity + Hub + Newsletter&utm _ campaign = 5a71915c29 − Hub _ Daily _ Newsletter&utm _ medium = email&utm_term=0_f0cf60cdae-5a71915c29-58476953

5 Altbach, P.G. *The Past, Present, and Future of the Research University*. http://siteresources. worldbank . org / EDUCATION / Resources / 278200 − 1099079877269 / 547664 − 1099079956815 / 547670 − 1317659123740 / Chapter1.pdf

Formal higher education will be driven by the "academia", led by professors and academic tutors, focusing on deliberate skills training, knowledge, know-how and expertise of the focus domain and its eco-system. In addition, amply interim assignments in corporations and organizations will be available. Every "student" will have to make a talent assessment and perform a Talent Development Project. The transformation of Higher Education will also encompass the faculty. Professors will also be increasingly learning from their students. Today the best example of practice oriented higher education is the "Fachhochschule" (University of Applied Sciences and Arts), a type of higher education that emerged from the traditional Engineering schools, highly popular in Germany, Switzerland and Austria, focused on practical knowledge or industry-oriented studies.[6]

Corporations and other nonacademic organizations, led by executives and professional coaches, will drive post-formal Higher Education. The main aim is to deepen the domain expertise by exposure to corresponding practice; deliberate training of core skills in particular, with respect to the core competencies; development of core competencies and deployment within the focus domain. This will lead to talent and personality development with supervision by academic tutors, based on specific Talent Development Projects. This allows also improving the skills of collaboration. In such manner, the Higher Education Institutions will be ready to better prepare students for a transformed and increasingly challenging workplace. Development of everyone goes on her/his specific individual pace and progress. The milestones of progress are achievements.

In order to prepare and maintain talent in this fast-changing context, it will need new competencies. Competencies not only to deal with the new technology but also to deal with a VUCA type environment (Volatile, Uncertain, Complex, and Ambiguous). Here are some key competences to not feel stressed and obsolete:

- Competences for being connected in this digital and virtual world
- Competences to deal constantly with a changing work environment.
- Competences to collaborate with smart machines
- Competences to being resilient

INTERESTING TO KNOW

ON TRANSFORMATION AND OBSOLESCENCE

A new survey of 32,500 workers in 19 countries paints a picture of a global workforce that sees the shift to remote working as just the tip of the iceberg. Reflecting the fact, the COVID-19 pandemic has accelerated a number of workforce trend. 60% are worried that automation is putting many jobs at risk; 48% believe "traditional employment won't be around in the future" and 39% think it is likely that their job will be obsolete within 5 years.

Source: Khan (2021) Ten work skills which are obsolete in 2022 . https://libraryofcareer.com/advice/ten-work-skills-which-are-obsolete-in-2022/

---

6 https://en.wikipedia.org / wiki / Fachhochschule # Switzerland becoming obsolete in the future

TABLE 9.1 What you need to know in order to DE-STRESS

Obsolete skills/ competences	Skills /Competences that will become obsolete in the next 5–10 years	Jobs that are becoming obsolete	Top soft Skills / Competences that employers seek in 2022
Read and write in cursive	Taxi drivers	Travel agent	Time management
Dial a rotary phone	Bank tellers	Cashier	Decision making
Sewing	Telemarketer	Fast food cook	Collaboration
Navigate with a map or a compass	Watch repairman	Mail carrier	Emotional Intelligence
Drive a standard shift car	Bus drivers	Bank teller	Creativity and Resilience
Replace a flat tire	Printing press	Textile worker	Adaptability/ Change management

In sum, our world is in midst of digitalization and is fast shifting towards a world dominated by virtualization and artificial intelligence. People will work and live in collaboration with smart machines. This will lead to awkward distortions and disruptive contextual changes. We are at the dawn of a deep transformation with sizable scope that the world has never seen before; it is a world with fully developed virtual realities equipped with artificial intelligence. It is a journey into the big unknown and the bad news is that there is no way of going back. To cope with this deep transformation without being excessively stressed, we will need a life-long education that encompasses various forms and multiple levels of learning and applications. The new landscape will embed four pillars that encompass education: learning, research, development and deployment.

Advances in AI, cognitive computing and automation mean employers should equip workers with more than technical skills. Skills such as creativity, leadership, and critical thinking might be more important than ever. Disruption lies ahead. Driven by accelerating connectivity, new talent models and cognitive tools, work is changing. As robotics, AI, the gig economy, and crowds grow, jobs are being reinvented, creating the "augmented workforce." We must reconsider how jobs are designed and work to adapt and learn for future growth.

Table 9.1 suggests that in the next few years some jobs will disappear, some skills and competences will become obsolete, and the new demands on behalf of employer is a mix of hard and soft skills. In addition to skills in operating new technology, management such as technology design and programming will require skills such as creativity, authenticity and initiative, critical thinking, flexibility, complex problem solving, persuasion and negotiation and emotional intelligence. These mixes of skills are hard to find, and even harder to teach. While 38% of organizations say it is difficult to train in-demand technical skills, 43% said it is even harder to teach the soft skills they need.[7]

7 Manpower Group: Will My Skills be Obsolete in the Future? Out with the old skills, in with the new. www.manpowergroup.com/workforce-insights/world-of-work/will-my-skills-be-obsolete-in-the-future

Will Collaborative Intelligence Create More Stress or De-stress?[8]

The collaboration of humans with smart machines and programs is and will create new solutions way beyond our imagination, leading to meaningful life quality enhancing products, services, and experiences! Plainly speaking, digital platforms enable us to leverage collective human intelligence. The first attempt of collaboration and co-creation of humans and intelligent machines is popping up in the Internet of Things daily. Soon we will see the emergence of "Meta-Intelligence": it will represent a merger of human intelligence with AI, leveraging collective intelligence with the computational power of intelligent machines, the Internet of Things, the cloud and virtual reality. This will be the era of the Meta-Mind, which will lead us towards the "Fusion-Mind", when advancements in technology will allow us to merge an enhanced human mind with "Advanced General Artificial Intelligence" (hereafter AGAI) based entities. It is argued that this will be a process of "symbiosis" rather than replacement.

Research by McKinsey has gone as far as to describe AI as contributing to a transformation of society "happening ten times faster and at 300 times the scale" of the Industrial Revolution.[9]

The technological singularity, a term used by Kurzweil, is the moment when machines reach a level of intelligence that exceeds that of humans. He has set the year of 2045 for the "Singularity", which is when we will multiply our effective intelligence a billion-fold by merging with the intelligence we have created.[10] Let's, explore a couple of possibilities and examine how it may affect us physically and emotionally.

Will Robots Be Your Friends or Your Foes?

In light of the ongoing and rapid development of innovative technologies, two intriguing issues arise: do people have more positive or more negative attitudes toward robots with high (versus low) mental capabilities and do attitudes toward robots can make a difference if people look at them as an opportunity or a threat.

Although we are quite a long way off developing the computing power or the algorithms for fully autonomous AI, it may happen within the next 30 or 40 years. The hope is that human will remain in control of technology, and it will help us solve many of the world's problems. However, no one really knows what will happen if machines become more intelligent than humans. They may help us, ignore us or destroy us. If you have a positive outlook of life you may believe AI will have a positive influence on our future lives,

---

8 Section based on: Raich, M., Dolan, S.L., Cisullo, C., and Richley, B. (2019) Beyond Collaborative Intelligence We Can See a Meta-Mind Society Surfacing and We Can Dream of a Ω-Mind?, *The European Business Review*, September www.europeanbusinessreview.com/beyond-collaborative-intelligence-we-can-see-a-meta-mind-society-surfacing-and-we-can-dream-of-a-%cf%89-mind/

9 Dobbs, R., James, M., Jonathan, W. (2015) The Four Global Forces Breaking all the Trends. McKinsey Global Institute. Quoted in *Artificial Intelligence. The Road Ahead in Low and Middle-Income Countries.* June 2017,

10 https://futurism.com/kurzweil-claims-that-the-singularity-will-happen-by-2045/

And vice versa, a negative attitude towards the development of robots in the future, can bring pessimism and stress. The potential consequences of creating something that can match or surpass human intelligence might be frightening. As these lines are being written, the President of Russia is threatening to use his nuclear arsenal to achieve his non rational goals. Imagine that robots will manage this decision independently. In the short term, there is the danger that robots will take over millions of human jobs, creating a large underclass of unemployed people. This could mean large-scale poverty and social unrest. In the long term, machines might decide the "world would be better without humans".

Martin Ford's influential 2016 book, "Rise of the Robots", painted a bleak picture of a jobless future where automation takes over.[11] While his predictions might serve as a warning, there is also a view that interaction with our robotic friends could introduce a new harmony between man and machine. In the book, Ford says the jobs under threat are "routine, repetitive or predictable… from fast-food workers to taxi drivers, to financial analysts to radiologists". And to the latter, Robots can be very useful (from automatic pilots to elder care, to agriculture, and many other).

In sum, are robots job stealers of productivity enhancers? According to the International Federation of Robotics, China is the fastest growing market for robots and is anticipated to install more manufacturing robots than any other country. While certain jobs are being replaced, other jobs will likely be created. It is anticipated that millions of jobs will be created or adapted to design, build and maintain many of the machines that will be used in the economy. With this context in mind, robot advocates argue that automation is more likely to cause job transformation rather than job replacement. This is the idea behind the concept of "Churning". The bad news is that some people lose their jobs as the economy evolves and changes, and some companies go bankrupt. There are real victims and tragic stories. But the good news is that other jobs are created, and entrepreneurs start new businesses.

If future jobs require more complex skill sets, it could be difficult for lower-skilled, less-educated workers to access opportunities. And as automation begins to drive down the cost of labour, workers are at risk of entering a "human vs. machine" battle for the lowest wages.

The New Working Models and New Paradigms[12]

A new model or organizing is emerging and some call it the "cyber-enterprise" and its functionality in a business context that is (and will) constantly generate disruption due to rapid technological advances and a shift in the definition of work.

The cyber-enterprise is, and will be, operating in this fast-changing context driven by artificial intelligence. I argue that cyber-reality will change the fundamental roles of all stakeholders, be they employees, suppliers, customers, investors, partners, associations, or governmental agencies, and will require corresponding changes in the governing bodies of organizations.

---

11 Ford, M., (2016) *Rise of the Robots: Technology and the Threat of a Jobless Future*, Basic Books
12 This section is based on a paper we published in 2020 and is called: The Cyber-Organisation and the New World of Work, The European Business Review, March-April. Authors included> Mario Raich, Simon L. Dolan, Dave Ulrich and Alaudio Cisullo.

Today, we are living in a world in transition and transformation(1). There are three powerful converging megatrends that may explain the shaping of the new world of work: *globalization, digitalization* and *creation /destruction*. Add to this the rise in cyber-reality, artificial intelligence (AI), global connectivity, as well as hybrid reality, hybrid work and business entity, and, finally, new, disruptive technologies like quantum computing, blockchain, neurotech and robotics, and you will understand that a new form of cyber-organization is emerging. It is not a luxury; it is a vital necessity in order to survive and sustain business.

However, these new structures of organizations will create a chain of reactions that will impact the way we do business.

The Rising Stress in Emerging and Odd Occupations – the Case of Elite Professional Athletes[13]

> Only when athletes are able to focus their thinking and control their emotions can they maximize their abilities to successfully master their sport.
> **(Dolan and Espejo, 2021)**

Why are elite athletes more susceptible to stress?
Can sports athletes be prepared to better cope with stress? can meltdown be prevented?
How do elite athletes cope with performance anxiety?
What are the symptoms of chronic stress in athletes?
Are there diagnostic tools readily available to identify chronic accumulated stress?
Can we develop resilience in top performance athletes?

Some professions that require constant top performance because they are subject to instant public scrutiny have been and most likely will be stress inducing. There are two events that have caught the public attention in 2021. First was the very sad exposure of the breakdown of **Simone Biles** that was undiagnosed (or ignored) and eventually lead to a breakdown; the early signs and symptoms of chronic stress were not clear to her, to her technical coaches and even to friends and family members surrounding her. What a pity. This story is heart breaking but hardly unique. More elite athletes, as well as top performers (arts, music, entertainment, etc.) are reporting mental health ailments such as anxiety, depression, psychiatric conditions and eating disorders. The exact percentage of Olympic athletes with mental health concerns isn't clear, since it hasn't been recorded. One thing is certain, tope level athletes need absolutely engage in three simultaneous activities:

1. **Emotion-Focused Coping (EFC)**: Using emotion regulation and other mindfulness techniques to calm "fight or flight" stress responses.

2. **Problem-Focused Coping (PFC)**: Actively troubleshooting and problem-solving to counteract stressful stimuli in a specific context.

---

[13] This section is based on a paper we have published recently Dolan, S.L., and Espejo, S.M. (2021) Breakthrough or Breakdown? Diagnosing Chronic Stress and Risk Factors in Elite Athletes in View of Preventing Meltdowns and Enhancing Top Performance. *The European Business Review*, August.

3. **Avoidance Coping (AC):** Using avoidant strategies to disengage physically or psychologically block out a source of stress.

Furthermore, the latest studies in neuroscience and psychology show that 80% of the athlete's performance is mental, which implies that if they do not prepare and train their mind, they will never achieve their 100%. The brain is just one more muscle and as such must be trained; the brain directs the show.

However, in order to do all that, the first step for the athlete (or his/her coaches) is to develop this level of consciousness. Thus, a valid and reliable diagnostic tool is really needed (some think like the stress map that was introduced in Chapter 7). Wellness coaches and other mental health professionals will be aware of the importance of training elite athletes, ever since the breakthrough message contained in the best-selling book of one of the co-founders of the coaching profession, Timothy Gallway (1972) who wrote "***The inner Game of Tennis***".[14] The message of the inner game is simple: "***focus on the present moment, the only one you can really live in***". In his book, Gallway asserts that "*Freedom from stress does not necessarily involve giving up anything, but rather being able to let go of anything, when necessary, and knowing that one will still be all right*". And finally, in this classical book it is suggested that almost every human activity involves both the outer and inner games.

There are always external obstacles between us and our external goals, whether we are seeking wealth, education, reputation, friendship, peace on earth or simply something to eat for dinner. In the end our obstacles are always there; the very mind we use in obtaining our external goals is easily distracted by its tendency to worry, regret, or generally model the situation, thereby causing difficulties from within. Freedom from stress happens in proportion to our responsiveness to our true selves, allowing every moment possible to be an opportunity for self to be what it is and enjoy the process. As far as we can see, this is a lifelong learning process. The true question is how do we get to this point? How do we develop to reach this state? What is the extent that coaches and those surrounding us can help us get there? And most importantly, what tool (s) are available to help us diagnose the outer and inner noises that generate stress and prevent us from focusing on the here and now (and nothing else).

A professional athlete should always ask himself/herself: what is the mental and/or physical price to pay in order to become professionally successful? Figure 9.2 may help this reflection.

Quadrant A: Breakthrough and resilience – This is an ideal case. This is the quadrant that most athletes opt for. It means that the athlete is able to reach record performance and feels mentally positively and complete. Some people refer to this state as a ***state of flow***. It is that sense of fluidity between the athlete body and mind, where he/she is totally absorbed by and deeply focused on the professional task or challenges, beyond the point of distraction. The state of flow was popularized by positive psychologists Mihaly Csikszentmihalyi and Jeanne Nakamura when the person become fully immersed in whatever he/she were doing. Csikszentmihalyi and Nakamura reached this conclusion by interviewing a variety of self-actualized, high-performing people including mountain climbers, chess players, surgeons and ballet

---

14 Gallway, T., (1972) *The Inner Game of Tennis*. https://theinnergame.com/

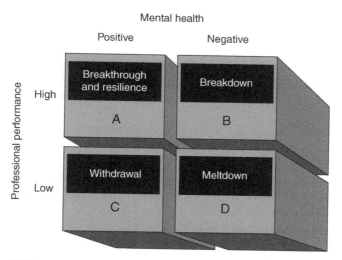

FIGURE 9.2 Bi-dimensional outcomes of professional athlete success of failure.

dancers.[15] Mind you, the flow mental state is generally less common during periods of relaxation and makes itself present during challenging and engaging activities. But if is it happening during multiple moments of competition it can be inferred as a state of true resilience.

Quadrant B: Breakdown – Breakdown happens when the athlete realize that he/she pays the mental prize of sustaining high performance continuously. There are many studies that show that high performing individuals that lacks the resources to overcome the continuous demands on them, end up overwhelmed and they breakdown. Breakdown can be manifested in several forms but the most common is burnout and depression. Depression is not about having an off day. It is more substantial and negatively affects how the athletes feels, thinks, and acts, and eventually diminishing their ability to function well professionally but also at home. And there is also the case of minor mental breakdowns; when athletes over-think sport situations to the point where fear and anxiety disrupts the natural execution of sport skills – the problem is a mental breakdown. For example, when you see an athlete become upset after a bad play and loses focus in the plays that immediately follow, the athlete is suffering from poor emotional coping skills – or a mental breakdown.

Quadrant C: Withdrawal – This is the quadrant very typical to many athletes. We all know that top performance in many sports is determined by the length of time spent playing the sport, the competitive level achieved, and the amount of time spent in training and competition. Obviously, there are distinct types of sports, some that do not necessarily have an age expiry (i.e., Golf). But this is the exception. More elite high-performance athletes are aware of their expiry capacity and prefer to withdraw from a single competition (or from the sector altogether) before it affects their mental state. And there is also a partial withdraw that avoids excessive stress. For example,

---

15 For an interesting interview on the secrets of Flow, see this TED video: www.ted.com/talks/mihaly_csikszentmihalyi_flow_the_secret_to_happiness

Japanese tennis player and the world number 1, Naomi Osaka, withdrew from a post-match press conference citing high stress, which also invited her a huge fine and ire, but solidarity from fellow athletes has been coming which shows empathy to her condition. And again, this was the case of Simon Biles, a celebrated athlete and medal-winning, high-profile gymnast who has decided to withdraw even before the competition as she perceived a low performance result. Withdraw happened even before the act

Quadrant D: Meltdown – this is the worst-case scenario hence you really loose it all. Obviously in the long term may require professional health assistant in order to climb back to normal life. In meltdown situation, the athlete throws the towel and decided to not to go back to competition anymore. But there are also episodes of partial meltdown, that become chronic if they are repeated. And again, because we are living these days through the Olympic experience, lets quote a phrase from the media:

Greater lifetime stress made athletes more susceptible to future stressors. Research suggests that elite athletes are at increased risk of poor mental health, partly due to the intense demands associated with top-level sport. Despite growing interest in the topic, the factors that influence the mental health and well-being of elite athletes remain unclear. From a theoretical perspective, the accumulation of stress and adversity experienced over the life course may be an important factor.

In order to help the elite athlete to cope with this pressure and prevent crackdown, a mix of two critical elements will be needed: 1) a good coaching process (psychologically as well as technically), and 2) a good diagnostic tool that will help the coach build and prepare the athlete for enduring resilience.

Effective coaching requires not only the establishment of a satisfactory relationship but also adequate physical, technical, mental and tactical preparation of the athletes. Supportive coaching is used to refer to a broad and multi-faceted coaching style that incorporates distinct yet interrelated emotional/relational and structural/instrumental components of effective coaching. Supportive coaching can play a positive role in providing guidance in the goal striving process and nurturing of athletic and mental skills. It can be seen as a resource likely to make athletes more capable of problem solving and preparing them to cope with the stress inherent to sport competitions. Task-involving motivational climate are positively correlated with task-oriented coping. By contrast, an environment which includes an ego-motivated coaching culture may provide athletes with an unsupportive coaching style. As a result of an unsupportive environment, athletes experience excessive pressure from coaches, favoritism, and greater time spent with the best athletes are important risk factors for impaired self-regulation. This is shown by associations between ego-involving motivation climate and the use of disengagement-oriented coping in the sport domain.[16]

There is ample research suggesting that holistically young aspiring top athletes are at risk of developing burnout, as they face not only high physical demands but also psychological pressure to reach the elite level. Burnout appears to be linked to chronic emotional and interpersonal stressors in a person's relationship with their work. In athletes, burnout is associated with negative outcomes such as performance impairment, reduced enjoyment, depressed mood and, potentially sport termination.

---

16 Nicolas, M., Gaudreau, P., and Franche, V. (2011). Perception of Coaching Behaviors, Coping, and Achievement in a Sport Competition. *Journal of Sport & Exercise Psychology,* 33(3), 460–468.

Optimists perceive their life as less stressful than pessimists, which may be why they are less likely to burnout exhaustion is a central component to burnout and is related to stress associated with intense training and competition demands. Reduced sense of athletic accomplishment is manifested in a perception of low ability with regard to performance and skill level. Sport devaluation manifests itself in a loss of motivation, with the athlete ceasing to care about his or her previously beloved sport.

So, the role of a psychological coach is essential in preventing stress and burnout in athletes. An effective, proactive, and preventive approach to stress management adopted by the coach seeks to make changes in the macro environment (organization culture), the microenvironment (task redesign), or in the athlete perceptions of control (for example, enhanced decision-making opportunities). Organizations and official delegation management team are recommended to proactively address the underlying causes of the stressors, establish effective mechanisms to recognize and respond to stressor warning signs and to implement systematic learning, un-learning and re-learning in order to get rid of habits and behaviors that can eventually become counterproductive. The **stress map tool** (Chapter 7) can aid the coach in pinpointing and diagnosing the Achilles points and develop effective preventive strategies. Further interventions should focus on moderating external pressures for the athlete and monitoring and modifying their training demands.

Unlike machines, humans do not simply follow algorithms that lead to perfect solutions. Coaches generally do a good job of teaching sport skills, but when athletes are called to execute the skills in which they have learned in competitive situations, they often fall to pressure – and end up choking as a result. Making things worse, most athletes go back to only practicing the physical elements of a sport skill, and often disregard the importance of being able to control nerves and emotions (mental skills) the next time they feel pressure in a competitive situation.

Technostress and Virtustress – the Impact of Technology, Virtuality and the Metaverse on Mental Health

If we look at the world today, waves of new applications which employ artificial intelligence are being introduced across all spectrums of life – work, business and leisure. People are using various AI applications in daily activities and work tasks without even being aware of them. Research by McKinsey has gone as far as describing AI as contributing to a transformation of society "happening ten times faster and at 300 times the scale" of the Industrial Revolution.[17]

Several authors see AI as the new driver of growth. Purdy and Daugherty argue that AI has the potential to overcome the physical limitations of capital and labor, and open new sources of value and growth.[18] A report entitled "How AI Boosts Industry

---

[17] Dobbs, R., Manyika, J., and Woetzel, J. (2015) The Four Global Forces Breaking all the Trends, McKinsey Global Institute. Quoted in *Artificial Intelligence. The Road Ahead in Low and Middle-Income Countries*. June 2017, https://webfoundation.org/docs/2017/07/AI_Report_WF.pdf

[18] Purdy, M., and Daugherty, P. Why Artificial Intelligence is the Future of Growth, www.accenture.com/t20170927T080049Z__w__/us-en/_acnmedia/PDF-33/Accenture-Why-AI-is-the-Future-of-Growth.PDFla=en

Profits and Innovation", published by Accenture Research and Frontier Economics, claims that AI technologies have the potential to increase productivity by 40 percent or more by 2035. Accordingly, they will increase economic growth by an average of 1.7 percent across 16 industries, with information and communication, manufacturing and financial services leading all industries.

AI is already enabling a wave of innovation across many sectors of the global economy. By and large, it helps businesses use resources more efficiently. Pokémon Go went viral in 2016 using elements of augmented reality mobile game.

All these innovations, gadgets, games virtual opportunities, can be fun but if not managed properly, can create Technostress, virtu-stress and alike. Studies have already shown that this constant checking on mail, WhatsApp, Instagram and alike increases stress levels considerably. In one study, nearly 20 percent of participants said that technology was a substantial source of stress and anxiety. There is evidence that constant checkers experience a considerably higher amount of stress than those who rarely use technology or check social media.

Technostress has been defined as the negative psychological link between people and the introduction of new technologies. Where ergonomics is the study of how humans react to and physically fit with machines in their environment, technostress is a result of altered habits of work and collaboration that are being brought about due to the use of modern information technologies at office and home situation. People experience technostress when they cannot adapt to or cope with information technologies in a healthy manner. They feel compulsive about being connected and sharing constant updates, feel forced to respond to work-related information in real-time, and engage in almost habitual multi-tasking. They feel compelled to work faster because information flows faster and have little time to spend on sustained thinking and creative analysis.

Technostress is "a modern disease of adaptation caused by an inability to cope with the new technologies in a healthy manner. Some of the earliest technostress scholarly studies in the field of Management Information Systems show that technostress is an undesirable phenomenon spawned by use of computing and communication devices such as computers, tablets, and smartphones. Recent research also suggests that technostress is dependent on gender, age, and technology literacy. Women experience lower technostress than men, older people experience less technostress at work than younger people and those with greater computer literacy experience lower technostress

Technology is getting more pervasive and increasingly demands our attention, which risks disrupting our healthy and balanced lives. Often, it's the first thing we look at, speak to or hear in the morning and the last thing we scroll on at night. In fact, many are now linking the prolific decline in mental health to our **"always-on"** lifestyles. Because all that will increase exponentially in the future, we need to combat this negative impact with an uprising of technology aimed squarely at improving our mental well-being.

Here are a couple of ideas for combatting the hidden stressors of technology. These may work today but perhaps can be extended to the future:

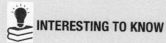

INTERESTING TO KNOW

NINE SIGNS AND SYMPTOMS OF TECHNOLOGY ADDICTION OF TEENAGERS

1. *It is hard for my child to stop using screen media.*
2. *The amount of time my child wants to use screen media keep increasing.*
3. *My child sneaks using screen media.*
4. *My child needs more intense and novel games and apps to reach the same level of satisfaction.*
5. *When my child has had a bad day, screen media seems to be the only thing that helps him [or] her feel better.*
6. *My child thinks obsessively about their game or phone when not using it.*
7. *My child's screen media use causes problems for the family.*
8. *My child's academics, activities or health are suffering because of electronics.*
9. *My child is becoming more and more isolated.*

Source: www.sandstonecare.com/resources/substance-abuse/technology-addiction

- Use creative boundaries to prevent anxious feelings over smartphone. Healthy boundaries can include not using it during a meal, when you're in a social situation, before bedtime, or in the bathroom. It might also mean creating set time limits for how long you spend on your phone or a particular app. Distance yourself from your phone and occupy your time with things that bring you joy – such as a hobby, going for a walk, spending time with loved ones, focusing on work, or hitting the gym.
- Avoid using trivial texts and messages when you are nervous or anxious. Everything can wait.
- Check from time to time if you did not become an addict to technology. If this is the case, ensure to take pauses, to seek compensatory behaviours, and awareness can generate creative solution to cut the addiction. Technology addiction is like any other type of addiction: it is defined as the kind of impulse control disorder in which you are exposed to the harmful effects of technology because of excessive use of computers, internet, video games and mobile devices. And addiction can be harmful to children. In Spain there was a sad story of a 14-year-old child that killed his parents and brother for being barred from using the game console for three days.

The Recipe for De-stress in the Future – Principles of Resilience[19]

Developing the Internal Compass – The 3E Triaxial Model of Values

For the past 40 years or so I have been studying values. Values, I claim are the best indicator to understand our behaviour. Values can be served as our compass when our behavior is aligned with our world view and definition of success.[20] In contrast, when our lives and behaviour are incongruent with our values, it results in stress, in poor performance, in all types of illnesses and alike.

So, developing a compass (individually and/or organization wide) is becoming a necessity. Over the years, I have developed the concept of "Managing by Values" model that may help organizations handle this VUCA world by developing a value-based configurational compass. In our book, we describe the evolution of the school of thought in management due to the increasing complexity in the environments that organizations operate in. Table 9.2 summarizes this evolution that started with MBI (Managing by Instructions) to MBO (Managing by Objectives) and finally to MBV (Managing by Values). The evolution is driven by the need to manage environmental and intra-organizational complexities which is characteristic of the future.[21] A very similar approach was developed in relationship to the internal compass of individuals.[22]

In the early twentieth century, Management by Instruction (MBI) was an appropriate and adequate way to run an organization. Change happened at a slower pace and therefore the way things were done in the past worked well enough to pass on to others. By the 1960s, change was accelerating to the point where more flexibility of action was required by managers. Thus, the introduction of Management by Objectives (MBO) enabled managers to agree on a direction and to choose their own strategy. As changes in the environment began to intensify (e.g., global competition, impact of technology, global economic crisis, etc.), MBO proved to be an insufficient strategy for managing in an interconnected and fast-paced VUCA world. Managing by Values (MBV) aims to help us create a set of values that directs us towards being productive, ethical and, all in all, satisfied human beings. The model argues that a full, balanced and healthy life needs to include three groups of values: *the economic pragmatic group*, *the ethical-social group* and *the emotional-developmental group*; this

---

19 This section is inspired by three recent papers we have published recently: 1) Garti A., and Dolan S.L. (2021) Using the Triaxial Model of Values to Build Resilience in a COVID-19 VUCA World. *The European Business Review*, January; Raich, M., and Dolan, S.L. (2022) The Art of Life Design. *Kindai Management Review*, 2 April, and Dolan, S.L., and Brykman, K. (2022) The Use of Dopamine to Enhance Resilience in a Post COVID-19 Era: Lessons From Recent Discoveries in Neuroscience that Helps Sustain Vigilance and Productivity in Life and Work. *The European Business Review*, January.

20 Read more in my latest book: The secrets of coaching and leading by values. 2020 Routledge The Secret of Coaching and Leading by Values: How to Ensure Alignment (routledge.com)

21 Dolan S., Garcia S., and Auerbach, A. (2003). Understanding and Managing Chaos in Organizations, *International Journal of Management*; (20)1:23–20.; Dolan, S.L., and Richley, B. (2006). Management by Values (MBV): A New Philosophy for a New Economic Order, *Handbook of Business Strategy*, 7(1).

22 Dolan S.L. (2011) *Coaching by values: how to succeed in the life of business and the business of life*, iUniverse.

TABLE 9.2 Translating values through MBV-MBO-MBI: Illustrative examples

Ax is	Economic pragmatic	Emotional-developmental		Ethical-Social
MBV	Transformability	Creativity	Vitality	Engagement
MBO	(1) Embracing VUCA; (2) creating fundamentally new system using the power of VUCA.	Finding solutions that are compatible in the VUCA world.	(1) Creating small pleasures daily; and (2) Capturing fulfilling experiences.	(1) Maintaining existing support systems; (2) creating new support systems.
Examples of Organisational MBI	Converting to agile management (McKinsey, 2020a).	See the Special Edition of the Innovation Update, which highlights how UN entities are leveraging innovative approaches to respond to the COVID-19 pandemic.2		An organisation was forced to work remotely. Every Monday, the mangement sends a cake to every employee's house; and at 9:00, all employees were invited to a Zoom engagement of coffee and cake before starting the week.
Examples of personal MBI	A sports coach who lost his income due to the closure of this gym because of COVID-19 limitations. He can create a hybrid fitness programme that allows a quick transition between training in the gym, training in the park, and remote workouts. A programme with colatility that addresses the uncertainty of the era.	Due to social distance restrictions, restaurants are closed. My spouse complains that it is impossible to enjoy life today. Icooked usa specialmeal and set the tablewith candles and flowers.		We now work from. To maintain friendships at work, I call my colleagues and talk to them daily.

Source: Garti and Dolan: Using the Triaxial Model of Values to Build Resilience in a COVID-19 VUCA World 2021. The European Business Review January. Used with permission.

is the essence of the 3Es Triaxial Model of Values. We will use these three groups of values to develop the concept of resilience.

Resilience was originally introduced by Holling (1973); he stated: "*Resilience determines the persistence of relationships within a system and is a measure of the ability of these systems to absorb changes of state variables, driving variables, and parameters, and still persist*" (p 17).[23] Others have proposed a variety of definitions for "resilience" but, all agree that nd concluded that there are two distinct meanings of resilience. In the first, resilience is defined as the time required for a system to return to an equilibrium point following a disturbance event. The second defines resilience as the amount of disturbance that a system can absorb before changing to another stable regime (i.e. de-stress), which is controlled by a different set of variables and characterised by a different structure. In order to enhance resilience the organizations need to incorporate the capacity of social–ecological systems to cope with, adapt to, and shape change, and learn to live with uncertainty and surprise. Managing by value with the

---

23 Holling, C.S. (1973). Resilience and stability of ecological systems. *Annual review of ecology and systematics*, 4(1), 1–23.

FIGURE 9.3 Dolan 3Es triaxial model of values: A compass for de-estress.
Source: Illustration in Garti & Dolan 2021 (Op. Cit.) used with permission.

three groups of the 3Es Triaxial Model encourages developing values which will help build the capacity to cope with, adapt to, and shape change, and learn to live with this future VUCA era (Figure 9.3).

The economic pragmatic group deals with values that direct behaviour in an effective manner which is instrumental to achieving our goals in life or at work. This group includes values such as excellence, planning, diligence, efficiency, etc. Developing resilience means having transformability as an economic-pragmatic value. Transformability is the capacity to create a fundamentally new system when ecological, economic or social (including political) conditions make the existing system untenable. This value should be the answer to our need for control and certainty. Instead of trying and failing, controlling and predicting a VUCA life, which may lead to stress, desperation and the development of "learned helplessness", we should embrace the volatility, uncertainty, complexity and ambiguity of the situation, be creative and derive a new system. Instead of waiting for our life to "return to normal", we have to transform our way of thinking and see the VUCA world as the next normal.

In my writing I argue that "**creativity**" is an important component of the emotional-developmental axis. In this VUCA situation, people often do not consider this value group seriously. They are so busy in the struggle merely to survive that they block the constructive emotional development. The underlying values in this axis are oriented towards constructing a life filled with interest, with passion and with creativity, despite the fact that this last is difficult to define. Creativity in the VUCA world can be viewed as a new sense of coping, adapting and solving novel problems. In this environment, creativity needs to be viewed out of the box; hence, it needs to surpass inhibitions, overcome the traditional way of the past of relying on experience, and break away from habitual assumptions and routines. The clear indicator of the need for creative solutions is apparent in the ongoing experience with the continuing waves of COVID-19 infections. Having succeeded in the first wave is not a guarantee that the same remedies will work again in the second wave. Actually, the facts show that many countries are failing in generating this creative solution in the next round, and the pandemic is becoming worse. That may be the reason that children are more creative than adults (Runco, 2014); they transform our way of thinking and see the VUCA world as the new normal, and are not bound in their imagination to the previous "normal" life.

Another emotional-developmental value that is required precisely in a VUCA period is **vitality**. Vitality is one's conscious experience of possessing energy, enthusiasm, spirit, and aliveness. Vitality will bring resilience, since vitality is our psychological survival ally. By vitality, we intend to create the small pleasures on a daily basis and capture the corresponding fulfilling experiences. Vitality can be instrumental and enhance resilience only when it breaks away from yesterday's world (which no longer exists) and tackles the new VUCA world positively, yet realistically.

The third axis in the 3Es Triaxial Model is the ethical-social group of values. This group deals with relationships, values that direct behavior of thoughtfulness, influence, loyalty, tolerance, etc. Developing resilience during a VUCA era means having engagement as one of the top ethical-social values. A VUCA era (like the COVID-19 that we have experimented) generates an extreme amount of ongoing stress. According to what we have seen in previous chapters, an acute or prolonged (chronic) stress can be mitigated by having strong social and ethical basis hence it may filter the stress reaction. And, if stress was defined throughout this book as causing "wear and tear" to the body (physically) or the soul (emotionally), any strategy addressed to minimize the wear and tear can be considered de-stress and enhance resilience. I should insist that ample research shows that having a support system in place plays a critical factor in de stressing people. The COVID-19 pandemic required us to implement social distance, for which developing and maintaining our support systems was difficult albeit essential. Thus, attempts were done by resilient people to replace physical social support with virtual one, which seems to be effective to some degree, but not for everyone.

In reference to Table 9.2 it is important to note that objectives must be understood in light of the values and not as stand-alone, otherwise we return to MBO of the sixties. The objectives interpret the spirit of value. They are flexible and come to serve the value. They are the means, and value is the goal. The instructions that follow are examples of ways in which the objectives that translate the essence of the value can be implemented. They should not be seen as instructions, as in MBI.

In summary, the resilience value system is recommended as a compass for living in a VUCA world. To be more specific, we propose to use the Values Pie chart.[24] The Values Pie integrates the 3Es Triaxial Model and the "behave your values" model, as has been described in this section, and creates a clearer picture for the way one wants to build resilience. The Values Pie has four ingredients. (1) The correct portion of each axis in the value system. Remember that in the Triaxial Model, the pie has to contain all three axes divided in any way that suits the system. (2) Each slice of the

24 Garti, A., and Dolan, S.L. (2019) Managing by Values (MBV). *The European Business Review*.

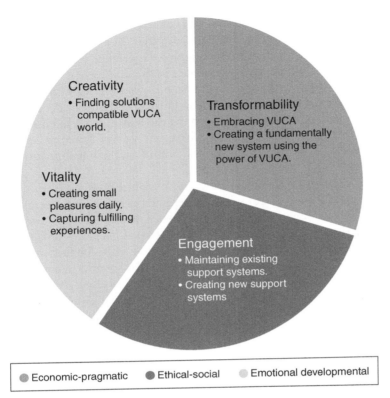

FIGURE 9.4 The resilience Value Pie – Refining our compass.
Source: Garti & Dolan (2021) op. cit. Used with permission.

pie contains the values of that axis. (3) The size of the font of each value expresses the importance of the value for the Values Pie owner. A value that is expressed in a small font represents a relative less important value compared to a value that is expressed in a bigger font. (4) Each value has its objectives (MBO). Given that the Values Pie portrays a holistic view of the axes distribution, the values that are in each axis show their importance and their objectives. The Resilience Values Pie recommended for living in a VUCA era is displayed in Figure 9.4.

Positive Psychology, Hormones and DNA Issues Connected to Combatting Stress?

Intelligent Use of Principles from Positive Psychology Helps to De-stress[25]

Another interesting angle to de-stress and build resilience has been inspired by Seligman and colleagues and the positive psychology movement.[26] The premise of

---

25 This section is based on a paper we have recently published in The *European Business Review*, and entitled: The Use of Dopamine to Enhance Resilience in a Post COVID-19 Era: Lessons From Recent Discoveries in Neuroscience that Helps Sustain Vigilance and Productivity in Life and Work, Dolan & Brykman, Op cit, 2022

26 Dr. Seligman's books have been translated into more than 45 languages and have been best sellers both in America and abroad. Among his better-known works are Flourish (Free Press, 2011), Authentic

positive psychology is that well-being can be defined, measured and taught. Well-being includes positive emotions, intense engagement, good relationships, meaning, and accomplishment (PERMA). Questionnaires can measure it. Trainers can teach it. Achieving it not only makes people more fulfilled but makes corporations more productive, soldiers more resilient, students more engaged, marriages happier. Seligman even came up with a formula:

$$H = S + C + V$$

Happiness (**H**) equals your genetic set point (S) plus the circumstances of your life, plus factors under voluntary control (**V**). Unlike previous promises of happiness, positive psychology insists it is evidenced-based, using the resources of contemporary social science – surveys, longitudinal studies, meta-analyses, animal experiments, brain imaging, hormone measuring, and case studies. Most recently, Seligman has turned to big data analyses of postings on social media websites (e.g., Facebook). He and his team have created a curriculum of positivity. They have measured the impact of training and the surprising benefits of learned optimism. The conclusions of positive psychology can validate experience and offer hope, in a sense, that:

- Genetics shape mood and personality, but only in part.
- Human beings can change and improve.
- Moods matter but can be altered by understanding circadian rhythm.
- Individuals have signature strengths that can be identified and employed.
- Flow moments exist and can be cultivated.
- Other people matter.
- Strong social bonds are crucial.
- Marriage and religion contribute to well-being.
- Positivity improves health, work, creativity, and relationships.
- Intrinsic adaptation to both the good and bad is useful
- Optimism is a learned skill.
- Happiness requires effort.
- Happiness is contagious.

So, Resilience has emerged from this stream of research in positive psychology. The construct of **Resilience**, represent the opposite pole of stress – the focus is on de-stress, on positive adjustment to inherent life challenges, resulting in a healthy, productive and happy self.

In this section we focus on the essence of individual resilience, and more specifically approached from the angle of neuroscience. The aim is to advance the proposition that some hormones are playing an important role in creating a sustainable resilience. More specifically, neurotransmitters, like dopamine, seem to help spark the chemical

Happiness (Free Press, 2002), Learned Optimism (Knopf, 1991), What You Can Change & What You Can't (Knopf, 1993), The Optimistic Child (Houghton Mifflin, 1995), Helplessness (Freeman, 1975, 1993) and Abnormal Psychology (Norton, 1982, 1988, 1995, with David Rosenhan).

messengers that keep us alert and on task. Dopamine in particular, seems to have a biological connection to motivation, focus and resilience.

In more clinical terms, resilience is the ability to adapt to difficult situations. When stress builds, or adversity and trauma strike, you still experience anger, grief, anxiety and pain, but you are able to keep functioning, sometimes even flourishing because of it. The Mayo clinic offers the following tips for becoming more resilient:[27]

- Get connected
- Make every day meaningful
- Learn from experience
- Remain hopeful
- Take care of yourself
- Be proactive

Now, that we understand what resilience entails, we turn to the latest discoveries from neuroscience that explains why some people are more resilient than others. The field of neuroscience places the focus on the role of Dopamine. Dopamine is known as the pleasure-and-reward neurotransmitter. It helps create a feeling of enjoyment and a sense of reward and accomplishment when we get something done. It motivates performance and builds positive habits.

Research undertaken at the Huberman Lab at Stanford University, proposes that Dopamine, in its role as chemical messenger in our brain, has the ability to help us create, stay focused and complete projects with extreme efficiency.[28] Huberman has concluded that Dopamine helps us feel more motivated, energized, happy, alert, and in control. It so follows that Dopamine would fuel resilience by stimulating support seeking, persistence over challenges, and positive mood to execute activities. In a series of videos on Apple Podcasts, which reviews the research on Dopamine consequences, Dr Huberman and his colleagues presents 14 tools to show how to control dopamine release to increase motivation and focus and reduce addiction and depression. They also explain why dopamine stacking with chemicals and behaviours inevitably leads to states of underwhelm and poor performance. They further explore how to achieve sustained increases in baseline dopamine, compounds that protect dopamine neurons (e.g., caffeine) from specific sources. Finally, they describe non-prescription supplements for increasing dopamine – both their benefits and risks – and synergy of pro-dopamine supplements with those that increase acetylcholine. While we focus in this section on Dopamine, worth mentioning that other hormones affect our moods and conduct (see Figure 9.5), but describing them all in detail is beyond the scope of this section.

While recent research in neuroscience suggest that Norepinephrine creates more energy and concentration, and Serotonin improves memory, Dopamine seems to be the de-stress hormone. It seems that Dopamine begins kicking in before we obtain

---

27 See: www.mayoclinic.org/tests-procedures/resilience-training/in-depth/resilience/art-20046311
28 Huberman Lab: Controlling Your Dopamine For Motivation, Focus & Satisfaction | Episode 39 https://podcasts.apple.com/us/podcast/controlling-your-dopamine-for-motivation-focus-satisfaction/id1545953110?i=1000536717492 Watch: https://podcasts.apple.com/us/podcast/controlling-your-dopamine-for-motivation-focus-satisfaction/id1545953110?i=1000536717492 .

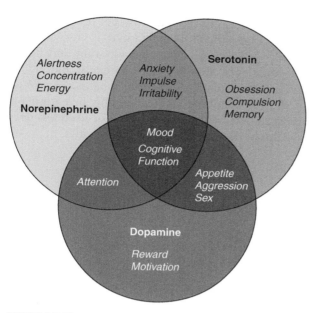

FIGURE 9.5 The road to de-stress using the moods and conduct hormones.

rewards. This is important because it means that its real job is to encourage us to act, either to achieve something good or to avoid something bad. Essentially, dopamine affects how our brain decides whether a goal is worth the effort in the first place. When our brain recognizes that something important is about to happen, dopamine kicks in. Researchers have found that dopamine spikes occur during moments of high stress – like when soldiers with PTSD hear gunfire.[29]

Researchers from Vanderbilt University correlated dopamine levels with resilience by mapping the brains of "go-getters" and "slackers". They found that people willing to work hard had higher dopamine levels in the striatum and prefrontal cortex – two areas known to impact motivation and reward. Among slackers, dopamine was present in the anterior insula, an area of the brain involved in emotion and risk perception.

Similar research from Brown University assessed the role of dopamine in influencing how the brain evaluates whether a mental task is worth the effort by measuring natural dopamine levels while choosing between memory tasks of varying difficulties. More difficult mental tasks were rewarded with more money, and those with higher dopamine levels in a region of the striatum called the caudate nucleus were more likely to focus on the benefits (the money) and choose the difficult mental tasks. Those with lower dopamine levels were more sensitive to the perceived cost, or task difficulty. Next, the participants completed experiments after taking either an inactive placebo, methylphenidate (a stimulant drug typically used to treat ADHD), or sulpiride (an antipsychotic medication that, at low doses, increases dopamine levels).

---

29 An important note: low dopamine correlates with feelings of hopelessness, worthlessness and even depression. Perhaps the bad news, then, is that Dopamine can also play a role in addictive behaviors. Its deficiency can impair our ability to manage stress, focus attention, finish tasks, and maintain motivation. Other downsides including self-isolation and self-destructive thoughts and behaviors.

Increasing dopamine boosted how willing people with low, but not high, Dopamine synthesis capacity were to choose more difficult mental tasks.

Dopamine, thus, seems to help us know exactly what we want and how to get it: it helps us access our self-confidence, rational, self-awareness, and our critical thinking. Dopamine also helps us focus intently on the task at hand and take pride in achievement: it enhances our strategic thinking, masterminding, inventing, problem solving, envisioning, and pragmatism. We may feel overly alert or need less sleep than other people. Dopamine also seems to support the following activities:

- Reward and pleasure centres.
- Attention and learning.
- Sleep and overall mood.
- Behavior and cognition.
- Movement and emotional responses.
- Voluntary movement, motivation, and reward.

By contrast, research in neuroscience shows that Dopamine depletion can result in a variety of issue in various systems in the body. Early warning signs are loss of energy, fatigue, sluggishness, memory loss, or depression. Other early symptoms include:

Hard time self-motivating
Cravings for chocolate
Easily distracted
Shiny object syndrome (easily distracted)
Not feeling fulfilled when you accomplish a task
Looking for quick fixes
Addictive tendencies (Alcohol, drugs, work, exercise, emotional eating, social media, gambling, shopping)
Having a hard time focusing and staying on task
Self-sabotage
Self-isolation
Feelings of hopelessness or worthlessness
Feeling tired in the morning
Having a shorter temper than usual
Don't feel like going out but feel good when you do

Avoiding or Using Some Hormones as an Important Facet of De-stress and a Combat Against Premature Aging?[30]

In the previous chapter we have also defined stress as aging, or more specifically premature aging. Obviously, increasing life span without disease is sought by most people.

---

30 This section is based on our paper: Dolan, S.L., and Raich (2021) A Voyage Into Premature Aging: The Role of Chronic Stress and its Principal Correlates, *The European Business Review*, November. www.europeanbusinessreview.com/a-voyage-into-premature-aging-the-role-of-chronic-stress-and-its-principal-correlates/

Researchers have tweaked multiple pathways to give rodents long and healthy lives. For example, restricting calorie intake in mice or introducing mutations in nutrient-sensing pathways shows extended lifespans by as much as 50%. And these "Methuselah mice" are more likely than the control mice to die without any apparent diseases. Post-mortems reveal that tumours, heart problems, neurodegeneration and metabolic disease are generally reduced or delayed in long-lived mice. In other words, extending lifespan also seems to increase "health-span", or the time lived without chronic age-related conditions. These insights have hardly made a dent in human medicine. The current tools for extending healthy life – better diets and regular exercise – are effective, but there is lot of room for improvements, especially in adding psycho-social factors to the generic algorithm of life expansion. All in all, the latter is the prime objective of this short section.

A series of recent studies are raising a powerful probability for the existence of an aging hormone or an aging enzyme. The problem is that this hormone is in increased production in one of five people. In those who are under stress, it seems to be almost non-existent. Additional studies are needed to reach a personal conclusion for reducing stress and perhaps, by doing so, will lead to a reduction of premature aging.

From a biological angle, aging is associated with a decrease in the regeneration capacity of the skeletal muscles after an acute injury – resulting in a decrease in physical strength and physiological abilities. A recent article in NATURE proposes a new factor that you may well have never heard of. The authors state that genetic studies have identified a powerful aging suppressant hormone called "***Klotho***". The document reviews important studies conducted on the mysterious hormone. And, while most of the studies on the subject were conducted at this stage only on mice, one of the most fascinating academic works focused specifically on a group of women. There, they report on a study including 90 mothers who were defined as living with "high emotional stress" and another 88 women who lead a more relaxed life. All women were generally healthy and in their 30s or 40s. Among the women who faced high mental stress, there was a significantly lower rate of this hormone. Dr Eric Perth, from the University of California, San Francisco who led the study, said, "*Our findings suggest that the which we now know is very important for health, may be associated with mental stress and even premature illness and death*".[31]

Klotho is a transmembrane protein that, in addition to other effects, provides some control over the sensitivity of the organism to insulin, and appears to be involved in aging. Its discovery was documented in 1997 by Makoto Kuro-o, et. al. The name of the gene comes from Klotho or Clotho, one of the Moirai, or Fates, in Greek mythology. In experiments with mice, Klotho-deficient mice, manifest a syndrome resembling accelerated human ageing and display extensive and accelerated arteriosclerosis.[32]

With all these findings, it will probably take a long time before such experiments are carried out in humans and before we understand exactly if and how this hormone affects

---

[31] Note: Perth stressed that his research was purely observational and did not prove a cause-and-effect relationship between high levels of stress and a decrease in the rate of this hormone, and certainly did not prove that such a link affects the acceleration of aging.

[32] Kuro-o, M., Matsumura, Y., Aizawa, H., Kawaguchi, H., Suga, T., Utsugi, T., Ohyama, Y., Kurabayashi, M., Kaname, T., Kume, E., Iwasaki, H., Iida, A., Shiraki-Iida, T., Nishikawa, S., Nagai, R., and Nabeshima, Y.I. (Nov 1997) Mutation of the Mouse Klotho Gene Leads to a Syndrome Resembling Ageing. *Nature*, 390 (6655), 45–51. Bibcode:1997Natur.390...45K. doi:10.1038/36285. PMID 9363890. S2CID 4428141.

the rate of aging and the risk of developing various diseases. Of course, until then, no one will recommend taking certain supplements without control – there is one conclusion that perhaps should be considered seriously: *Reducing chronic stress will certainly prolong life via the production of the Klotho hormone or via other etiological paths.*

A 2012 study found that work-related exhaustion can have a harmful effect on critical DNA in the cells. Researchers measured the length of DNA sections called telomeres and found that individuals with the most job stress had the shortest telomere – when telomeres become too short, the cells can die or become damaged. Those who did not experience work exhaustion had longer telomeres. Telomere shortening has been linked to Parkinson's, type 2 diabetes, cardiovascular disease, and cancer, the study notes. Chronic stress has been shown to contribute to the development of Alzheimer's disease, and recent research has shown that greater stress may be the reason that some women's brains age more prematurely than men. Researchers based in UC Berkeley, discovered that the pattern of gene activation and deactivation that occurs as the brain ages seemed to progress more quickly in women; the scientist states, "*A higher stress load could be driving the female brain towards faster aging-related decline*".[33]

Aside from the chemical-hormonal changes, it has been fairly well documented that people under stress neglect to take care of themselves; they are known to eat poorly, to exercise less, to drink more, and rely excessively on medication. All of those things eventually show up on your body and affects the aging process. Experts in nutrition insist that developing healthy habits (eating, sleeping, being active) is critical de-stress actions to aging well. Resilient people do regular exercise which protects the aging brain, and conversely, sleep deprivation can accelerate aging. As you get older, and wish to maintain your resiliency, good nutrition becomes increasingly important in how the body ages.

Combating Premature Aging by Avoiding the Risk of Inflammation

There are many studies connecting chronic stress with inflammatory processes resulting in higher microglial activation and expression of proinflammatory markers. More importantly, the higher inflammatory response seen in stressed animals was associated with a higher rate of death of dopamine, the most characteristic feature seen in Parkinson's disease. In total, stress seems to be an important risk factor in the degenerative processes leading to real diseases such as Parkinsons and naturally implies premature aging.

Furthermore, following the demonstrated association of employee burnout or vital exhaustion with several risk factors for cardiovascular disease (CVD) and CVD risk, research by Toker et Al,, shows the possibility that one of the mechanisms linking burnout with CVD morbidity is microinflammation; they pointed out the role of C-reactive protein (hs-CRP) and fibrinogen concentrations in the etiology. Their

---

[33] Ahola, K., Siren, I., Kivimaki, M., Ripatti, S., Aromaa, A., Lonnqvist, J., and Hovatta, I. (2012) Work-Related Exhaustion and Telomere Length: A Population-Based Study, *PLOSONE* https://doi.org/10.1371/journal.pone.0040186; Slezak, M., "Stress May Cause Women's Brains to Age Prematurely, www.newscientist.com/article/dn22107-stress-may-cause-womens-brains-to-age-prematurely/?ignored=irrelevant

sample included 630 women and 933 men, all apparently healthy, who underwent periodic health examinations. The authors controlled for possible confounders including two other negative affective states: depression and anxiety. In women, burnout was positively associated with hs-CRP and fibrinogen concentrations, and anxiety was negatively associated with them. In men, depression was positively associated with hs-CRP and fibrinogen concentrations, but not with burnout or anxiety. Thus, they have concluded that burnout, depression, and anxiety are differentially associated with microinflammation biomarkers, dependent on gender.[34]

Stress, Epigenetic and Premature Aging

The word "epigenetics" is derived from the Greek word "epi", meaning "over" or "above", and in this case, over or above the genome. This area of research involves the study of how our behaviors and environment can cause changes that affect the way our genes work. Genes are made of a molecule called DNA. Epigenetic changes are vital to normal biological functioning and can affect natural cycles of cellular death, renewal, and senescence. Different lifestyle and behavioural factors such as diet, sleep, exercise, smoking, and drinking alcohol can also affect the composition and location of the chemical groups that bind to our DNA. Environmental factors such as stress and trauma may also have an impact.

So, what is the link between epigenetics, psychological stress and aging? researchers conclude that psychosocial stress – especially when chronic, excessive, or occurring early in life – has been associated with accelerated aging and increased disease risk. Among molecular mechanisms linking stress and aging, the author reviews evidence on the role of epigenetics, biochemical processes that can be set into motion by stressors and in turn influence genomic function and complex phenotypes, including aging-related outcomes. There is emerging evidence, together with work examining related biological processes, that shed light on the epigenetic and more broadly, molecular underpinnings of the long-hypothesized connection between stress and aging.

Epigenetics can also mark accurate chronological time versus biological time. Our chronological age is based on our birthdate, but biological age means the true age that our cells, tissues, and organ systems appear to be, based on biochemistry. Our epigenome is affected by our environment and experiences over time, similar to how rings on the inside of a tree can tell us the tree's age and mark when it has encountered damage or stress.

A UCLA team discovered an epigenetic clock that allows us to measure the age of all human tissues. Past models of biological versus chronological age were based on an analysis of telomeres. These are structures at the end of chromosomes that keep them from tangling with each other and play an important role in DNA replication during cell division. One of the most promising, Nobel Prize-winning epigenetic techniques uses a harmless virus to introduce special genes called Yamanaka factors (after the researcher who discovered them) to undo the epigenetic programming of mature

---

[34] Toker, S.S., Shapira, A., Berliner, I., Shlomo Melamed, S., and Samuel (2005) The Association Between Burnout, Depression, Anxiety, and Inflammation Biomarkers: C-Reactive Protein and Fibrinogen in Men and Women. *Journal of Occupational Health Psychology*, 10(4), 344–362

cells. This process transforms the mature cells back into their younger stem cell form. Having those younger cells in place has been shown to regenerate some function lost to age, illness, or injury.[35]

In sum, resilience is not a trait that you are either born with or without. It's a set of behaviours, thoughts, and actions that can be learned and developed. When you break it down to the physical level in your brain, resilience is a neuroplastic process. It's really about how well your brain handles the unexpected aspects that life brings. So, being resilient doesn't mean that you don't experience hard times. In fact, intense emotional pain, extreme trauma and severe adversity are common in people who are considered very resilient. The road to resilience most often involves considerable hardship. That's how we often build and demonstrate our resilience.

Resilience means an adaptation in the face of adversity and the ability to bounce back from these circumstances without being overly influenced by negative emotions. Dopamine seems to be a neurotransmitter that enables the bouncing back rapidly and productively. Most people display a degree of resilience (and mobilization of the dopamine neurotransmitter) but recurrent episodes of stressful life and work events can deplete our dopamine reserves, making us less resilient.

This does not suggest that we need to administer dopamine like a supplement in order to be more resilient. As already mentioned, there are some issues of side effects and dependency. Thus, more research is needed in order to tune up and optimize the administering of dopamine in order to de stress and enhance resilience.

The Role of Spirituality and Broader Life Values for Leaders as a Form to De-stress

Life values are in essence represent everything that makes our life easier, better, meaningful, and happier. It also reflects our world view, like the importance of healthy ecosystems, the importance of health in general, the importance of friendship, the importance of care (to people, to the environment, etc.). Also, spiritual values like love and trust should perhaps be considered more important than pure materialist values. At the risk of being utopian, the following "to do" list can serve people to engage in more meaningful activities that one of its byproducts is becoming de-stressed:

- Make yourself, others, and future generations happy
- Preserve a habitable world for future generations
- Take care of something of importance
- Fulfill meaningful duties
- Leave a meaningful legacy behind and make the world a better place
- Create new things, knowledge, artifacts, works of art, etc.-
- Educate people around you; instill values for the next generation
- Develop your and others talents
- Facilitate progress towards peace

35 Zannas, A.S. (2019 Dec) Epigenetics as a Key Link Between Psychosocial Stress and Aging: Concepts, Evidence, Mechanisms, *Dialogues Clin Neurosci*, 21(4), 389–396. (https://pubmed.ncbi.nlm.nih.gov/31949406/)

- Serve others to heal; become a mentor and a coach
- Become more spiritual

Times of crisis may also be times of enlightenment with potential for change and growth.

It is often a time we begin to question our deeds, priorities and the way we live and work. Major (and often painful) life events, such as loss of a loved one, breakup of one's family, illness or redundancy, can be viewed as opportunities as much as challenges. These are the moments to examine the "dark night of the soul"; these events tend to bring forth a need to engender meaning, and the insights that follow. Often profound spiritual encounters such as a near-death experience or a personal epiphany incident may also have that transformative power and quality.

A life of meaning develops when we use our strengths for the purpose of something larger than oneself. A "meaningful life" comes from serving others and may include attending to the family, caring for other people, volunteer activities or purposeful work. The visionary person can help others to these paths to happiness, though the empowerment of pleasure, engagement and meaningfulness.

In the work settings, a review of more than 150 studies connected with successful leadership can teach us a lesson on the relationships between general life values and spiritual values and leadership success. It showed that there is a consistency between spiritual values and practices and effective leadership. Values that have long been considered spiritual virtues, such as compassion, contemplation, and meditation, have been demonstrated to be related to leadership success. Similarly, practices traditionally associated with spirituality practiced in daily life, such as prayer, have also been proposed to be connected to leadership effectiveness. All of the following actual applications of beliefs have been emphasized in many spiritual traditions (faiths), and they have also been found to be crucial leadership skills: showing respect for others, demonstrating fair treatment, expressing caring and concern, listening responsively, recognizing the contributions of others, and engaging in reflective practice.

In sum, spirituality can be used as a framework for workplace organizational values. In the framework we propose that spiritual values do not demonstrate a direct instrumentality like the 3E Triaxial model of values (i.e., they do not impact directly on organizational effectiveness), but they establish an enabling platform upon which the other, instrumental, values may be aligned. In the short term, an organization and a leader may do without them; in the longer term, this becomes a near impossibility.[36]

Values represent the nucleus of an organization, the DNA of its culture. All meaning and behaviors orbit around them. If an organization wishes to use people only as extensions of its machines and technologies, then do not expect them to innovate and become exemplary citizens of your enterprise. At the other extreme, we do not assume organizations will develop cultures of having solely fun; this is a fantasy that no organization can afford, though work and play is entirely possible and most desirable.

However, if an organizational culture can be designed where body and spirit are united, then alignment with the vision and mission of the organization can be

---

[36] For more, see: Dolan, S.L., and Altman, Y. (2012) Managing by Values: The Leadership Spirituality connection. *People and Strategy*, 35(4), 20–26.

engineered. Coaching by values is the methodology of facilitating managing by values that explains the processes of generating an organization wide dialogue and designing a value alignment.

A spiritually friendly workplace respects people's deepest beliefs, allows and encourages them to wear their faiths (including nonfaith) on their sleeves and incorporate these values in what they do and how they go about their work, giving expression – a voice – to their innermost values.

While some may feel uneasy about using words such as "spirituality" and "spiritual" when discussing workplace values, it is important to remember that "spiritual" and "religious" are not synonymous. Spirituality is not defined by an explicit set of religious beliefs or practices. The "experiencing of life", as an existential agenda is often missing from the pages of management journals. No matter how broad the perceptions of spirituality may be, all definitions in some way or another utilize the ideas expressed through the term "interconnectedness".

Thus, it is proposed to use a quadriaxial model to serve as the link between the instrumental values of the real business world and the spiritual needs for experiencing life that sustains it (see Figure 9.6).

I contend that talking about spirituality and for the profit organizations is risky business. Leaders in the business world and, these days, in the public sector, too, are normally judged by hard-number figures, added value and wealth creation. But surely, leadership is in itself a risky business, and a visionary leader does not shy away from taking risks – because following a vision is inherently risky.

Nonetheless, we are all spiritual beings. Unleashing the whole capability of the individual – mind, body, and spirit, gives enormous power to the organization.

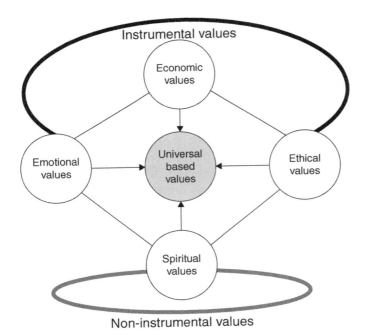

FIGURE 9.6 Towards a universal value-based organizations.

Spirituality unlocks the real sense of significance of the organization's purpose. Such leaders, and organizations create a de-stress culture.

How Can Spirituality Help You to De-stress?

Spirituality has many benefits for stress relief and overall mental health. It can help you:

- **Feel a sense of purpose**. Cultivating your spirituality may help uncover what's most meaningful in your life. By clarifying what's most important, you can focus less on the unimportant things and eliminate stress.
- **Connect to the world.** The more you feel you have a purpose in the world, the less solitary you feel even when you're alone. This can lead to a valuable inner peace during difficult times.
- **Release control**. When you feel part of a greater whole, you realize that you aren't responsible for everything that happens in life. You can share the burden of tough times as well as the joys of life's blessings with those around you.
- **Expand your support network**. Whether you find spirituality in a church, mosque or synagogue, in your family or in nature walks with a friend, this sharing of spiritual expression can help build relationships.
- **Lead a healthier life**. People who consider themselves spiritual appear to be better able to cope with stress and heal from illness or addiction faster.

Combining stress management (as we discussed in earlier chapters) and spiritual principles can be a healthy outlet for self-growth and learning to handle anything that comes your way.

Chapter Summary and Postscript

Today's world is best described by the concept of VUCA (volatility, uncertainty, complexity, ambiguity). The coronavirus pandemic has created unprecedented disruption and stress at the personal level as well as for organizations and their workforces. Entire countries are affected by it as well. Only with time will we learn and understand the real devastation that has happened (and is still growing strongly).

The pace of change and transformation is accelerating, and people are lost, people are stressed, people wonder what the future would look like. There are numerous articles, papers, books and even TV documentaries on the suffering, the stress and the devastation, and many point to a very bleak future. At the macro level, "it is upending entire sectors, industries and even countries. And, at the very personal level, it is affecting people's physical and mental health, as well as their livelihoods. True, there are no definite answers about how long the disruption will last and when stability and clarity be established. We have described the factors and the drivers of this new world.

Against this gloomy background, we are attempting to propose a focus on positivity by creating hope. We have chosen to focus on the concept of de stress and resilience. These concepts can apply to individuals, to teams, organizations, or an entire community. Building a resilient workforce in an organization, for example, is one of the best defenses against adversity, helplessness and even numbness in a VUCA world.

Resilient organizations are those that can successfully bounce back and grow from adverse experiences. Resilient people do the same. Thus, business leaders over the past twenty years have adopted the US Army War College's concept of VUCA as a way to describe the massive change and disruptions that have continually rocked organizations, markets, and governments around the world. VUCA has become the new normal, especially in light of COVID-19, and leaders have realized that there is little we can do to change these kinds of external factors; we can only prepare and respond by strengthening the internal compass/factors.

The understanding of the configurations of our values on can lead to the emergence of a targeted, resilience-based behaviour. In the chapter, we move from the abstract theory of resilience to the concrete way of illustrating the value-driven compass. By adopting the behaviours and strategies of these highly resilient people, we can create an entire workforce that will become better equipped to face adversity with a positive outlook, recover quickly and contribute in innovative and creative ways to driving value, even in such volatile times.

 ACTION: THE FUTURE OF WORK READINESS QUIZ

The Future of Work Readiness Quiz is an instrument that captures your perception on where we are heading in terms of work in the future, as well as your respective level of readiness for it. Following the "Escape room Simulation" we hope that you are better prepared for confronting the future and we wish to reassess your preparedness. The quiz includes projected scenarios, work patterns, anticipated changes in the business context, the environment, the preferences, the needs of knowledge workers, and other relevant issues.

The current version of the quiz includes 10 categories that, albeit somewhat overlapping, capture the fundamental challenges we will face in working in the future. These were based on data assembled in the last couple of years at the Global Future of Work Foundation. These are:

- The impact of technology and cyber-age on the future of work/jobs
- The type of work that people will be performing
- Where will people work and what locations they consider desirable
- Work and Non-Work (leisure) – the new mix of activities in a typical day (meetings, private work, etc.)
- Portfolio employment
- The social context in which work will take place
- The physical context in which work will take place
- The mix of skills and education that knowledge workers will need
- Perspectives on productivity and the factors that contribute to them
- Work and life satisfaction in the future

Note: *This quiz is designed to do a quick inventory that can lead to self-assessment. We hope that it will stimulate your understanding about how the workplace is evolving and how individual patterns of work are changing. It may also provide insight into the level of readiness that you have for this type of work future. The Future of Work Readiness Quiz is currently undergoing validation studies. Please give yourself 20 to 25 minutes to complete the quiz.*

Any suggestions for adding items or improving the quiz can be sent to: Prof. Simon L. Dolan, President – "The Global Future of Work Foundation". Email: simon@globalfutureofwork.com

GENERAL INSTRUCTIONS

In the next couple of pages, you are requested to complete the information. There are 10 categories. In each category there are three items/questions that you are asked to assess. It is your perception that counts.

USE THE FOLLOWING SCALE TO ASSESS THE LEVEL OF READINESS PER ITEM:

*No or marginally = **0***
*A little bit = **1***
*Yes, or significantly = **2***
*Definitely, or very significantly = **3***

CATEGORY 1: THE IMPACT OF TECHNOLOGY, AI AND THE CYBER-AGE ON THE FUTURE OF WORK/JOBS

Item	Agreement *Just indicate an overall **yes (Y)** or **No (N)** for each statement*	Am I ready for it? *(You may add comments in addition to the score)*	Score
New technologies in the cyber-age will have a major impact on the nature of jobs in the future			
New technology in the cyber-age will replace many people in doing their jobs			
New technology will produce a form of slavery of humans to the pace of the machines			
Total number of "YES":		**My personal total score is:**	

CATEGORY 2: THE TYPE OF WORK THAT PEOPLE WILL BE PERFORMING

Item	Agreement *Just indicate an overall **yes (Y)** or **No (N)** for each statement*	Am I ready for it? *(You may add comments in addition to the score)*	Score
Most manual work will be replaced and performed by robotics and machines			
Machines will replace human as workers, even in non-manual work			
People will compete with machine equipped with artificial intelligence for work			
Total number of "YES":		**My personal total score is:**	

CATEGORY 3: WHERE WILL PEOPLE WORK AND WHAT LOCATIONS THEY CONSIDER DESIRABLE

Item	Agreement *Just indicate an overall **yes (Y)** or **No (N)** for each statement*	Am I ready for it? *(You may add comments in addition to the score)*	Score
People will have the choice to work from home or from the office			
Companies will not have offices and employees providing services locally will work from all parts of the world.			
People work will be from any mobile connected place, home, car, street, etc.			
Total number of "YES":		**My personal total score is:**	

CATEGORY 4: WORK AND NON-WORK (LEISURE) – THE NEW MIX OF ACTIVITIES IN A TYPICAL DAY (*MEETINGS, PRIVATE WORK, ETC.*)

Item	Agreement Just indicate an overall **yes (Y)** or **No (N)** for each statement	Am I ready for it? (You may add comments in addition to the score)	Score
Most people will not be able to separate work from non-work (leisure)			
The ratio between hours spent at work and hours at leisure will change – people will spend less time at work and more in leisure			
Work and leisure activities will be so interwoven that it will be impossible to tell the difference			
Total number of "YES":		**My personal total score is:**	

CATEGORY 5: PORTFOLIO EMPLOYMENT

Item	Agreement Just indicate an overall **yes (Y)** or **No (N)** for each statement	Am I ready for it? (You may add comments in addition to the score)	Score
Only few people will work full time for the same employer/employment			
Portfolio employment (multiple jobs) will become the rule (not the exception)			
People will no longer stick to one career – career changes will become the norm			
Total number of "YES":		**My personal total score is:**	

CATEGORY 6: THE SOCIAL CONTEXT IN WHICH WORK WILL TAKE PLACE

Item	Agreement Just indicate an overall **yes (Y)** or **No (N)** for each statement	Am I ready for it? (You may add comments in addition to the score)	Score
Most work will be deal with tools and technology rather than directly with other people			
People will work in teams only occasionally			
Communications between people will be via internet, smart phones and other technologies rather than face-to-face			
Total number of "YES":		My personal total score is:	

CATEGORY 7: THE PHYSICAL CONTEXT IN WHICH WORK WILL TAKE PLACE

Item	Agreement Just indicate an overall **yes (Y)** or **No (N)** for each statement	Am I ready for it? (You may add comments in addition to the score)	Score
People will not have physical workspace			
For most people, office space will be shared			
Office context and architecture will be permanently changing (decor, furniture, etc.)			
Total number of "YES"		My personal total score is	

CATEGORY 8: THE MIX OF SKILLS AND EDUCATION THAT KNOWLEDGE WORKERS WILL NEED

Item	Agreement Just indicate an overall **yes (Y)** or **No (N)** for each statement	Am I ready for it? (You may add comments in addition to the score)	Score
People-related skills such as communication, interpersonal, team working, and customer-service skills will be highly demanded			
Mastering conceptual skills such as collecting and organizing information will be highly demanded			

Item	Agreement Just indicate an overall **yes (Y)** or **No (N)** for each statement	Am I ready for it? (You may add comments in addition to the score)	Score
Skills like problems solving, creativity and innovation would become a must			
Total number of "YES":		**My personal total score is:**	

CATEGORY 9: PERSPECTIVES ON PRODUCTIVITY AND THE FACTORS THAT CONTRIBUTE TO THEM

Item	Agreement Just indicate an overall **yes (Y)** or **No (N)** for each statement	Am I ready for it? (You may add comments in addition to the score)	Score
Advances in machine and robotics will help make productivity higher			
Artificial intelligence will help boost productivity rather than human intelligence			
The focus on productivity will be on effectiveness rather than on efficiency			
Total number of "YES":		**My personal total score is:**	

CATEGORY 10: WORK AND LIFE SATISFACTION IN THE FUTURE

Item	Agreement Just indicate an overall yes (Y) or No (N) for each statement	Am I ready for it? (You may add comments in addition to the score)	Score
Most people will be better trained but not necessarily more satisfied at work			
While economies and technologies improve, life satisfaction will not improve respectfully			
The future generation will never be able to attain the level of satisfaction of the old generation			
Total number of "YES":		**My personal total score is:**	

Template for identifying your preparedness zone

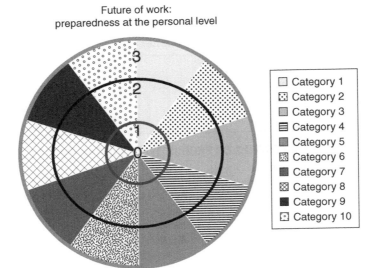

Category	Domain and impact of the future of work
1	Technology and cyber age including collective intelligence
2	The type of work that people will be performing
3	Location and life of work
4	The work and non-work ratio and relationships
5	Permanent part time and portfolio employment
6	The social context of work
7	The physical context in which work will take place
8	The mix of skills and education that knowledge workers will need
9	Productivity and the factors that contribute to them
10	Work and life satisfaction

IMAGE 9.1 Template was developed by Prof. Dolan for the Global Future of Work Foundation. Copyrights permission granted by the GFWF.

Instructions
1 *Calculates your score for each of the 10 categories (the range is between 0–3)*
2 *Place the results on the template. Connect the dots to see your preparedness total zone*

Interpretation:
By and large, the more area that your template is covered, the better you are prepared to the future of work. Nonetheless, you may have some dimension that you are better prepared then other. Evaluate and reevaluate the results and thinks about the validity of this assessment. Sometimes, it is better to do it jointly with a work team, hence aggregate preparedness can give an idea to the extent that you team is prepared for the future of work.

Index

ACTH 28, 30, 97
actionable trust zone 121, 122
acute stress and chronic stress 43
Adnane, Belout 14
aetiology of stress 64
African Proverb 4
age and stress 80
agreeableness 54, 60, 62–3
Albert, Bandura 69
ambiguity of roles 45, 46
Anat, Garti 5–7, 14, 15, 123, 127, 159, 228–32
Andre, Arsenault 6, 9–10, 12, 14, 33, 37–9, 44, 59, 89, 109, 145
antecedents of stress 90
Arie, Shirom 1, 6, 11, 239
assertiveness 62, 71, 191, 193–5, 197, 198
autogenous training (Schultz) 176–7
Avi, Liran 114, 184, 185, 186
Avishai, Landau 15, 134
avoidance coping (AC) 222

The big five personality traits 60
biofeedback-assisted relaxation 183
biological consequences of stress 33–4
The Blue Ocean Strategy 110
BOCA conditions 106
Bonnie, Richley 6, 13, 73, 219, 228

Cary, Cooper 1, 10, 12
change management skills 200
chronic work stress 15
coaching by values 9, 110, 228, 242

cognitive reconstruction 189
collaborative intelligence 213, 219
combatting obsolescence 215
conflict management 132, 140, 171
conflict of roles 46
conscientiousness 54, 60–2
consequences of occupational stress 94
COVID-19 1, 10, 18, 73, 78, 93, 138, 144, 183, 188, 214, 217, 228, 229, 231, 232, 244
culture reengineering 110
cyberness 14, 210
cyber-organization 215, 221

David, Alonso 6, 15, 113
density (of stress) 145, 147–50, 152
diathesis-stress model 42–3
digital leadership 111–12
Digital Online Value Audit (DOVA) 15
Dolan and Arsenault's Model 37
Dolan & Arsenault personality classification 59
Dolan 3Es triaxial model of values 230

education and stress 62
effort-reward imbalance model 40–2
emotion-focused coping (EFC) 221
epigenetic 239–40
Eric, Gosselin 6, 10, 14, 123
extraversion 54, 60, 62
extrinsic sources of stress 91

family triangle synchronization 5, 7, 123, 127, 133
flow (state of) 144
future of higher education 215

gender and stress 78
General Adaptation Syndrome (GSA) 27, 29–31
global future of work (foundation) 1, 5, 6, 14, 15, 19, 210, 211, 244, 245, 250
group stressors 45, 47

Hans, Selye x, 22, 25–9, 31–3, 37, 80
hardiness 69–70, 80
hierarchical level and stress 82
human resource practices 172
humour and laughter therapy 184

individual stressors 45, 46
internal vs. external locus of control 57
International Labor Office (ILO) 1, 16, 24, 29
intra-organizational stressors 45
intrinsic sources of stress 91

Javier, De Pablo 15
job characteristics model 40
jobs-demand-control 40, 41

Karasek Job Demands Model 41
Karl, Menninger 35
Kawamura Kristine 6, 14, 211
Klotho 237, 238
Kurt, Lewin 73

Laura, Moncho xv
leaders and stress 105–6
leadership and trust 115
life stress and adaptation 88
Linus, Pauling 12, 187
locus of control 54, 56–9, 175
Lucien, Abenhaim 6, 12

Mario, Raich 14, 80, 81, 162, 210, 219, 220, 228, 236
management by instruction (MBI) 228
management by objectives (MBO) 174, 228
managing by values (MBV) 13, 73, 110, 228, 231, 242
managing triangle disagreements 132

Maslach Burnout Inventory (MBI) 13
Mayo Clinic 6, 31, 203, 234
MBV-MBO-MBI 229
meditation 74, 176–83, 241
meta sources of stress 145, 146, 148
metaverse 216, 225
mindfulness 179, 182–4, 221
most stressful jobs 93, 94

National Institute for Occupational Safety and Health (NIOSH) 13–15, 21, 49
neuroticism 54, 60, 63, 64, 90
non-specific response (Selye) 23, 27–9

occupational stress xiii, 1, 2, 5, 10, 12, 13, 89, 90, 94, 95, 162–6
openness 54, 60–2, 70, 115
organizational strategies to "de-stress" 162
organizational stressors 45, 47, 205

pandemic 1, 3, 4, 10, 17, 23, 24, 79, 93, 138, 144, 183, 188, 209, 214, 215, 217, 243
physical pathologies derived from stress 96
pills to boost intelligence 214
positive psychology 232, 233
positive thought 76, 184, 189–91
premature aging 19, 80, 81, 236–9
principles of resilience 228
problem-focused coping (PFC) 221
progressive muscle relaxation (Jacobson) 176
psycho-toxicology of work 6
psychological contract (with yourself) 126–8, 140, 150
Pythagoras triangle 68, 69

quality of work life (QWL) 7–11, 14, 21, 25, 166

Ramon, Valle 6
relaxation techniques 161, 176, 177, 184, 191, 203
resilience 1, 3, 5, 7–9, 15, 70, 107, 109, 123, 127, 133, 139, 161, 207, 218, 221–4, 228–235, 240, 244
resistance to change 168, 200
resilience value pie 232
Riane, Eisler 14, 210

Richard, Lazarus 36
Ron, Burke 1, 6, 12, 59
Rotter, J. B. 56, 109
rumination 107

Salvador, Garcia 6, 10, 13, 69, 71, 73, 75, 110, 229
Schuler Randall xiii, 6
self-efficacy 54, 69, 70, 90
self-esteem 1–5, 7, 9, 12, 14, 31–3, 36, 42, 46, 53, 54, 64–7, 69, 71–8, 82, 83, 85, 86, 117, 145, 194, 196, 197, 203, 204
Shay, Tzafrir 5, 115, 123–43, 146
signs and symptoms of your stress 147
six biggest meditation Gurus 180
social support 38, 41, 59, 82, 90, 109, 124–6, 145, 146, 158, 172, 192, 231
spillover context 123
spirituality 177, 181, 210, 240–3
stages in occupational stress management 165
stress and immune system 96, 97
stress and strain 26
stress audit 101–4, 206, 207
stress definition 22
stress different models 25
stress, emotions and diseases 33
stress-less leader *vs.* toxic leader 119
stress management 15, 22, 78, 79, 89, 101, 109, 147, 149, 150, 152, 162, 164, 165, 168, 208, 225, 243
stress map viii, xv, 1, 5, 60, 90, 109, 134, 144–60, 222, 225
stress modulators 145, 149, 159
stressors of the future 212
stress & performance 88
stress prone personality 54
stress prone traits 54
Susan, Jackson 1, 13

technology addiction of teenagers 227
Thích Nhất Hạnh 182
time management 161, 169, 197, 199, 218

time thieves 198
T lymphocytes 34
toxicity at work 6
toxic leader 5, 35, 101, 117–19
transactional model of stress 3, 6, 36
triaxial model of values 13, 73, 101, 202, 228–30, 241
triaxial PIR model of leader competences 113
type A personality 3, 54, 56, 58, 90, 146, 153
type A/B/C personality 54–6
type B pattern of behavior 55
type C pattern of behavior 55
Tzafrir and Dolan's RCH model of trust 117

value compass 210–12
value congruence 73, 83–5
value of values 115, 145, 154, 155
vitamin C 185–8
vitamin D 188
volatile, uncertain, complex and ambiguous (VUCA) 1, 19, 108, 217, 228–32, 243, 244

Walter, Canon 25, 26
wear and tear 2, 27, 44, 83, 89, 109, 147, 231
WHO 12, 13, 26, 27, 209
work–family conflict (WFC) 123–43
work–family triangle relationship 5, 127
work–family triangle synchronization (WFTS) 5, 127, 133, 137–40
workplace stress 5, 23–4, 39–43, 53, 209–50
work stress during the pandemic 17–18

yoga 177, 178, 180, 182, 185, 186, 208

zinc and curcumin 188
ZINQUO xv, 6, 81, 113, 147–8, 160

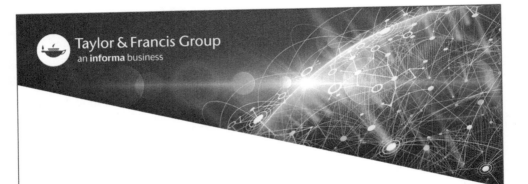